SOCIAL PSALMIST,

OR

HYMNS, SELECTED

FOR

THE PRIVATE USE AND SOCIAL MEETINGS

OF

EVANGELICAL CHRISTIANS.

NEW-YORK:
NEWMAN & IVISON,
199 BROADWAY.
1852.

STEREOTYPED BY SMITH AND WRIGHT,
COR. FULTON AND GOLD STREETS,
NEW YORK.

J. Bedford, Print. 138 Fulton st.

HYMNS.

THE SCRIPTURES.

---

1. C. M.
The Bible suited to our Wants.

1 FATHER of mercies! in thy word
What endless glory shines!
For ever be thy name adored,
For these celestial lines.

2 Here, the fair tree of knowledge grows,
And yields a free repast;
Sublimer sweets than nature knows
Invite the longing taste.

3 Here, the Redeemer's welcome voice
Spreads heavenly peace around;
And life, and everlasting joys
Attend the blissful sound.

4 Oh! may these heavenly pages be
My ever dear delight;
And still new beauties may I see,
And still increasing light.

5 Divine instructor, gracious Lord!
Be thou for ever near;
Teach me to love thy sacred word,
And view my Saviour there.

2. L. M.
Prophecy and Inspiration.

1 'T WAS by an order from the Lord,
The ancient prophets spoke his word;
His spirit did their tongues inspire,
And warmed their hearts with heavenly fire.

2 Great God! mine eyes with pleasure look
On the dear volume of thy book;
There my Redeemer's face I see,
And read his name who died for me.

3 Let the false raptures of the mind
Be lost, and vanish in the wind;
Here I can fix my hope secure;
This is thy word, and must endure.

3.

C. M.

The Holy Scriptures.

1 LADEN with guilt, and full of fears,
  I fly to thee, my Lord!
And not a glimpse of hope appears,
  But in thy written word.

2 The volume of my Father's grace
  Does all my grief assuage;
Here I behold my Saviour's face,
  Almost in every page.

3 Here, consecrated water flows,
  To quench my thirst of sin;
Here, the fair tree of knowledge grows;—
  No danger dwells therein.

4 This is the judge that ends the strife,
  Where wit and reason fail;—
My guide to everlasting life,
  Through all this gloomy vale.

5 Oh! may thy counsels, mighty God!
  My roving feet command;
Nor I forsake the happy road
  That leads to thy right hand.

4.

L. M.

A Saviour seen in the Scriptures.

1 NOW let my soul, eternal King!
To thee its grateful tribute bring;
My knee, with humble homage, bow,
My tongue perform its solemn vow.

2 All nature sings thy boundless love,
In worlds below, and worlds above;
But, in thy blessed word, I trace
Diviner wonders of thy grace.

3 There, what delightful truths I read!
There, I behold the Saviour bleed:
His name salutes my listening ear,
Revives my heart, and checks my fear.

4 There Jesus bids my sorrows cease,
And gives my lab'ring conscience peace;
Raises my grateful passions high,
And points to mansions in the sky.

5 For love like this, Oh! let my song,
Through endless years, thy praise prolong;
Let distant climes thy name adore,
Till time and nature are no more.

5. C. M.

Revelation welcomed.

1 HAIL, sacred truth! whose piercing rays
Dispel the shades of night;
Diffusing, o'er the mental world,
The healing beams of light.

2 Jesus! thy word, with friendly aid,
Restores our wandering feet;
Converts the sorrows of the mind
To joys divinely sweet.

3 Oh! send thy light and truth abroad,
In all their radiant blaze;
And bid th' admiring world adore
The glories of thy grace.

6. L. M.

The Blessings of the new Covenant

1 GOD, in the gospel of his Son,
Makes his eternal counsels known;
Where love in all its glory shines,
And truth is drawn in fairest lines.

2 Here, sinners of an humble frame
May taste his grace, and learn his name;
May read, in characters of blood,
The wisdom, power and grace of God.

3 Here, faith reveals, to mortal eyes,
A brighter world beyond the skies;
Here, shines the light which guides our way
From earth to realms of endless day.

4 Oh! grant us grace, almighty Lord!
To read and mark thy holy word,
Its truths with meekness to receive,
And by its holy precepts live.

5 May this blest volume ever lie
Close to my heart, and near mine eye,—
Till life's last hour my soul engage,
And be my chosen heritage.

7.

L. M.

A written Revelation.

1 LET everlasting glories crown
Thy head, my Saviour, and my Lord!
Thy hands have brought salvation down,
And writ the blessings in thy word.

2 In vain the trembling conscience seeks
Some solid ground to rest upon;
With long despair the spirit breaks,
Till we apply to Christ alone.

3 How well thy blessed truths agree!
How wise and holy thy commands!
Thy promises—how firm they be!
How firm our hope and comfort stands!

4 Should all the forms that men devise
Assault my faith, with treacherous art,
I'd call them vanity and lies,
And bind the gospel to my heart.

8.

L. M.

The Power of Truth.

1 THIS is the word of truth and love,
Sent to the nations from above;
Jehovah here resolves to show
What his almighty grace can do.

2 This remedy did wisdom find,
To heal diseases of the mind;—
This sovereign balm, whose virtues can
Restore the ruined creature, man.

3 The gospel bids the dead revive,—
Sinners obey the voice, and live;
Dry bones are raised, and clothed afresh,
And hearts of stone are turned to flesh.

4 May but this grace my soul renew,
Let sinners gaze, and hate me too;
The word that saves me doth engage
A sure defence from all their rage.

GOD.

9. L. M.
Existence of God.

1 THERE is a God!—all nature speaks,
Through earth, and air, and sea, and skies;
See!—from the clouds his glory breaks,
When earliest beams of morning rise!

2 The rising sun, serenely bright,
Throughout the world's extended frame,
Inscribes, in characters of light,
His mighty Maker's glorious name.

3 Ye curious minds, who roam abroad,
And trace creation's wonders o'er!
Confess the footsteps of your God;
Bow down before him and adore.

10. C. M.
Creation and Providence.

1 LORD! when my raptured thought surveys
Creation's beauties o'er,
All nature joins to teach thy praise,
And bid my soul adore.

2 Where'er I turn my gazing eyes,
Thy radiant footsteps shine;
Ten thousand pleasing wonders rise,
And speak their source divine.

3 On me thy providence hath shone
With gentle, smiling rays;
Oh! let my lips and life make known
Thy goodness and thy praise.

4 All-bounteous Lord! thy grace impart;
Oh! teach me to improve
Thy gifts, with ever-grateful heart,
And crown them with thy love.

11.

H. M.

Perfections of God's Government.

1 THE Lord Jehovah reigns;
His throne is built on high;
The garments he assumes
Are light and majesty:
His glories shine with beams so bright,
No mortal eye can bear the sight.

2 The thunders of his hand
Keep the wide world in awe;
His wrath and justice stand
To guard his holy law:
And where his love resolves to bless,
His truth confirms and seals the grace.

3 Through all his perfect work,
Surprising wisdom shines;
Confounds the powers of hell,
And breaks their cursed designs:
Strong is his arm—and shall fulfill
His great decrees—his sovereign will.

4 And can this mighty King
Of glory condescend,—
And will he write his name,
My Father and my Friend?
I love his name,—I love his word:
Join, all my powers! and praise the Lord.

12.

C. M.

God, the Creator.

1 ETERNAL Wisdom! thee we praise,
Thee the creation sings;
With thy loved name, rocks, hills, and seas,
And heaven's high palace rings.

2 How wide thy hand hath spread the sky!
How glorious to behold!
Tinged with a blue of heavenly dye,
And starred with sparkling gold.

3 Thy glories blaze all nature round,
And strike the gazing sight,
Through skies, and seas, and solid ground,
With terror and delight.

4 Infinite strength, and equal skill,
Shine through the worlds abroad;

Our souls with vast amazement fill,
  And speak the builder—God.

5 But still, the wonders of thy grace
  Our softer passions move;
Pity divine, in Jesus' face,
  We see, adore, and love.

13. C. M.

God's eternal Dominion.

1 GREAT God! how infinite art thou!
  What worthless worms are we!
Let the whole race of creatures bow,
  And pay their praise to thee.

2 Thy throne eternal ages stood,
  Ere seas or stars were made:
Thou art the ever-living God,
  Were all the nations dead.

3 Eternity, with all its years,
  Stands present in thy view;
To thee there 's nothing old appears—
  Great God! there 's nothing new.

4 Our lives through various scenes are drawn,
  And vexed with trifling cares;
While thine eternal thought moves on
  Thine undisturbed affairs.

5 Great God! how infinite art thou!
  What worthless worms are we!
Let the whole race of creatures bow,
  And pay their praise to thee.

14. H. M.

Praise from all Creation.

1 ANGELS! assist to sing
  The honors of your God;
Touch every tuneful string,
  And sound his name abroad:
Come, pour the trembling notes along;
And swell the grand immortal song.

2 And, ye of meaner birth!
  Your joyful voices raise;
Inhabitants of earth!
  Your great Creator praise:
Let your hosannas joyful rise,
And shake the earth and pierce the skies.

3 Let day and dusky night,
  In solemn order, join
His praises to recite,
  And speak his power divine:
Let every hill and every vale
Re-echo with the sacred tale.

4 Let every creature sing
  The honors of our God;
Touch every tuneful string,
  And spread his praise abroad:
Come, pour the trembling notes along;
And swell the universal song.

15.

L. M.

Majesty of God.

1 COME, O my soul! in sacred lays,
Attempt thy great Creator's praise;
But Oh! what tongue can speak his fame?
What mortal verse can reach the theme?

2 Enthroned amidst the radiant spheres,
He glory, like a garment, wears;
To form a robe of light divine
Ten thousand suns around him shine.

3 In all our Maker's grand designs,
Omnipotence with wisdom shines;
His works, through all his wondrous frame,
Bear the great impress of his name.

4 Raised on devotion's lofty wing,
Do thou, my soul! his glories sing;
And let his praise employ thy tongue,
Till listening worlds repeat the song.

16.

7s.

Praise for temporal Mercies.

1 PRAISE to God!—immortal praise,
For the love that crowns our days:
Bounteous scource of every joy!
Let thy praise our tongues employ.

2 All that spring, with bounteous hand,
Scatters o'er the smiling land;—
All that liberal autumn pours
From her rich, o'erflowing stores;—

3 These to that dear source we owe,
Whence our sweetest comforts flow;
These, through all my happy days,
Claim my cheerful songs of praise.

4 Lord! to thee my soul should raise
Grateful, never-ending praise;
And, when every blessing 's flown,
Love thee for thyself alone.

17.

S. M.

Praise to the Creator.

1 ALMIGHTY Maker, God!
How wondrous is thy name!
Thy glories, how diffused abroad,
Through all creation's frame!

2 Nature, in every dress,
Her humble homage pays;
And does, a thousand ways, express
Her undissembled praise.

3 My soul would rise and sing
Her great Creator too;
Fain would my tongue adore my King,
And pay the homage due.

4 Let joy and worship spend
The remnant of my days,
And oft to God my soul ascend,
In grateful songs of praise.

18.

H. M.

Rejoicing in God.

1 TO your Creator, God,
Your great preserver, raise,
Ye creatures of his hand!
Your highest notes of praise:
Let every voice
Proclaim his power,
His name adore,
And loud rejoice.

2 Let every creature join
To celebrate his name,
And all their various powers
Assist th' exalted theme:

Let nature raise,
From every tongue,
A general song
Of grateful praise.

3 But Oh! from human tongues
Should nobler praises flow;
And every thankful heart
With warm devotion glow:
Your voices raise
Above the rest;
Ye highly blest!
Declare his praise.

4 Assist me, gracious God!
My heart, my voice inspire,
Then shall I grateful join
The universal choir:
Thy grace can raise
My heart, my tongue,
And tune my song
To lively praise.

19.

C. M.

Wonders of God's Love.

1 YE humble souls! approach your God
With songs of sacred praise;
For he is good, supremely good;
And kind are all his ways.

2 All nature owns his guardian care,
In him we live and move;
But nobler benefits declare
The wonders of his love.

3 He gave his Son, his only Son
To ransom rebel-worms;
'T is here he makes his goodness known,
In its diviner forms.

4 To this dear refuge, Lord! we come,
'T is here our hope relies;—
A safe defence, a peaceful home,
When storms of trouble rise.

5 Thine eye beholds, with kind regard,
The souls that trust in thee;
Their humble hope thou wilt reward,
With bliss divinely free.

6 Great God! to thine almighty love,
What honors shall we raise?
Not all th' angelic songs above
Can render equal praise.

20.

C. M.

The glory of God in Creation.

1 THE God of nature and of grace
In all his works appears;
His goodness through the earth we trace,
His grandeur in the spheres.

2 Behold this fair and fertile globe,
By him in wisdom planned!
'T was he who girded, like a robe,
The ocean round the land.

3 Lift to the arch of heaven your eye;
Thither his path pursue;
His glory, boundless as the sky,
O'erwhelms the wondering view.

4 How excellent, O Lord! thy name,
In all creation's lines!
Spread through eternity, thy fame
With rising lustre shines.

5 These lower works that swell thy praise,
High as our thoughts can tower,
Are but a portion of thy ways,—
The hiding of thy power.

6 Millions before thy presence stand,
Who feel, while they adore,
Fulness of joy, at thy right hand,
And pleasures evermore.

21.

11s.

The Mercy of God.

1 THY mercy my God! is the theme of my song,
The joy of my heart, and the boast of my tongue;
Free grace hath alone, from the first to the last,
Secured my affections, and bound my soul fast.

2 Thy mercy, has vanquished my obdurate heart,
That wonders to feel its own hardness depart:

Dissolved by thy goodness, I fall to the ground,
And weep to the praise of the mercy I 've found.

3 The door of thy mercy stands open all day,
To the poor and the needy, who knock by the way;
No sinner shall ever a place be denied,
Who comes seeking mercy through Jesus that died.

4 Thy mercy in Jesus exempts me from hell;
Its glories I 'll sing, and its wonders I 'll tell:
'T was Jesus, my friend, when he hung on the tree,
Who opened the fountain of mercy for me.

22.

S. M.

God, all and in all.

1 MY God, my life, my love!
To thee, to thee I call;
I cannot live, if thou remove,
For thou art all in all.

2 To thee, and thee alone,
The angels owe their bliss;
They sit around thy gracious throne,
And dwell where Jesus is.

3 Not all the harps above
Can make a heavenly place,
If God his residence remove,
Or but conceal his face.

4 Nor earth, nor all the sky,
Can one delight afford;
No, not a drop of real joy.
Without thy presence, Lord!

5 Thou art the sea of love,
Where all my pleasures roll,
The circle, where my passions move,
And centre of my soul.

23.

C. M.

Confiding in God.

1 TO thee, my God! my heart shall bring
The lively, grateful song;
Attending kings shall hear me sing,
With rapture on my tongue.

2 Amid the glories of thy name,
Thy truth exalted shines;

A faithful God thy words proclaim,
  In everlasting lines.

3 When, in the day of deep distress,
  To thee, my God! I cried,
With strength divine, thy powerful grace
  My fainting soul supplied.

4 Thou, Lord! wilt all my hopes fulfill,
  To thee the work belongs;
Let endless mercy guide me still,
  And tune my grateful songs.

24.

C. M.

The Mercy-Seat.

1 DEAR Father! to thy mercy-seat
  My soul for shelter flies:
'T is here I find a safe retreat,
  When storms and tempests rise.

2 My cheerful hope can never die,
  If thou, my God! art near;
Thy grace can raise my comforts high,
  And banish every fear.

3 My great Protector, and my Lord!
  Thy constant aid impart;
Oh! let thy kind, thy gracious word
  Sustain my trembling heart.

4 Oh! never let my soul remove
  From this divine retreat;
Still let me trust thy power and love,
  And dwell beneath thy feet.

25.

C. M.

Prayer for quickening Grace.

1 PERMIT me, Lord! to seek thy face,
  Obedient to thy call;
To seek the presence of thy grace,
  My strength, my life, my all!

2 All I can wish is thine to give:
  My God! I ask thy love,—
That greatest boon I can receive,—
  The bliss of heaven above.

3 To heaven my restless heart aspires;
  Oh! for a quickening ray,

To wake and warm my faint desires,
  And cheer the tiresome way.

4 The path to thy divine abode
  Through a wild desert lies;
A thousand snares beset the road,—
  A thousand terrors rise.

5 Satan and sin unite their art
  To keep me from my Lord:
Dear Saviour! guard my trembling heart,
  And guide me by thy word.

6 My Guardian, my almighty Friend!
  On thee my soul would rest;
On thee alone my hopes depend;
  Be near, and I am blest.

26.

H. M.

Perpetual Praise.

1 TO thee, great Source of light!
  My thankful voice I'll raise;
And all my powers unite
  To celebrate thy praise;
And, till my voice is lost in death,
May praise employ my every breath.

2 And when this feeble tongue
  Lies silent in the dust,
My soul shall dwell among
  The spirits of the just;
Then, with the shining hosts above,
In nobler strains I'll sing thy love.

27.

C. M.

God's Presence is Light in Darkness.

1 MY God! the spring of all my joys,
  The life of my delights;
The glory of my brightest days,
  And comfort of my nights.

2 In darkest shades, if he appear,
  My dawning is begun;
He is my soul's sweet morning-star,
  And he my rising sun.

3 The opening heavens around me shine,
  With beams of sacred bliss,

While Jesus shows his heart is mine,
And whispers I am his.

4 My soul would leave this heavy clay,
At that transporting word;
Run up with joy the shining way,
T' embrace my dearest Lord.

5 Fearless of hell and ghastly death,
I 'd break through every foe;
The wings of love, and arms of faith,
Should bear me conqueror through.

28. S. M.

God, my Creator and Benefactor.

1 MY Maker and my King!
To thee my all I owe;
Thy sovereign bounty is the spring
Whence all my blessings flow.

2 The creature of thy hand,—
On thee alone I live;
My God! thy benefits demand
More praise than life can give.

3 Shall I withhold thy due?
And shall my passions rove?
Lord! form this wretched heart anew,
And fill it with thy love.

4 Oh! let thy grace inspire
My soul with strength divine;
Let all my powers to thee aspire
And all my days be thine.

29. C. M.

Thanks for Providence and Grace.

1 ALMIGHTY Father, gracious Lord,
Kind guardian of my days!
Thy mercies let my heart record
In songs of grateful praise.

2 In life's first dawn, my tender frame
Was thine indulgent care;
Long ere I could pronounce thy name,
Or breathe the infant prayer.

3 Yet I adore thee, gracious Lord!
For favors more divine;—

That I have known thy sacred word,
  Where all thy glories shine.

4 When blest with that transporting view,
  That Jesus died for me,
For this sweet hope, what praise is due,
  O God of grace! to thee?

5 Now shall my joyful powers unite,
  In more exalted lays,
Till I shall join the sons of light,
  In everlasting praise.

30.

L. M.

Imploring divine Influence.

1 MY God! whene'er my longing heart
Its grateful tribute would impart,
In vain my boldest thoughts arise,—
I sink to earth, and losé the skies.

2 Thy name inspires the harps above,
With harmony, and praise, and love;
That grace, which tunes th' immortal strings,
Looks kindly down on mortal things.

3 Oh! let thy grace guide every song,
And fill my heart and tune my tongue;
Then shall the strain harmonious flow,
And heaven's sweet work begin below

31.

C. M.

Thanks for providential Favors.

1 WHEN all thy mercies, O my God!
  My rising soul surveys,
Transported with the view, I 'm lost
  In wonder, love, and praise.

2 Unnumbered comforts, on my soul,
  Thy tender care bestowed,
Before my infant heart conceived
  From whom those comforts flowed.

3 When in the slippery paths of youth,
  With heedless steps, I ran,
Thine arm, unseen, conveyed me safe,
  And led me up to man.

4 Ten thousand thousand precious gifts
  My daily thanks employ;

Nor is the least a cheerful heart,
That tastes those gifts with joy.

5 Through every period of my life,
Thy goodness I'll pursue;
And after death, in distant worlds,
The glorious theme renew.

6 Through all eternity, to thee
A joyful song I'll raise:
But Oh! eternity's too short
To utter all thy praise.

32. L. M.

Song of Gratitude and Praise.

1 GOD of my life! through all my days,
I'll tune the grateful notes of praise;
The song shall wake with opening light,
And warble to the silent night.

2 When anxious cares would break my rest,
And griefs would tear my throbbing breast,
The notes of praise, ascending high,
Shall check the murmur and the sigh.

3 When death o'er nature shall prevail,
And all the powers of language fail,
Joy through my swimming eyes shall break,
And mean the thanks I cannot speak.

4 But Oh! when that last conflict's o'er,
And I am chained to earth no more,—
With what glad accents shall I rise
To join the music of the skies.

5 Then shall I learn th' exalted strains
That echo through the heavenly plains,
And emulate, with joy unknown,
The glowing seraphs round thy throne.

33. 8s and 7s.

Praise to Jehovah.

1 SAINTS! with pious zeal attending,
Now a grateful tribute raise;
Joyful songs, to heaven ascending,
Join the universal praise.

2 Round Jehovah's footstool kneeling,
Lowly bend with contrite souls;

Here his milder grace revealing,
Here his wrath no thunder rolls.

3 Every secret fault confessing,
Deed unholy—thought of sin,—
Seize, Oh! seize the proffered blessing,—
Grace from God, and peace within.

4 Heart and voice with rapture swelling,
Still the song of glory raise;
On the theme immortal, dwelling,
Join the universal praise.

34.

L. M.

Retirement and Devotion.

1 MY God! permit me not to be
A stranger to myself and thee;
Amidst a thousand thoughts I rove,
Forgetful of my highest love.

2 Why should my passions mix with earth,
And thus debase my heavenly birth?
Why should I cleave to things below,
And let my God, my Saviour, go?

3 Call me away from flesh and sense;
One sovereign word can draw me thence;
I would obey the voice divine,
And all inferior joys resign.

4 Be earth, with all her scenes, withdrawn:
Let noise and vanity be gone;
In secret silence of the mind,
My heaven—and there my God, I find.

35.

C. M.

God, our Refuge.

1 DEAR refuge of my weary soul!
On thee, when sorrows rise,—
On thee, when waves of trouble roll,
My fainting hope relies.

2 To thee I tell each rising grief,
For thou alone canst heal;
Thy word can bring a sweet relief,
For every pain I feel.

3 But Oh! when gloomy doubts prevail,
I fear to call thee mine;

The springs of comfort seem to fail,
And all my hopes decline.

4 Hast thou not bid me seek thy face?
And shall I seek in vain?
And can the ear of sovereign grace
Be deaf when I complain?

5 No,—still the ear of sovereign grace
Attends the mourner's prayer:
Oh! may I ever find access
To breathe my sorrows there!

6 Thy mercy-seat is open still:
Here let my soul retreat;
With humble hope attend thy will,
And wait beneath thy feet.

36.

C. M.

Thirsting after God.

1 WHEN fainting in the sultry waste,
And parched with thirst extreme,
The weary pilgrim longs to taste
The cool refreshing stream:—

2 So longs the weary, fainting mind,
Oppressed with sins and woes,
Some soul-reviving spring to find,
Whence heavenly comfort flows.

3 Oh! may I thirst for thee, my God!
With ardent, strong desire;
And still, through all this desert road,
To taste thy grace aspire.

4 Then shall my prayer to thee ascend,
A grateful sacrifice;
My mourning voice wilt thou attend,
And grant me full supplies.

37.

C. M.

God, as seen in Nature.

1 I SING th' almighty power of God,
That made the mountains rise,
That spread the flowing seas abroad,
And built the lofty skies.

2 I sing the wisdom that ordained
The sun to rule the day;

The moon shines full at his command,
And all the stars obey.

3 I sing the goodness of the Lord,
That filled the earth with food;
He formed the creatures with his word,
And then pronounced them good.

4 Lord! how thy wonders are displayed,
Where'er I turn mine eye!
If I survey the ground I tread,
Or gaze upon the sky!

5 There 's not a plant nor flower below,
But makes thy glories known;
And clouds arise, and tempests blow,
By order from thy throne.

6 Creatures that borrow life from thee,
Are subject to thy care;
There 's not a place where we can flee,
But God is present there.

38.

C. M.

Rejoicing in God, our Father.

1 COME, shout aloud the Father's grace,
And sing the Saviour's love;
Soon shall you join the glorious theme,
In loftier strains above.

2 God, the eternal, mighty God,
To dearer names descends;
Calls you his treasure and his joy,
His children and his friends.

3 My Father, God! and may these lips
Pronounce a name so dear?
Not thus could heaven's sweet harmony
Delight my listening ear.

4 Thanks to my God for every gift
His bounteous hands bestow;
And thanks eternal for that love
Whence all those comforts flow.

39.

L. M

Perfections of God in his Government.

1 JEHOVAH reigns—his throne is high,
His robes are light and majesty;

His glory shines, with beams so bright,
No mortal can sustain the sight.

2 His terrors keep the world in awe;
His justice guards his holy law;
His love reveals a smiling face;
His truth and promise seal the grace.

3 Through all his works his wisdom shines,
And baffles Satan's deep designs;
His power is sovereign to fulfill
The noblest counsels of his will.

4 And will this glorious Lord descend
To be my father and my friend?
Then let my songs with angels join:
Heaven is secure, if God be mine.

40.

C. M.

God, all in all.

1 MY God, my portion and my love,
My everlasting all!
I 've none but thee in heaven above,
Or on this earthly ball.

2 What empty things are all the skies,
And this inferior clod!
There 's nothing here deserves my joys:
There 's nothing like my God.

3 In vain the bright, the burning sun
Scatters his feeble light:
'T is thy sweet beams create my noon;
If thou withdraw,—'t is night.

4 How vain a toy is glittering wealth,
If once compared with thee!
Or what 's my safety, or my health,
Or all my friends to me?

5 Were I possessor of the earth,
And called the stars my own,—
Without thy graces and thyself,
I were a wretch undone.

6 Let others stretch their arms like seas,
And grasp in all the shore;
Grant me the visits of thy face,
And I desire no more.

41.

L. M.

God's Condescension.

1 UP to the Lord, who reigns on high,
And views the nations from afar,
Let everlasting praises fly,
And tell how large his bounties are.

2 He over-rules all mortal things,
And manages our mean affairs:
On humble souls the King of kings
Bestows his counsels and his cares.

3 Our sorrows and our tears we pour
Into the bosom of our God;
He hears us in the mournful hour,
And helps us bear the heavy load.

4 Oh! could our thankful hearts devise
A tribute equal to thy grace—
To the third heaven our songs should rise,
And teach the golden harps thy praise.

42.

S. M.

Exhortation to Praise.

1 STAND up, and bless the Lord,
Ye people of his choice!
Stand up, and bless the Lord your God,
With heart, and soul, and voice.

2 Though high above all praise,
Above all blessing high,
Who would not fear his holy name,
And laud, and magnify?

3 Oh! for the living flame
From his own altar brought,
To touch our lips, our souls inspire,
And wing to heaven our thought.

4 God is our strength and song,
And his salvation ours;
Then be his love in Christ proclaimed,
With all our ransomed powers.

5 Stand up, and bless the Lord,—
The Lord, your God, adore,
Stand up, and bless his glorious name,
Henceforth, for evermore.

43.

L. M.

Men not comparable with God.

1 SHALL the vile race of flesh and blood
Contend with their Creator, God?
Shall mortal worms presume to be
More holy, wise, or just, than he?

2 Behold! he puts his trust in none
Of all the spirits round his throne;
Their natures, when compared with his,
Are neither holy, just nor wise.

3 But how much meaner things are they,
Who spring from dust, and dwell in clay!
Touched by the finger of thy wrath,
We faint, and vanish like the moth.

4 Almighty Power! to thee we bow;
How frail are we—how glorious thou!
No more the sons of earth shall dare,
With an eternal God, compare.

44.

L. M.

Praise to God.

1 PRAISE, everlasting praise, be paid
To him, who earth's foundation laid:
Praise to the God, whose strong decrees
Sway the creation, as he please.

2 Praise to the goodness of the Lord,
Who rules his people by his word;
And there, as strong as his decrees,
He sets his kindest promises.

3 Whence, then, should doubts and fears arise?
Why trickling sorrows drown our eyes?
Slowly, alas! our mind receives
The comforts that our Maker gives.

4 Oh! for a strong, a lasting faith,
To credit what th' Almighty saith;
T' embrace the message of his Son,
And call the joys of heaven our own.

5 Then, should the earth's old pillars shake,
And all the wheels of nature break,
Our steady souls would fear no more,
Than solid rocks when billows roar.

45.

C. M.

Goodness of God seen in his Works.

1 HAIL, great Creator, wise and good!
To thee our songs we raise;
Nature, through all her various scenes,
Invites us to thy praise.

2 At morning, noon, and evening mild,
Fresh wonders strike our view;
And while we gaze, our hearts exult,
With transports ever-new.

3 Thy glory beams in every star
Which gilds the gloom of night;
And decks the smiling face of morn,
With rays of cheerful light.

4 The lofty hill—the humble lawn,
With countless beauties shine;
The silent grove—the awful shade,
Proclaim thy power divine.

5 And while, in all thy wondrous ways,
Thy varied love we see;
Oh! may our hearts, great God! be led
Through all thy works to thee.

46.

L. M.

Wisdom and Knowledge of God.

1 AWAKE, my tongue! thy tribute bring
To him, who gave thee power to sing;
Praise him, who is all praise above,—
The source of wisdom and of love.

2 How vast his knowledge—how profound!
A depth, where all our thoughts are drowned!
The stars he numbers;—and their names
He gives to all those heavenly flames.

3 Through each bright world above, behold
Ten thousand thousand charms unfold:
Earth, air, and mighty seas combine,
To speak his wisdom all divine.

4 But in redemption, Oh! what grace!—
Its wonders, Oh! what thought can trace!
Here wisdom shines for ever bright;—
Praise him, my soul! with sweet delight.

47.

C. M.

Sovereignty and Dominion of God.

1 KEEP silence, all created things!
And wait your Maker's nod;
My soul stands trembling, while she sings
The honors of her God.

2 Life, death, and hell, and worlds unknown,
Hang on his firm decree;
He sits on no precarious throne,
Nor borrows leave to be.

3 Chained to his throne, a volume lies,
With all the fates of men,
With every angel's form and size,
Drawn by th' eternal pen.

4 His providence unfolds his book,
And makes his counsels shine;
Each opening leaf, and every stroke,
Fulfills some deep design.

5 My God! I would not long to see
My fate, with curious eyes,—
What gloomy lines are writ for me,
Or what bright scenes may rise.

6 In thy fair book of life and grace,
Oh! may I find my name,
Recorded in some humble place,
Beneath my Lord—the Lamb.

48.

H. M.

Faithfulness of God.

1 THE promises I sing,
Which sovereign love hath spoke;
Nor will th' eternal King
His words of grace revoke:
They stand secure
And steadfast still;
Not Zion's hill
Abides so sure.

2 The mountains melt away,
When once the Judge appears;
And sun and moon decay,
That measure mortal years;

But still the same,
In radiant lines,
The promise shines
Through all the flame.

3 Their harmony shall sound
Through my attentive ears,
When thunders cleave the ground,
And dissipate the spheres;
Mid all the shock
Of that dread scene,
I stand serene;—
Thy word, my rock.

49.

C. M

The glories of Redemption.

1 FATHER! how wide thy glory shines!
How high thy wonders rise!
Known through the earth by thousand signs,—
By thousand through the skies.

2 Those mighty orbs proclaim thy power,
Their motions speak thy skill;
And on the wings of every hour,
We read thy patience still.

3 But when we view thy strange design
To save rebellious worms,
Where vengeance and compassion join,
In their divinest forms,—

4 Here the whole Deity is known;
Nor dares a creature guess,—
Which of the glories brightest shone,
The justice, or the grace.

5 Now the full glories of the Lamb
Adorn the heavenly plains:
Bright seraphs learn Immanuel's name,
And try their choicest strains.

6 Oh! may I bear some humble part,
In that immortal song:
Wonder and joy shall tune my heart,
And love command my tongue.

50.

S. M.

The God of Mercy and Justice.

1 THE Lord on high proclaims
His Godhead from his throne;—

"Mercy and justice are the names,
By which I will be known.

2 "Ye dying souls, that sit
In darkness and distress!
Look from the borders of the pit,
To my recovering grace."

3 Sinners shall hear the sound;
Their thankful tongues shall own,—
Our righteousness and strength is found
In thee, the Lord, alone.

4 In thee shall Israel trust,
And see their guilt forgiven;
God will pronounce the sinners just,
And take the saints to heaven.

51. C. M.

Almighty Power and Majesty of God.

1 THE Lord, our God, is full of might,
The winds obey his will;
He speaks,—and, in his heavenly height,
The rolling sun stands still.

2 Rebel, ye waves! and o'er the land
With threatening aspect roar;
The Lord uplifts his awful hand,
And chains you to the shore.

3 Howl, winds of night! your force combine;
Without his high behest,
Ye shall not, in the mountain-pine,
Disturb the sparrow's nest.

4 His voice sublime is heard afar,
In distant peals it dies;
He yokes the whirlwind to his car,
And sweeps the howling skies.

5 Ye nations! bend—in reverence bend,
Ye monarchs! wait his nod,
And bid the choral song ascend
To celebrate your God.

52. C. M.

God, holy, just, and sovereign.

1 HOW should the sons of Adam's race
Be pure before their God?

If he contend in righteousness,
  We fall beneath his rod.

2 Strong is his arm, his heart is wise;
  What vain presumers dare,
Against their Maker's hand to rise,
  Or tempt th' unequal war?

3 Mountains, by his almighty wrath,
  From their old seats are torn;
He shakes the earth, from south to north,
  And all her pillars mourn.

4 He bids the sun forbear to rise—
  Th' obedient sun forbears:
His hand with sackcloth spreads the skies,
  And seals up all the stars.

5 He walks upon the stormy sea,
  Flies on the stormy wind:
There 's none can trace his wondrous way,
  Or his dark footsteps find.

53. C. M.

The divine Purpose and Providence.

1 GOD moves in a mysterious way,
  His wonders to perform;
He plants his footsteps in the sea,
  And rides upon the storm.

2 Deep, in unfathomable mines
  Of never-failing skill,
He treasures up his bright designs,
  And works his sovereign will.

3 Ye fearful saints! fresh courage take;
  The clouds ye so much dread
Are big with mercy, and shall break
  In blessings on your head.

4 Judge not the Lord by feeble sense,
  But trust him for his grace;
Behind a frowning providence,
  He hides a smiling face.

5 His purposes will ripen fast,
  Unfolding every hour;
The bud may have a bitter taste,
  But sweet will be the flower.

6 Blind unbelief is sure to err,
And scan his work in vain:
God is his own interpreter,
And he will make it plain.

54.

C. M.

Love of God.

1 COME, ye that know and fear the Lord!
And raise your soul above;
Let every heart and voice accord,
To sing that—God is love.

2 This precious truth his word declares,
And all his mercies prove;
While Christ, th' atoning Lamb, appears,
To show that—God is love.

3 Behold his loving-kindness waits,
For those who from him rove,
And calls of mercy reach their hearts,
To teach them—God is love.

4 The work begun is carried on,
By power from heaven above;
And every step, from first to last,
Proclaims that—God is love.

5 Oh! may we all, while here below,
This best of blessings prove;
Till warmer hearts, in brighter worlds,
Shall shout that—God is love.

55.

C. M.

The Sovereignty of God.

1 THY way, O God! is in the sea;
Thy paths I cannot trace,
Nor comprehend the mystery
Of thine unbounded grace.

2 Here the dark veils of flesh and sense
My captive soul surround;
Mysterious deeps of providence
My inward thoughts confound.

3 As, through a glass, I dimly see
The wonders of thy love,
How little do I know of thee,
Or of the joys above!

4 Though but in part I know thy will,
 I bless thee for the sight:
When will thy love the whole reveal
 In glory's clearer light?

5 In rapture shall I then survey
 Thy providence and grace;
And spend an everlasting day
 In wonder, love, and praise.

56.

7s.

Universal Praise to God.

1 SONGS of praise the angels sang,
Heaven with hallelujahs rang,
When Jehovah's work begun,—
When he spake, and it was done.

2 Songs of praise awoke the morn,
When the Prince of peace was born;
Songs of praise arose, when he
Captive led captivity.

3 Heaven and earth must pass away,—
Songs of praise shall crown that day:
God will make new heavens and earth,—
Songs of praise shall hail their birth.

4 And shall man alone be dumb,
Till that glorious morning come?
No!—the church delights to raise
Psalms, and hymns, and songs of praise.

5 Saints below, with heart and voice,
Still in songs of praise rejoice,
Learning here, by faith and love,
Songs of praise to sing above.

6 Borne upon their latest breath,
Songs of praise shall conquer death;
Then, amid eternal joy,
Songs of praise their powers employ.

57.

C. M.

A faithful God.

1 BEGIN, my tongue! some heavenly theme,
 And speak some boundless thing,—
The mighty works, or mightier name
 Of our eternal King.

2 Tell of his wondrous faithfulness,
And sound his power abroad;
Sing the sweet promise of his grace,
And the performing God.

3 Proclaim—"Salvation from the Lord,
For wretched, dying men;"
His hand has writ the sacred word,
With an immortal pen.

4 Engraved as in eternal brass,
The mighty promise shines,
Nor can the powers of darkness raze,
Those everlasting lines.

5 His word of grace is sure and strong,
As that which built the skies:
The voice that rolls the stars along
Speaks all the promises.

6 Oh! might I hear thy heavenly tongue
But whisper,—"Thou art mine;"
Those gentle words should raise my song,
To notes almost divine.

58.

7s.

Thanksgiving.

1 SWELL the anthem, raise the song;
Praises to our God belong:
Saints and angels! join to sing
Praises to the heavenly King.

2 Blessings from his liberal hand
Flow around this happy land:
Guarded by his watchful eye,
Peace and freedom we enjoy.

3 Here, beneath a virtuous sway,
May we cheerfully obey,
Never feel oppression's rod,
Ever own and worship God.

4 Hark! the voice of nature sings
Praises to the King of kings;
Let us join the choral song,
And the grateful notes prolong.

59.

C. M.

Endless Praise.

1 YES—I will bless thee, O my God!
Through all my mortal days,

And to eternity prolong
 Thy vast, thy boundless praise.

2 Nor shall my tongue alone proclaim
 The honors of my God;
My life, with all its active powers,
 Shall spread thy praise abroad.

3 Not death itself shall stop my song,
 Though death will close my eyes:
My thoughts shall then to nobler heights
 And sweeter raptures rise.

4 There shall my lips in endless praise
 Their grateful tribute pay:
The theme demands an angel's tongue,
 And an eternal day.

60.

L. M.

God acknowledged in national Blessings.

1 GREAT God of nations! now to thee
 Our hymn of gratitude we raise;
With humble heart, and bending knee,
 We offer thee our song of praise.

2 Thy name we bless, Almighty God!
 For all the kindness thou hast shown
To this fair land the pilgrims trod,—
 This land we fondly call our own.

3 Here, Freedom spreads her banner wide,
 And casts her soft and hallowed ray;—
Here, thou our fathers' steps didst guide
 In safety, through their dangerous way,

4 We praise thee, that the gospel's light,
 Through all our land, its radiance sheds;
Dispels the shades of error's night,
 And heavenly blessings round us spreads.

5 Great God! preserve us in thy fear;
 In dangers still our guardian be;
Oh! spread thy truth's bright precepts here,—
 Let all the people worship thee.

61.

L. P. M.

National Praise and Prayer.

1 WITH grateful hearts, with joyful tongues,
To God we raise united songs;
 His power and mercy we proclaim:

Through every age, Oh ! may we own,
Jehovah here has fixed his throne,—
And triumph in his mighty name.

2 Long as the moon her course shall run,
Or men behold the circling sun,
Lord ! in our land, support thy reign ;
Crown her just counsels with success,
With truth and peace her borders bless,
And all thy sacred rights maintain.

CHRIST.

62.

C. M.

Christ's Nativity.

1 MORTALS ! awake ; with angels join,
And chant the solemn lay :
Joy, love, and gratitude, combine
To hail th' auspicious day.

2 In heaven the rapturous song began,
And sweet seraphic fire
Through all the shining legions ran,
And strung and tuned the lyre.

3 Swift, through the vast expanse, it flew,
And loud the echo rolled ;
The theme, the song, the joy was new,
'T was more than heaven could hold.

4 Down through the portals of the sky
Th' impetuous torrent ran ;
And angels flew, with eager joy,
To bear the news to man.

5 Hark ! the cherubic armies shout,
And glory leads the song ;
Good will and peace are heard throughout
Th' harmonious heavenly throng.

6 With joy the chorus we repeat—
"Glory to God on high !"
Good-will and peace are now complete ;
Jesus is born to die.

63.

8s and 7s.

Christ, the Saviour, born.

1 HAIL, thou long-expected Jesus!
Born to set thy people free;
From our sins and fears release us,
Let us find our rest in thee.

2 Israel's strength and consolation,
Hope of all the saints, thou art;
Long-desired of every nation,
Joy of every waiting heart.

3 Born, thy people to deliver,—
Born a child, yet God our King,—
Born to reign in us for ever,—
Now thy gracious kingdom bring.

4 By thine own eternal Spirit,
Rule in all our hearts alone;
By thine all-sufficient merit,
Raise us to thy glorious throne.

64.

C. M

The Redeemer's Message.

1 HARK the glad sound! the Saviour comes,—
The Saviour, promised long:
Let every heart prepare a throne,
And every voice a song.

2 On him the Spirit, largely poured,
Exerts his sacred fire;
Wisdom, and might, and zeal, and love,
His holy breast inspire.

3 He comes,—the pris'ners to release,
In Satan's bondage held;
The gates of brass before him burst—
The iron fetters yield.

4 He comes,—the broken heart to bind,
The bleeding soul to cure;
And, with the treasures of his grace,
T' enrich the humble poor.

5 Our glad hosannas, Prince of peace!
Thy welcome shall proclaim;
And heaven's eternal arches ring
With thy beloved name.

65.

S. M.

The Nativity of Christ

1 BEHOLD the grace appear—
  The blessing promised long!
Angels announce the Saviour near,
  In their triumphant song:—

2 "Glory to God on high,
  And heavenly peace on earth;
Good-will to men—to angels joy,
  At the Redeemer's birth.

3 In worship so divine
  Let saints employ their tongues;
With the celestial hosts we join,
  And loud repeat their songs:—

4 "Glory to God on high,
  And heavenly peace on earth;
Good-will to men—to angels joy,
  At our Redeemer's birth."

66.

7s.

Songs of the Angels.

1 HARK! the herald-angels sing,—
"Glory to the new-born King;
Peace on earth, and mercy mild,—
God and sinners reconciled."

2 Joyful, all ye nations! rise,
Join the triumph of the skies;
With th' angelic host, proclaim,—
"Christ is born in Bethlehem."

3 Mild he lays his glory by,
Born that man no more may die;
Born to raise the sons of earth;
Born to give them second birth.

4 Hail! the heaven-born Prince of peace!
Hail! the Sun of righteousness!
Light and life to all he brings,
Risen with healing in his wings.

5 Let us then with angels sing,—
"Glory to the new-born King;
Peace on earth, and mercy mild,—
God and sinners reconciled."

67.

H. M.

Joy at Immanuel's Birth.

1 HARK! hark!—the notes of joy
Roll o'er the heavenly plains,
And seraphs find employ
For their sublimest strains;
Some new delight in heaven is known;
Loud sound the harps around the throne.

2 Hark! hark!—the sounds draw nigh,
The joyful hosts descend;
Jesus forsakes the sky,
To earth his footsteps bend;
He comes to bless our fallen race;
He comes with messages of grace.

3 Bear, bear the tidings round;
Let every mortal know
What love in God is found,
What pity he can show;
Ye winds that blow! ye waves that roll!
Bear the glad news from pole to pole.

4 Strike, strike the harps again,
To great Immanuel's name;
Arise, ye sons of men!
And all his grace proclaim;
Angels and men! wake every string,
'T is God the Saviour's praise we sing.

68.

8s and 7s.

The Songs of Angels.

1 HARK! what mean those holy voices,
Sweetly sounding through the skies?
Lo! th' angelic host rejoices—
Heavenly hallelujahs rise.

2 Listen to the wondrous story
Which they chant in hymns of joy;—
"Glory in the highest, glory—
Glory be to God most high!

3 "Peace on earth, good-will from heaven,
Reaching far as man is found;
Souls redeemed, and sins forgiven;—
Loud our golden harps shall sound.

4 "Christ is born, the great Anointed;
Heaven and earth! his praises sing:
Oh! receive whom God appointed,
For your prophet, priest, and king.

5 "Hasten, mortals! to adore him;
Learn his name, and taste his joy;
Till in heaven ye sing before him,—
Glory be to God most high!"

69.

H. M.

The Birth of Christ.

1 HARK! what celestial notes,
What melody we hear!
Soft on the morn it floats,
And fills the ravished ear:
The tuneful shell,
The golden lyre,
And vocal choir
The concert swell.

2 Th' angelic hosts descend,
With harmony divine;
See how from heaven they bend,
And in full chorus join!
"Fear not," say they,
"Great joy we bring;—
Jesus, your King,
Is born to-day.

3 "He comes, from error's night,
Your wandering feet to save;
To realms of bliss and light,
He lifts you from the grave:
This glorious morn,
Let all attend;
Your matchless friend,
Your Saviour 's born.

4 "Glory to God on high!
Ye mortals! spread the sound,
And let your raptures fly,
To earth's remotest bound:
For peace on earth,
From God in heaven,
To man is given,
At Jesus' birth."

70.

8s and 7s.

The Incarnation

1 SHEPHERDS! hail the wondrous stranger;
Now to Bethle'm speed your way;
Lo! in yonder humble manger,
Christ, the Lord, is born to-day:—

2 Christ, by prophets long-predicted,
Joy of Israel's chosen race;
Light to Gentiles long-afflicted,
Lost in error's darkest maze.

3 Bright the star of your salvation,
Pointing to his rude abode!
Rapturous news for every nation:—
Mortals! now behold your God!

4 Glad, we trace th' amazing story,
Angels leave their bliss to tell;
Theme sublime, replete with glory—
Sinners saved from death and hell.

5 Love eternal moved the Saviour,
Thus to lay his radiance by;
Blessings on the Lamb for ever—
Glory be to God on high!

71.

7s.

The Star in the East.

1 SONS of men! behold from far,
Hail the long-expected star;—
Jacob's star, that gilds the night,
Guides bewildered nature right.

2 Never fear, that hence should flow
Wars or pestilence below:
Wars it bids, and tumults, cease,
Ushering in the Prince of peace.

3 Mild it shines on all beneath,
Piercing through the shades of death,—
Scattering error's wide-spread night,
Kindling darkness into light.

4 Nations all! far off and near,
Haste to see your God appear;
Haste, for him your hearts prepare,
Meet him manifested there.

72.
C. M.

Joy of Angels at the Saviour's Birth.

1 WHILE shepherds watched their flocks by night,
All seated on the ground,
The angel of the Lord came down,
And glory shone around.

2 "Fear not," said he, for mighty dread
Had seized their troubled mind,
"Glad tidings of great joy I bring,
To you and all mankind.

3 "To you, in David's town, this day,
Is born of David's line,
The Saviour, who is Christ, the Lord,
And this shall be the sign;—

4 "The heavenly babe you there shall find,
To human view displayed,
All meanly wrapped in swathing bands,
And in a manger laid."

5 Thus spake the seraph—and forthwith
Appeared a shining throng
Of angels, praising God, who thus
Addressed their joyful song:—

6 "All glory be to God on high,
And to the earth be peace;
Good-will henceforth from heaven to men,
Begin, and never cease!"

73.
8s, 7s and 4s.

Good Tidings of great Joy.

1 ANGELS! from the realms of glory,
Wing your flight o'er all the earth;
Ye, who sang creation's story,
Now proclaim Messiah's birth:
Come and worship—
Worship Christ, the new-born King.

2 Shepherds! in the field abiding,
Watching o'er your flocks by night,—
God with man is now residing,
Yonder shines the infant light:
Come and worship—
Worship Christ, the new-born King.

3 Sages! leave your contemplations—
Brighter visions beam afar;
Seek the great Desire of nations;
Ye have seen his natal star:
Come and worship—
Worship Christ, the new-born King.

4 Saints! before the altar bending,
Watching long in hope and fear,
Suddenly the Lord, descending,
In his temple shall appear:
Come and worship—
Worship Christ, the new-born King.

5 Sinners! wrung with true repentance,
Doomed for guilt to endless pains,
Justice now revokes the sentence,
Mercy calls you—break your chains:
Come and worship—
Worship Christ, the new-born King.

74.

11s and 10s.

Star of the East.

1 BRIGHTEST and best of the sons of the morning!
Dawn on our darkness, and lend us thine aid
Star of the East!—the horizon adorning—
Guide where the infant Redeemer is laid.

2 Cold on his cradle, the dew-drops are shining;
Low lies his head, with the beasts of the stall;
Angels adore him, in slumber reclining—
Maker, and Monarch, and Saviour of all.

3 Say, shall we yield him, in costly devotion,
Odors of Edom, and offerings divine?
Gems of the mountain, and pearls of the ocean,
Myrrh from the forest, or gold from the mine?

4 Vainly we offer each ample oblation,
Vainly with gold, would his favor secure;
Richer, by far, is the heart's adoration,—
Dearer to God, are the prayers of the poor.

5 Brightest and best of the sons of the morning!
Dawn on our darkness, and lend us thine aid;
Star of the east!—the horizon adorning—
Guide where our infant Redeemer is laid.

75.

C. M.

The Incarnation.

1 AWAKE, awake the sacred song
To our incarnate Lord!
Let every heart, and every tongue
Adore th' eternal Word.

2 That awful Word, that sovereign Power,
By whom the worlds were made,—
Oh! happy morn—illustrious hour!—
Was once in flesh arrayed.

3 Then shone almighty power and love,
In all their glorious forms,
When Jesus left his throne above,
To dwell with sinful worms.

4 To dwell with misery here below,
The Saviour left the skies,
And sunk to wretchedness and wo,
That worthless man might rise.

5 Adoring angels tuned their songs,
To hail the joyful day;
With rapture, then, let human tongues
Their grateful homage pay.

76.

C. M.

The Song of Angels.

1 ANGELS rejoiced and sweetly sung,
At our Redeemer's birth:
Mortals! awake; let every tongue
Proclaim his matchless worth.

2 Glory to God who dwells on high,
And sent his only Son
To take a servant's form, and die,
For evils we had done!

3 Good-will to men:—ye fallen race!
Arise, and shout for joy;
He comes with rich, abounding grace
To save, and not destroy.

4 Lord! send the gracious tidings forth,
And fill the world with light,
That Jew and Gentile, through the earth,
May know thy saving might.

5 Ye poor! who tremble at the word,
  Distressed, and helpless too,—
Oh! come and welcome to the Lord,
  For he was born for you.

77.

L. M.

The Star of Bethlehem.

1 WHEN, marshalled on the nightly plain,
  The glittering host bestud the sky;
One star alone, of all the train,
  Can fix the sinner's wandering eye.

2 Hark! hark!—to God the chorus breaks,
  From every host, from every gem;
But one alone the Saviour speaks,—
  It is the Star of Bethlehem.

3 Once on the raging seas I rode,
  The storm was loud, the night was dark,—
The ocean yawned—and rudely blowed
  The wind that tossed my foundering bark.

4 Deep horror then my vitals froze,
  Death-struck, I ceased the tide to stem;—
When suddenly a star arose,—
  It was the Star of Bethlehem.

5 It was my guide, my light, my all;
  It bade my dark forebodings cease;
And through the storm, and danger's thrall,
  It led me to the port of peace.

6 Now safely moored—my perils o'er,
  I'll sing, first in night's diadem,
For ever and for evermore,
  The Star—the Star of Bethlehem!

78.

C. M.

Christ's Commission.

1 COME, happy souls! approach your God,
  With new melodious songs;
Come, render to almighty grace
  The tributes of your tongues.

2 So strange, so boundless was the love,
  That pitied dying men,
The Father sent his equal Son
  To give them life again.

3 Thy hands, dear Jesus! were not armed
With a revenging rod;
No hard commission to perform
The vengeance of a God.

4 But all was mercy, all was mild,
And wrath forsook the throne,
When Christ, on the kind errand, came,
And brought salvation down.

5 Here, sinners! you may heal your wounds,
And wipe your sorrows dry;
Trust in the mighty Saviour's name,
And you shall never die.

6 See, dearest Lord! our willing souls
Accept thine offered grace;
We bless the great Redeemer's love,
And give the Father praise.

79. C. M.

Christ's Compassion to the Weak.

1 WITH joy we meditate the grace
Of our High-Priest above;
His heart is made of tenderness,
His bowels melt with love.

2 Touched with a sympathy within,
He knows our feeble frame;
He knows what sore temptations mean
For he has felt the same.

3 But spotless, innocent, and pure,
The great Redeemer stood;
While Satan's fiery darts he bore,
And did resist to blood.

4 He, in the days of feeble flesh,
Poured out his cries and tears,
And, in his measure, feels afresh
What every member bears.

5 Then let our humble faith address
His mercy and his power;
We shall obtain delivering grace,
In the distressing hour.

80. C. M.

God glorified in the Gospel.

1 THE Lord, descending from above,
Invites his children near;

While power, and truth, and boundless love,
  Display their glories here.

2 Here, in thy gospel's wondrous frame,
  Fresh wisdom we pursue;
A thousand angels learn thy name,
  Beyond whate'er they knew.

3 Thy name is writ in fairest lines,—
  Thy wonders here we trace;
Wisdom through all the mystery shines,—
  And shines in Jesus' face.

4 The law its best obedience owes
  To our incarnate God;
And thy revenging justice shows
  Its honors in his blood.

5 But still the lustre of thy grace
  Our warmer thoughts employs,
Gilds the whole scene with brighter rays,
  And more exalts our joys.

81.

L. M.

Peace and Hope through Christ's Intercession.

1 HE lives—the great Redeemer lives!
What joy the blest assurance gives!
And now, before his Father-God,
Pleads the full merits of his blood.

2 Repeated crimes awake our fears,
And justice, armed with frowns, appears;
But, in the Saviour's lovely face,
Sweet mercy smiles—and all is peace.

3 In every dark, distressful hour,
When sin and Satan join their power,
Let this dear hope repel the dart—
That Jesus bears us on his heart.

4 Great Advocate, almighty Friend!
On thee our humble hopes depend:
Our cause can never, never fail,
For Jesus pleads, and must prevail.

82.

C. M.

Praise to the Saviour.

1 OH! for a thousand tongues to sing
  My dear Redeemer's praise!

The glories of my God and King,
  The triumphs of his grace!

2 My gracious Master and my God!
  Assist me to proclaim,
To spread, through all the earth abroad,
  The honors of thy name.

3 Jesus—the name that calms my fears,
  That bids my sorrows cease;
'T is music to my ravished ears;
  'T is life, and health, and peace.

4 He breaks the power of reigning sin,
  He sets the pris'ner free;
His blood can make the foulest clean;
  His blood availed for me.

5 Let us obey, we then shall know,
  Shall feel our sins forgiven;
Anticipate our heaven below,
  And own, that love is heaven.

83.

L. M.

Hosannas to Christ.

1 WHAT are those soul-reviving strains
That echo thus from Salem's plains!
What anthems loud, and louder still,
Sweetly resound from Zion's hill?

2 Lo! 't is an infant chorus sings
Hosanna to the King of kings:
The Saviour comes, and babes proclaim
Salvation, sent in Jesus' name.

3 Nor these alone their voice shall raise,
For we will join this song of praise:
Still Israel's children forward press
To hail the Lord, their righteousness.

4 Proclaim hosannas loud and clear:
See David's son and Lord appear!
Glory and praise on earth be given,—
Hosanna in the highest heaven.

84.

C. M.

Jesus, my Trust.

1 JESUS! I love thy charming name,
  'T is music to mine ear;

Fain would I sound it out so loud,
That earth and heaven should hear.

2 Yes,—thou art precious to my soul,
My joy, my hope, my trust;
Jewels, to thee, are gaudy toys,
And gold is sordid dust.

3 All my capacious powers can wish,
In thee most richly meet;
Nor to mine eyes is light so dear,
Nor friendship half so sweet.

4 Thy grace still dwells upon my heart,
And sheds its fragrance there;—
The healing balm of all its wounds,
The cordial of its care.

5 I 'll speak the honors of thy name,
With my last lab'ring breath;
Then, speechless, clasp thee in mine arms,—
The antidote of death.

85.

C. M.

God reconciled in Christ.

1 DEAREST of all the names above,
My Jesus and my God!
Who can resist thy heavenly love,
Or trifle with thy blood?

2 'T is by the merits of thy death,
The Father smiles again;
'T is by thine interceding breath,
The Spirit dwells with men.

3 Till God in human flesh I see,
My thoughts no comfort find;
The holy, just, and sacred Three,
Are terrors to my mind.

4 But, if Immanuel's face appear,
My hope, my joy begins;
His name forbids my slavish fear,
His grace removes my sins.

5 While Jews on their own law rely
And Greeks of wisdom boast;—
I love th' incarnate mystery,
And there I fix my trust.

86.

C. P. M.

The Excellency of Christ.

1 OH! could I speak the matchless worth,—
Oh! could I sound the glories forth,
Which in my Saviour shine;
I 'd soar and touch the heavenly strings,
And vie with Gabriel while he sings,
In notes almost divine.

2 I 'd sing the characters he bears,
And all the forms of love he wears,
Exalted on his throne;
In loftiest songs of sweetest praise,
I would, to everlasting days,
Make all his glories known.

3 Soon the delightful day will come,
When my dear Lord will bring me home,
And I shall see his face;
Then, with my Saviour, brother, friend,
A blest eternity I 'll spend—
Triumphant in his grace.

87.

C. M.

Christ, the living Fountain.

1 THERE is a fountain filled with blood,
Drawn from Immanuel's veins;
And sinners, plunged beneath that flood,
Lose all their guilty stains.

2 The dying thief rejoiced to see
That fountain in his day;
And there may I, though vile as he,
Wash all my sins away.

3 Dear dying Lamb! thy precious blood
Shall never lose its power,
Till all the ransomed church of God
Be saved, to sin no more.

4 E'er since, by faith, I saw the stream
Thy flowing wounds supply,
Redeeming love has been my theme,
And shall be, till I die.

5 Then in a nobler, sweeter song,
I 'll sing thy power to save,
When this poor lisping, stammering tongue
Lies silent in the grave.

88.

C. M.

Sun of Righteousness.

1 RISE, glorious Sun! supremely bright
  Diffuse thy rays abroad;
Scatter the shades of gloomy night,
  And show the heavenly road.

2 With healing in thy wings, arise
  On this dark soul of mine;
Oh! pour thy glories from the skies,
  And give me life divine.

3 Though thorns and briers, pits and snares,
  Beset the path I go,
One ray of thine dispels my fears,
  And guides me safely through.

89.

S. M.

Christ, suffering for our Sins

1 LIKE sheep we went astray,
  And broke the fold of God;
Each wandering in a different way,
  But all the downward road.

2 How dreadful was the hour,
  When God our wanderings laid,
And did at once his vengeance pour
  Upon the shepherd's head!

3 How glorious was the grace,
  When Christ sustained the stroke!
His life and blood the shepherd pays,
  A ransom for the flock.

4 But God shall raise his head,
  O'er all the sons of men,
And make him see a numerous seed
  To recompense his pain.

5 "I 'll give him," saith the Lord,
  "A portion with the strong;
He shall possess a large reward,
  And hold his honors long."

90.

L. M.

The Teaching of Jesus.

1 HOW sweetly flowed the gospel's sound
  From lips of gentleness and grace,

While listening thousands gathered round,
And joy and reverence filled the place!

2 From heaven he came, of heaven he spoke,
To heaven he led his foll'wers' way;
Dark clouds of gloomy night he broke,
Unveiling an immortal day.

3 Come, wanderers! to my Father's home,
Come, all ye weary ones! and rest:—
Yes, sacred Teacher! we will come,
Obey, and be for ever blest.

4 Decay, then, tenements of dust!
Pillars of earthly pride! decay;
A nobler mansion waits the just,
And Jesus has prepared the way.

91. S. M.

Preserving Grace.

1 TO God, the only-wise,
Our Saviour and our King,
Let all the saints, below the skies,
Their humble praises bring.

2 'T is his almighty love,
His counsel and his care,
Preserves us safe from sin and death,
And every hurtful snare.

3 He will present our souls,
Unblemished and complete,
Before the glory of his face,
With joys divinely great.

4 Then all the chosen seed
Shall meet around the throne;
Shall bless the conduct of his grace,
And make his wonders known

5 To our Redeemer-God,
Wisdom, with power, belongs;
Immortal crowns of majesty,
And everlasting songs.

92. L. M.

Love of Christ.

1 I WAS a traitor doomed to die,
Bound to endure eternal pains;

When Jesus saw me from on high,
Was moved by love, and broke my chains.

2 Did melting pity stoop so low,
The Lord from heaven pour out his blood,
To save our rebel-race from wo,
And be our advocate with God?

3 Infinite mercy! boundless love!
Stand in amaze, ye rolling skies!
The Son of God, his grace to prove,
Hangs on a tree, and groans, and dies!

93.

S. M.

The Light of the World.

1 HOW heavy is the night
That hangs upon our eyes,
Till Christ, with his reviving light,
Over our souls arise!

2 Our guilty spirits dread
To meet the wrath of heaven:
But in his righteousness arrayed,
We see our sins forgiven.

3 Unholy and impure
Are all our thoughts and ways;
His hands infected nature cure,
With sanctifying grace.

4 The powers of hell agree
To hold our souls in vain:
He sets the sons of bondage free,
And breaks the cursed chain.

5 Lord! we adore thy ways
To bring us near to God;
Thy sovereign power, thy healing grace
And thine atoning blood.

94.

7s.

Sun of Righteousness.

1 CHRIST, whose glory fills the skies,—
Christ, the true, the only light,—
Sun of Righteousness! arise,
Triumph o'er the shades of night:
Day-spring from on high! be near,
Day-star! in my heart appear.

2 Dark and cheerless is the morn,
If thy light is hid from me;
Joyless is the day's return,
Till thy mercy's beams I see;
Till they inward light impart,—
Peace and gladness to my heart.

3 Visit, then, this soul of mine,
Pierce the gloom of sin and grief;
Fill me, Radiancy divine!
Scatter all my unbelief:
More and more thyself display,
Shining to the perfect day.

95.

C. M.

Praise to the Redeemer.

1 PLUNGED in a gulf of dark despair,
We wretched sinners lay,
Without one cheerful beam of hope,
Or spark of glimmering day.

2 With pitying eyes the Prince of grace
Beheld our helpless grief;
He saw, and—Oh! amazing love!—
He ran to our relief.

3 Down from the shining seats above,
With joyful haste he fled,
Entered the grave in mortal flesh,
And dwelt among the dead.

4 Oh! for this love let rocks and hills
Their lasting silence break;
And all harmonious human tongues
The Saviour's praises speak.

5 Angels! assist our mighty joys;
Strike all your harps of gold;
But when you raise your highest notes,
His love can ne'er be told.

96.

C. M.

Pearl of great Price.

1 YE glittering toys of earth! adieu;—
A nobler choice be mine;
A real prize attracts my view,—
A treasure all divine.

2 Begone, unworthy of my cares,
   Ye flattering baits of sense!
 Inestimable worth appears,—
   The pearl of price immense.

3 Should both the Indies, at my call,
   Their boasted stores resign,
 With joy I would renounce them all,
   For leave to call thee mine.

4 Should earth's vain treasures all depart,
   Of this dear gift possessed,
 I 'd clasp it to my joyful heart,
   And be for ever blessed.

5 Dear Sovereign of my soul's desires!
   Thy love is bliss divine;
 Accept the praise that grace inspires
   Since I can call thee mine.

97. C. M.

Christ, our Support in Death.

1 JESUS! the vision of thy face
   Hath overpowering charms:
 Scarce shall I feel death's cold embrace,
   While in the Saviour's arms.

2 And while ye hear my heart-strings break,
   How sweet the minutes roll!
 A mortal paleness on my cheek,
   And glory in my soul.

98. L. M.

Christ, our Wisdom and our Righteousness

1 BURIED in shadows of the night,
 We lie, till Christ restores the light;
 Wisdom descends to heal the blind,
 And chase the darkness of the mind.

2 Our guilty souls are drowned in tears,
 Till his atoning blood appears;
 Then we awake from deep distress,
 And sing the Lord, our righteousness.

3 Jesus beholds where Satan reigns,
 Binding his slaves in heavy chains:
 He sets the pris'ners free, and breaks
 The iron bondage from our necks

4 Poor helpless worms in thee possess
Grace, wisdom, power, and righteousness:
Thou art our mighty All—and we
Give our whole selves, O Lord! to thee.

99.

S. M.

All Things in Christ.

1 THOU very-present Aid
In suffering and distress!
The mind, which still on thee is stayed,
Is kept in perfect peace.

2 The soul, by faith reclined
On the Redeemer's breast,
Mid raging storms, exults to find
An everlasting rest.

3 Sorrow and fear are gone,
Whene'er thy face appears;
It stills the sighing orphan's moan,
And dries the widow's tears.

4 It hallows every cross,
It sweetly comforts me;
It makes me now forget my loss,
And lose myself in thee.

5 Jesus, to whom I fly,
Will all my wishes fill;
What though created streams are dry?
I have the fountain still.

6 Stripped of my earthly friends,
I find them all in one:
And peace, and joy which never ends,
And heaven, in Christ, begun.

100.

L. M.

The Mercy of God in Christ.

1 NOT to condemn the sons of men,
Did Christ, the Son of God, appear;
No weapons in his hands are seen,
No flaming sword, nor thunder there.

2 Such was the pity of our God,
He loved the race of man so well,
He sent his Son, to bear our load
Of sins, and save our souls from hell.

3 Sinners! believe the Saviour's word,
Trust in his mighty name and live;
A thousand joys his lips afford,
His hands a thousand blessings give.

101.

L. M.

Love of Christ in the Heart.

1 COME, dearest Lord! descend and dwell,
By faith and love in every breast;
Then shall we know, and taste, and feel,
The joys that cannot be expressed.

2 Come, fill our hearts with inward strength;
Make our enlarged souls possess,
And learn the height, and breadth, and length,
Of thine eternal love and grace.

3 Now to the God whose power can do
More than our thoughts and wishes know,
Be everlasting honors done
By all the church, through Christ, the Son.

102.

S. M.

Vital Union to Christ.

1 DEAR Saviour! we are thine
By everlasting bonds;
Our names, our hearts, we would resign;
Our hearts are in thy hands.

2 To thee we still would cleave,
With ever-growing zeal;
If millions tempt us Christ to leave,
Oh! let them ne'er prevail.

3 Thy Spirit shall unite
Our souls to thee, our head;
Shall form us to thine image brigh
That we thy paths may tread.

4 Death may our souls divide
From these abodes of clay;
But love shall keep us near thy side
Through all the gloomy way.

5 Since Christ and we are one,
Why should we doubt and fear?
If he in heaven hath fixed his throne,
He 'll fix his members there.

103.

C. M.

God's Love in Christ.

1 THE Saviour!—Oh! what endless charms
Dwell in the blissful sound!
Its influence every fear disarms,
And spreads sweet peace around.

2 Here pardon, life, and joys divine,
In rich effusion flow,
For guilty rebels lost in sin,
And doomed to endless wo.

3 Oh! the rich depths of love divine,
Of bliss a boundless store!
Dear Saviour! let me call thee mine;
I cannot wish for more.

4 On thee alone my hope relies,
Beneath thy cross I fall;
My Lord, my life, my sacrifice,
My Saviour, and my all!

104.

H. M.

Mission of Christ.

1 COME, every pious heart,
That loves the Saviour's name!
Your noblest powers exert
To celebrate his fame;
Tell all above, and all below,
The debt of love to him you owe.

2 He left his starry crown,
And laid his robes aside;
On wings of love, came down,
And wept, and bled, and died:
What he endured no tongue can tell,
To save our souls from death and hell.

3 From the dark grave he rose,—
The mansion of the dead;
And thence his mighty foes
In glorious triumph led;
Up through the sky the conqueror rode,
And reigns on high, the Saviour-God.

4 From thence he'll quickly come,—
His chariot will not stay,—

And bear our spirits home
  To realms of endless day:
There shall we see his lovely face,
And ever be in his embrace.

105.

C. M.

King of Saints.

1 COME, ye that love the Saviour's name,
  And joy to make it known!
The sovereign of your hearts proclaim,
  And bow before the throne.

2 Behold your King, your Saviour, crowned
  With glories all-divine;
And tell the wondering nations round,
  How bright these glories shine.

3 Infinite power and boundless grace,
  In him unite their rays;
Ye that have e'er beheld his face!
  Can ye forbear his praise?

4 When in his earthly courts we view
  The beauties of our King,
We long to love as angels do,
  And wish like them to sing.

5 And shall we long and wish in vain?
  Lord! teach our songs to rise;
Thy love can animate the strain,
  And bid it reach the skies.

106.

C. M.

A new Song to the Lamb.

1 BEHOLD the glories of the Lamb,
  Amidst his Father's throne!
Prepare new honors for his name,
  And songs, before unknown.

2 Let elders worship at his feet,
  The church adore around;
With vials full of odors sweet,
  And harps of sweeter sound.

3 Those are the prayers of all the saints,
  And these the hymns they raise:
Jesus is kind to our complaints,
  He loves to hear our praise.

4 Now to the Lamb, that once was slain,
Be endless blessings paid;
Salvation, glory, joy, remain
For ever, on thy head.

5 Thou hast redeemed our souls with blood,
Hast set the pris'ners free,
Hast made us kings and priests to God,
And we shall reign with thee.

107. C. M.

Asking the Presence of Christ.

1 COME, thou desire of all thy saints!
Our humble strains attend,
While, with our praises and complaints,
Low at thy feet we bend.

2 How should our songs, like those above,
With warm devotion rise!
How should our souls, on wings of love,
Mount upward to the skies!

3 Come, Lord! thy love alone can raise
In us the heavenly flame;
Then shall our lips resound thy praise
Our hearts adore thy name.

4 Dear Saviour! let thy glory shine
And fill thy dwellings here,
Till life, and love, and joy divine
A heaven on earth appear.

5 Then shall our hearts enraptured say,—
Come, great Redeemer! come,
And bring the bright, the glorious day,
That calls thy children home.

108. L. M.

Divinity of Christ proved by his Miracles.

1 BEHOLD! the blind their sight receive;
Behold! the dead awake and live;
The dumb speak wonders—and the lame
Leap, like the hart, and bless his name.

2 Thus doth th' eternal Spirit own
And seal the mission of the Son;
The Father vindicates his cause,
While he hangs bleeding on the cross.

3 He dies—the heavens in mourning stood!—
He rises, and appears a God;
Behold the Lord ascending high,—
No more to bleed—no more to die!

4 Hence, and for ever from my heart
I bid my doubts and fears depart;
And to those hands my soul resign,
Which bear credentials so divine.

109.

L. M.

Christ, our Righteousness.

1 JESUS! thy robe of righteousness
My beauty is,—my glorious dress:
Mid flaming worlds, in this arrayed,
With joy shall I lift up my head.

2 When, from the dust of death, I rise
To claim my mansion in the skies,
E'en then shall this be all my plea,—
"Jesus hath lived and died for me."

3 This spotless robe the same appears,
When ruined nature sinks in years;
No age can change its glorious hue;—
The robe of Christ is ever new.

4 Oh! let the dead now hear thy voice;
Now bid thy banished ones rejoice;
Their beauty this—their glorious dress,
Jesus, the Lord, our righteousness.

110.

L. M.

The example of Christ.

1 MY dear Redeemer, and my Lord!
I read my duty in thy word,
But in thy life the law appears,
Drawn out in living characters.

2 Such was thy truth, and such thy zeal,
Such deference to thy Father's will,—
Such love and meekness so divine,
I would transcribe and make them mine.

3 Cold mountains, and the midnight-air,
Witnessed the fervor of thy prayer;
The desert thy temptations knew,
Thy conflict, and thy vict'ry too.

4 Be thou my pattern ;—make me bear
More of thy gracious image here;
Then God, the judge, shall own my name,
Among the foll'wers of the Lamb.

111.

6s and 4s.

Worthy the Lamb.

1 GLORY to God on high!
Let heaven and earth reply—
" Praise ye his name!"
His love and grace adore,
Who all our sorrows bore;
And sing for ever more—
"Worthy the Lamb!"

2 Ye who surround the throne!
Cheerfully join in one,
Praising his name:
Ye who have felt his blood
Sealing your peace with God!
Sound his dear name abroad,—
"Worthy the Lamb!"

3 Join, all ye ransomed race!
Our Lord and God to bless;
Praise ye his name:
In him we will rejoice,
And make a joyful noise,
Shouting with heart and voice—
"Worthy the Lamb!"

4 Soon must we change our place,
Yet will we never cease
Praising his name:
To him our songs we 'll bring,
Hail him our gracious King,
And through all ages sing—
"Worthy the Lamb!"

112.

C. M.

Praise from Saints and Angels.

1 COME, let us join our cheerful songs,
With angels round the throne;
Ten thousand thousand are their tongues,
But all their joys are one.

2 "Worthy the Lamb that died," they cry
"To be exalted thus!"

"Worthy the Lamb," our lips reply,
"For he was slain for us!"

3 Jesus is worthy to receive
Honor and power divine;
And blessings, more than we can give,
Be, Lord! for ever thine.

4 Let all who dwell above the sky,
And air, and earth, and seas,
Conspire to lift thy glories high,
And speak thine endless praise.

5 The whole creation join in one,
To bless the sacred name
Of him who sits upon the throne,
And to adore the Lamb.

113.

L. M.

Blessing and Honor to the Lamb.

1 WHAT equal honors shall we bring
To thee, O Lord, our God, the Lamb!
When all the notes that angels sing
Are far inferior to thy name?

2 Worthy is he who once was slain,—
The Prince of peace, who groaned and died,—
Worthy to rise, and live, and reign,
At his almighty Father's side.

3 Honor immortal must be paid,
Instead of scandal and of scorn;
While glory shines around his head,
And a bright crown without a thorn.

4 Blessings for ever on the Lamb,
Who bore the curse for wretched men!
Let angels sound his sacred name,
And every creature say,—Amen.

114.

C. M.

Love to Christ desired.

1 THOU lovely source of true delight,
Whom I unseen adore!
Unveil thy beauties to my sight,
That I may love thee more.

2 Thy glory o'er creation shines;—
But in thy sacred word,

I read, in fairer, brighter lines,
  My bleeding, dying Lord.

3 'T is here, whene'er my comforts droop,
  And sin and sorrow rise,
Thy love, with cheering beams of hope,
  My fainting heart supplies.

4 But ah! too soon the pleasing scene
  Is clouded o'er with pain;
My gloomy fears rise dark between,
  And I again complain.

5 Jesus, my Lord, my life, my light!
  Oh! come with blissful ray;
Break radiant through the shades of night,
  And chase my fears away.

6 Then shall my soul with rapture trace
  The wonders of thy love:
But the full glories of thy face
  Are only known above.

115. L. M.

Christ, our High Priest and King.

1 NOW to the Lord, who makes us know
  The wonders of his dying love,
Be humble honors paid below,
  And strains of nobler praise above.

2 'T was he that cleansed our foulest sins,
  And washed us in his richest blood;
'T is he that makes us priests and kings,
  And brings us rebels near to God.

3 To Jesus, our atoning priest,
  To Jesus, our superior king,
Be everlasting power confessed,
  And every tongue his glory sing.

4 Behold! on flying clouds he comes,
  And every eye shall see him move:
Though with our sins we pierced him once,
  Then he displays his pard'ning love.

5 The unbelieving world shall wail,
  While we rejoice to see the day:
Come, Lord! nor let thy promise fail,
  Nor let thy chariot long delay.

116.

8s and 7s. Peculiar.

Christ, the Lamb, enthroned and worshiped.

1 HARK!—ten thousand harps and voices
Sound the note of praise above,
Jesus reigns, and heaven rejoices;—
Jesus reigns, the God of love:
See! he sits on yonder throne;
Jesus rules the world alone.

2 Jesus! hail! whose glory brightens
All above, and gives it worth;
Lord of life! thy smile enlightens,
Cheers, and charms thy saints on earth:
When we think of love like thine,
Lord! we own it love divine.

3 King of glory! reign for ever—
Thine an everlasting crown;
Nothing, from thy love, shall sever
Those whom thou hast made thine own;—
Happy objects of thy grace,
Destined to behold thy face.

4 Saviour! hasten thine appearing;
Bring—Oh! bring the glorious day,
When the awful summons hearing,
Heaven and earth shall pass away;—
Then, with golden harps, we 'll sing,—
"Glory, glory to our King."

117.

8s and 7s.

Praise to God, the Saviour.

1 MIGHTY God! while angels bless thee,
May a mortal lisp thy name?
Lord of men, as well as angels!
Thou art every creature's theme:
Lord of every land and nation!
Ancient of eternal days!
Sounded through the wide creation,
Be thy just and lawful praise.

2 For the grandeur of thy nature,—
Grand beyond a seraph's thought;—
For the wonders of creation,
Works with skill and kindness wrought;—
For thy providence, that governs
Through thine empire's wide domain,

Wings an angel, guides a sparrow ;—
Blessed be thy gentle reign.

3 For thy rich, thy free redemption,
Bright, though veiled in darkness long ;—
Thought is poor, and poor expression,
Who can sing that wondrous song ?
Brightness of the Father's glory !
Shall thy praise unuttered lie ?
Break, my tongue ! such guilty silence,
Sing the Lord who came to die :—

4 From the highest throne of glory,
To the cross of deepest wo,
Came to ransom guilty captives !—
Flow, my praise ! for ever flow :
Re-ascend, immortal Saviour !
Leave thy footstool, take thy throne,
Thence return and reign for ever ;—
Be the kingdom all thine own !

118.

S. M.

Moses and Christ.

1 THE law by Moses came ;
But peace and truth and love
Were brought by Christ, a nobler name,
Descending from above.

2 Amidst the house of God,
Their different works were done ;
Moses a faithful servant stood,
But Christ a faithful Son.

3 Then to his new commands
Be strict obedience paid ;
O'er all his Father's house he stands,
The sovereign and the head.

4 The man, who durst despise
The law that Moses brought—
Behold ! how terribly he dies
For his presumptuous fault.

5 But sorer vengeance falls
On that rebellious race;
Who hate to hear when Jesus calls,
And dare resist his grace.

119.

C. M.

Various Success of the Gospel.

1 CHRIST and his cross is all our theme;
The mysteries that we speak
Are scandal in the Jews' esteem,
And folly to the Greek.

2 But souls, enlightened from above,
With joy receive the word;
They see what wisdom, power, and love,
Shine in their dying Lord.

3 The vital savor of his name
Restores their fainting breath;
But unbelief perverts the same
To guilt, despair, and death.

4 Till God diffuse his graces down,
Like showers of heavenly rain,
In vain Apollos sows the ground,
And Paul may plant in vain.

120.

8s and 7s.

The Light of the World.

1 LIGHT of those whose dreary dwelling
Borders on the shades of death!
Come, and, by thy love revealing,
Dissipate the clouds beneath:
The new heaven and earth's Creator,
In our deepest darkness rise,—
Scattering all the night of nature,
Pouring eye-sight on our eyes.

2 Still we wait for thine appearing;
Life and joy thy beams impart,
Chasing all our fears, and cheering
Every poor benighted heart:
Come, and manifest thy favor
To the ransomed, helpless race;
Come, thou glorious God and Saviour!
Come, and bring the gospel-grace.

3 Save us, in thy great compassion,
O thou mild, pacific Prince!
Give the knowledge of salvation,
Give the pardon of our sins;
By thine all-sufficient merit,
Every burdened soul release;

Every weary, wandering spirit,
  Guide into thy perfect peace.

121.

H. M.

Christ, our King.

1 REJOICE! the Lord is King!—
  Your God and King adore;
Mortals! give thanks, and sing,
  And triumph evermore:
Lift up the heart,—lift up the voice,—
Rejoice aloud, ye saints! rejoice.

2 His kingdom cannot fail;
  He rules o'er earth and heaven;
The keys of death and hell
  Are to our Jesus given:
Lift up the heart,—lift up the voice,—
Rejoice aloud, ye saints! rejoice.

3 He all his foes shall quell,—
  Shall all our sins destroy,
And every bosom swell
  With pure seraphic joy:
Lift up the heart,—lift up the voice,—
Rejoice aloud, ye saints! rejoice.

4 Rejoice in glorious hope;
  Jesus, the judge, shall come,
And take his servants up
  To their eternal home:
We soon shall hear th' archangel's voice;
The trump of God shall sound,—Rejoice.

122.

L. M.

God, the Son, equal with the Father.

1 BRIGHT King of glory, dreadful God!
  Our spirits bow before thy seat;
To thee we lift an humble thought,
  And worship at thine awful feet.

2 A thousand seraphs, strong and bright,
  Stand round the glorious Deity;
But who, among the sons of light,
  Pretends comparison with thee?

3 Yet one there is, of human frame,—
  Jesus, arrayed in flesh and blood,—

Thinks it no robbery to claim
  A full equality with God.

4 Their glory shines with equal beams,
  Their essence is for ever one:
Though they are known by different names,
  The Father-God, and God, the Son.

5 Then let the name of Christ, our king,
  With equal honors be adored;
His praise let every angel sing,
  And all the nations own him—Lord.

123.

12s.

The Voice of free Grace.

1 THE voice of free grace cries—"Escape to the mountain!"
For Adam's lost race, Christ hath opened a fountain;
For sin and uncleanness, and every transgression,
His blood flows most freely, in streams of salvation.

CHORUS.

Hallelujah to the Lamb! he hath purchased our pardon,
We 'll praise him again, when we pass over Jordan.

2 Ye souls that are wounded! Oh! flee to the Saviour;
He calls you in mercy,—'t is infinite favor
Your sins are increasing,—escape to the mountain,—
His blood can remove them, it flows from the fountain.

3 O Jesus! ride onward, triumphantly glorious,
O'er sin, death and hell, thou art more than victorious;
Thy name is the theme of the great congregation,
While angels and saints raise the shout of salvation.

4 With joy shall we stand, when escaped to the shore;
With harps in our hands, we 'll praise him the more;
We 'll range the sweet plains on the bank of the river,
And sing of salvation for ever and ever!

124.

C. M.

Christ precious.

1 HOW sweet the name of Jesus sounds
  In a believer's ear!
It soothes his sorrows, heals his wounds,
  And drives away his fear.

2 It makes the wounded spirit whole,
And calms the troubled breast;
'T is manna to the hungry soul,
And, to the weary, rest.

3 Jesus!—my shepherd, husband, friend,
My prophet, priest, and king,
My Lord, my life, my way, my end,—
Accept the praise I bring.

4 Weak is the effort of my heart,
And cold my warmest thought,
But, when I see thee as thou art,
I 'll praise thee as I ought.

5 Till then, I would thy love proclaim,
With every fleeting breath;
And may the music of thy name
Refresh my soul in death.

125.

L. M.

Life in Christ.

1 WHEN sins and fears prevailing rise,
And fainting hope almost expires,
Jesus! to thee I lift mine eyes,—
To thee I breathe my soul's desires.

2 If my immortal Saviour lives,
Then my immortal life is sure;
His word a firm foundation gives;
Here let me build, and rest secure.

3 Here let my faith unshaken dwell,
For ever firm the promise stands;
Not all the powers of earth and hell
Can e'er dissolve the sacred bands.

4 Here, O my soul! thy trust repose;
If Jesus is for ever mine,
Not death itself—that last of foes—
Shall break a union so divine.

126.

L. M.

Communion with Christ.

1 OH! that I could for ever dwell,
Delighted at the Saviour's feet,
Behold the form I love so well,
And all his tender words repeat:—

2 The world shut out from all my soul,
  And heaven brought in with all its bliss:—
Oh! is there aught, from pole to pole,
  One moment, to compare with this?

3 This is the hidden life I prize,—
  A life of penitential love;
When most my follies I despise,
  And raise my highest thoughts above:

4 When all I am, I clearly see,
  And freely own, with deepest shame;
When the Redeemer's love to me
  Kindles within a deathless flame.

5 Thus would I live, till nature fail,
  And all my former sins forsake;
Then rise to God, within the veil,
  And of eternal joys partake.

127.

L. M.

Christ, the supreme God and King.

1 AROUND the Saviour's lofty throne,
  Ten thousand times ten thousand sing;
They worship him as God alone,
  And crown him—everlasting King.

2 Approach, ye saints! this God is yours;
  'T is Jesus, fills the throne above:
Ye cannot want, while God endures;
  Ye cannot fail, while God is love.

3 Jesus, thou everlasting King!
  To thee the praise of heaven belongs;
Yet, smile on us who fain would bring
  The tribute of our humble songs.

4 Though sin defile our worship here,
  We hope ere-long thy face to view;
And, when our souls in heaven appear,
  We 'll praise thy name as angels do.

128.

7s.

Jesus, the Refuge.

1 JESUS, lover of my soul!
  Let me to thy bosom fly,
While the billows near me roll,
  While the tempest still is high;

Hide me, O my Saviour! hide,
  Till the storm of life be past;
Safe into the haven guide;
  Oh! receive my soul at last.

2 Other refuge have I none,—
  Hangs my helpless soul on thee
Leave, ah! leave me not alone;
  Still support and comfort me:
All my trust on thee is stayed;
  All my help from thee I bring;
Cover my defenceless head,
  With the shadow of thy wing.

3 Plenteous grace with thee is found,—
  Grace to pardon all my sin;
Let the healing streams abound,
  Make and keep me pure within;
Thou of life the fountain art,
  Freely let me take of thee;
Spring thou up within my heart,
  Rise to all eternity.

129. L. M.

Christ, the only Refuge.

1 THOU only Sovereign of my heart,
  My refuge, my almighty friend!
And can my soul from thee depart,
  On whom alone my hopes depend?

2 Whither, ah! whither shall I go,
  A wretched wanderer from my Lord?
Can this dark world of sin and wo
  One glimpse of happiness afford?

3 Eternal life thy words impart,
  On these my fainting spirit lives;
Here sweeter comforts cheer my heart,
  Than all the round of nature gives.

4 Let earth's alluring joys combine;
  While thou art near, in vain they call;
One smile—one blissful smile of thine,—
  My dearest Lord! outweighs them all.

5 Low at thy feet my soul would lie,—
  Here safety dwells and peace divine;

Still let me live beneath thine eye,
For life—eternal life—is thine.

130.

C. M.

Jesus, seen of Angels.

1 BEYOND the glittering, starry skies,
Far as th' eternal hills,
There, in the boundless worlds of light,
Our dear Redeemer dwells.

2 Legions of angels round his throne,
In countless armies shine;
And swell his praise with golden harps,
Attuned to songs divine.

3 "Hail, glorious Prince of peace!" they cry,
"Whose unexampled love
Moved thee to quit these glorious realms,
And royalties above."

4 Through all his travels here below,
They did his steps attend;
Oft wondering how, or where, at last.
The mystic scene would end.

5 They saw his heart transfixed with wounds,
And viewed the crimson gore;
They saw him break the bars of death,
Which none e'er broke before.

6 They brought his chariot from above,
To bear him to his throne;
Clapped their triumphant wings, and cried,—
"The glorious work is done!"

131.

7s and 6s.

Praise to the Saviour.

1 TO thee, my God and Saviour!
My heart exulting sings,
Rejoicing in thy favor,
Almighty King of kings!
I'll celebrate thy glory,
With all thy saints above,
And tell the joyful story
Of thy redeeming love.

2 Soon as the morn, with roses,
Bedecks the dewy east,

And when the sun reposes
  Upon the ocean's breast;
My voice, in supplication,
  Well-pleased the Lord shall hear:
Oh! grant me thy salvation,
  And to my soul draw near.

3 By thee, through life supported,
  I 'll pass the dangerous road,
With heavenly hosts escorted,
  Up to thy bright abode;
Then cast my crown before thee,
  And, all my conflicts o'er,
Unceasingly adore thee:—
  What could an angel more?

132.

L. M.

Glory and Grace in Christ.

1 NOW to the Lord a noble song!
Awake, my soul! awake, my tongue!
Hosanna to th' eternal name,
And all his boundless love proclaim.

2 See where it shines in Jesus' face,—
The brightest image of his grace!
God, in the person of his Son,
Has all his mightiest works outdone.

3 Grace!—'t is a sweet, a charming theme;
My thoughts rejoice at Jesus' name:
Ye angels! dwell upon the sound;
Ye heavens! reflect it to the ground.

4 Oh! may I reach that happy place
Where he unveils his lovely face;
Where all his beauties you behold,
And sing his name to harps of gold.

133.

L. M.

The Presence of the Saviour.

1 LORD! what a heaven of saving grace
Shines through the beauties of thy face,
And lights our passions to a flame!
Lord! how we love thy charming name!

2 When I can say,—my God is mine,—
When I can feel thy glories shine,

I tread the world beneath my feet,
And all that earth calls good or great.

3 While such a scene of sacred joys
Our raptured eyes and souls employs,
Here we could sit and gaze away
A long, an everlasting day.

4 Well, we shall quickly pass the night,
To the fair coasts of perfect light;
Then shall our joyful senses rove
O'er the dear object of our love.

5 Send comforts down from thy right hand,
While we pass through this barren land,
And in thy temple let us see
A glimpse of love, a glimpse of thee.

134.

C. M.

Christ, our Example.

1 BEHOLD! where, in a mortal form,
Appears each grace divine:
The virtues, all in Jesus met,
With mildest radiance shine.

2 To spread the rays of heavenly light,
To give the mourner joy,
To preach glad tidings to the poor,
Was his divine employ.

3 Mid keen reproach and cruel scorn,
He, meek and patient, stood;
His foes, ungrateful, sought his life,
Who labored for their good.

4 When, in the hour of deep distress,
Before his Father's throne,
With soul resigned, he bowed, and said,—
"Thy will, not mine, be done!"

5 Be Christ our pattern, and our guide,
His image may we bear;
Oh! may we tread his holy steps,—
His joy and glory share.

135.

C. M.

The Glory of Christ in Heaven.

1 OH! the delights, the heavenly joys,
The glories of the place,

Where Jesus sheds the brightest beams
  Of his o'erflowing grace!

2 Sweet majesty and awful love
  Sit smiling on his brow;
And all the glorious ranks above,
  At humble distance bow.

3 Archangels sound his lofty praise,
  Through every heavenly street;
And lay their heavenly honors down,
  Submissive, at his feet.

4 This is the man, th' exalted man,
  Whom we, unseen, adore;
But when our eyes behold his face,
  Our hearts shall love him more.

5 Lord! how our souls are all on fire,
  To see thy blest abode;
Our tongues rejoice in tunes of praise
  To our incarnate God.

136.

H. M.

Prophet, Priest, and King.

1 JOIN all the glorious names
  Of wisdom, love, and power,
That ever mortals knew,
  That angels ever bore:
All are too mean to speak his worth,
Too mean to set my Saviour forth.

2 Great Prophet of our God!
  Our tongues would bless thy name;
By thee the joyful news
  Of our salvation came;—
The joyful news of sins forgiven,
Of hell subdued, and peace with heaven.

3 Jesus, our great High-Priest,
  Hath shed his blood and died;
My guilty conscience needs
  No sacrifice beside:
His precious blood did once atone,
And now it pleads before the throne.

4 O thou almighty Lord,
  Our conqueror and our King!

Thy sceptre and thy sword,
Thy reigning grace we sing;
Thine is the power; Oh! make us sit,
In willing bonds, beneath thy feet.

137.

L. M.
Loving-Kindness.

1 AWAKE, my soul! in joyful lays,
And sing thy great Redeemer's praise;
He justly claims a song from me;—
His loving-kindness,—Oh! how free!

2 He saw me ruined by the fall,
Yet loved me notwithstanding all;
He saved me from my lost estate;—
His loving-kindness,—Oh! how great!

3 When trouble, like a gloomy cloud,
Has gathered thick, and thundered loud,
He near my soul has always stood;—
His loving-kindness,—Oh! how good!

4 Soon shall I pass the gloomy vale—
Soon all my mortal powers shall fail;
Oh! may my last expiring breath
His loving-kindness sing in death.

5 Then let me mount, and soar away
To the bright world of endless day;
And sing, with rapture and surprise,
His loving-kindness in the skies.

138.

S. M.
Christ, our Sacrifice.

1 NOT all the blood of beasts,
On Jewish altars slain,
Could give the guilty conscience peace,
Or wash away the stain.

2 But Christ, the heavenly Lamb,
Takes all our sins away;—
A sacrifice of nobler name,
And richer blood than they.

3 My faith would lay her hand
On that dear head of thine,
While, like a penitent, I stand,
And there confess my sin.

4 My soul looks back to see
The burdens thou didst bear,
When hanging on th' accursed tree,—
And hopes her guilt was there.

5 Believing, we rejoice
To see the curse remove;
We bless the Lamb, with cheerful voice,
And sing his bleeding love.

139.

8s.

The Songs of Heaven.

1 YE angels! who stand round the throne,
And view my Immanuel's face,—
In rapturous songs make him known,
Tune—tune your soft harps to his praise:
He formed you the spirits you are,
So happy, so noble, so good;
When others sunk down in despair,
Confirmed by his power, ye stood.

2 Ye saints! who stand nearer than they,
And cast your bright crowns at his feet,—
His grace and his glory display,
And all his rich mercies repeat:
He snatched you from hell and the grave,
He ransomed from death and despair:
For you he was mighty to save,—
Almighty to bring you safe there.

3 Oh! when will the moment appear,
When I shall unite in your song?
I'm weary of lingering here,
And I to your Saviour belong:
I'm fettered, and chained here in clay,—
I struggle and pant to be free;
I long to be soaring away,
My God and my Saviour to see.

4 I long to put on my attire,—
Washed white in the blood of the Lamb;
I long to be one of your choir,
And tune my sweet harp to his name;
I long—Oh! I long to be there,
Where sorrow and sin bid adieu,—
Your joy and your friendship to share,—
To wonder, and worship with you.

140. H. M.

The Name of Christ a sweet Savor.

1 PRAISE to the Lord on high,
   Who spreads his triumphs wide!
While Jesus' fragrant name
   Is breathed on every side;
Balmy and rich the odors rise,
And fill the earth, and reach the skies.

2 Ten thousand dying souls
   Its influence feel—and live,
Sweeter than vital air
   The incense they receive:
They breathe anew, and rise and sing—
Jesus, the Lord, their conquering King.

3 But they, who scorn the grace
   That brings salvation nigh,
And turn away their face,
   Must faint, and fall, and die:
So sad a doom, ye saints! deplore,
For Oh! they fall to rise no more.

141. L. M.

Christ present with his People.

1 HOW sweet to leave the world awhile,
   And seek the presence of our Lord!
Dear Saviour! on thy people smile,
   And come, according to thy word.

2 From busy scenes we now retreat,
   That we may here converse with thee:
Ah! Lord! behold us at thy feet;—
   Let this the "gate of heaven" be.

3 "Chief of ten thousand!" now appear,
   That we by faith may see thy face:
Oh! speak, that we thy voice may hear,
   And let thy presence fill this place.

142. C. M.

Excellency of Christ.

1 INFINITE loveliness is thine,
   Thou glorious Prince of grace!
Thine uncreated beauties shine,
   With never-fading rays.

2 Sinners, from earth's remotest end,
   Come bending at thy feet;

To thee their prayers and songs ascend,
  In thee their wishes meet.

3 Millions of happy spirits live
  On thine exhaustless store;
From thee they all their bliss receive,
  And heaven can give no more.

4 Thou art their triumph and their joy,—
  They find their life in thee;
Thy glories will their tongues employ,
  Through all eternity.

143.

L. M.

Not ashamed of Christ.

1 JESUS! and shall it ever be—
A mortal man ashamed of thee?
Ashamed of thee, whom angels praise,
Whose glories shine through endless days?

2 Ashamed of Jesus!—sooner far
Let evening blush to own a star;
He sheds the beams of light divine,
O'er this benighted soul of mine.

3 Ashamed of Jesus—that dear friend
On whom my hopes of heaven depend?
No!—when I blush, be this my shame,—
That I no more revere his name.

4 Ashamed of Jesus?—yes, I may,
When I've no guilt to wash away,—
No tear to wipe,—no good to crave,—
No fears to quell,—no soul to save.

5 Till then—nor is my boasting vain—
Till then, I boast a Saviour slain!
And Oh! may this my glory be—
That Christ is not ashamed of me.

144.

S. M.

Christ's Mediation.

1 RAISE your triumphant songs
  To an immortal tune;
Let the wide earth resound the deeds
  Celestial grace has done.

2 Sing—how eternal love
  Its chief beloved chose,

And bade him raise our ruined race
  From their abyss of woes.

3 His hand no thunder bears,
  No terror clothes his brow,
No bolts to drive our guilty souls
  To fiercer flames below.

4 'T was mercy filled the throne,
  And wrath stood silent by,
When Christ was sent, with pardons, down
  To rebels doomed to die.

5 Now, sinners! dry your tears,
  Let hopeless sorrows cease;
Bow to the sceptre of his love,
  And take the offered peace.

6 Lord! we obey thy call;
  We lay an humble claim
To the salvation thou hast brought,
  And love and praise thy name.

145.

C. M.

Chief among ten thousand.

1 MAJESTIC sweetness sits enthroned
  Upon the Saviour's brow;
His head with radiant glories crowned,
  His lips with grace o'erflow.

2 No mortal can with him compare
  Among the sons of men;
Fairer is he, than all the fair
  Who fill the heavenly train.

3 He saw me plunged in deep distress,
  And flew to my relief;
For me he bore the shameful cross,
  And carried all my grief.

4 To him I owe my life and breath,
  And all the joys I have:
He makes me triumph over death,
  And saves me from the grave.

5 To heaven, the place of his abode,
  He brings my weary feet;
Shows me the glories of my God,
  And makes my joys complete.

6 Since from thy bounty I receive
Such proofs of love divine,
Had I a thousand hearts to give,
Lord! they should all be thine.

146.

C. M.

Love of Christ celebrated.

1 TO our Redeemer's glorious name
Awake the sacred song!
Oh! may his love—immortal flame—
Tune every heart and tongue.

2 His love, what mortal thought can reach?
What mortal tongue display?
Imagination's utmost stretch,
In wonder, dies away.

3 Dear Lord! while we adoring pay
Our humble thanks to thee,
May every heart with rapture say,—
"The Saviour died for me!"

4 Oh! may the sweet, the blissful theme,
Fill every heart and tongue,
Till strangers love thy charming name,
And join the sacred song.

147.

6s and 4s.

Christ, our Confidence.

1 MY faith looks up to thee,
Thou Lamb of Calvary!—
Saviour divine!
Now hear me, while I pray,
Take all my guilt away,
Oh! let me, from this day,
Be wholly thine.

2 May thy rich grace impart
Strength to my fainting heart,
My zeal inspire;
As thou hast died for me,
Oh! may my love to thee,
Pure, warm, and changeless be,—
A living fire.

3 While life's dark maze I tread,
And griefs around me spread,
Be thou my guide;

Bid darkness turn to day,
Wipe sorrow's tears away,
Nor let me ever stray
From thee aside.

4 When ends life's transient dream,
When death's cold sullen stream
Shall o'er me roll,
Blest Saviour! then, in love,
Fear and distrust remove;
Oh! bear me safe above,—
A ransomed soul.

148.

L. M.

Christ's Sufferings and Glory.

1 NOW for a tune of lofty praise
To great Jehovah's equal Son!
Awake, my voice! in heavenly lays,
Tell the loud wonders he hath done.

2 Sing—how he left the worlds of light,
And the bright robes he wore above,—
How swift and joyful was his flight,
On wings of everlasting love.

3 Deep in the shades of gloomy death,
Th' almighty captive pris'ner lay;
Th' almighty captive left the earth,
And rose to everlasting day.

4 Among a thousand harps and songs,
Jesus, the God, exalted reigns;
His sacred name fills all their tongues,
And echoes through the heavenly plains.

149.

7s.

The Rock of Ages.

1 ROCK of ages, cleft for me!
Let me hide myself in thee;
Let the water and the blood,
From thy wounded side that flowed,
Be of sin the perfect cure;
Save me, Lord! and make me pure.

2 Should my tears for ever flow,
Should my zeal no languor know,
This for sin could not atone,
Thou must save, and thou alone:

In my hand no price I bring;
Simply to thy cross I cling.

3 While I draw this fleeting breath,
When mine eye-lids close in death,
When I rise to worlds unknown,
And behold thee on thy throne,
Rock of ages, cleft for me!
Let me hide myself in thee.

150. C. M.

Christ, the Way, the Truth, and the Life.

1 THOU art the Way;—to thee alone
From sin and death we flee;
And he, who would the Father seek,
Must seek him, Lord! in thee.

2 Thou art the Truth;—thy word alone
True wisdom can impart;
Thou only canst instruct the mind,
And purify the heart.

3 Thou art the Life;—the rending tomb
Proclaims thy conquering arm;
And those who put their trust in thee
Not death nor hell shall harm.

4 Thou art the Way, the Truth, the Life;—
Grant us to know that Way,
That Truth to keep, that Life to win,
Which lead to endless day.

151. L. M.

Christ, the Physician of the Soul.

1 DEEP are the wounds which sin has made;
Where shall the sinner find a cure?
In vain, alas! is nature's aid;
The work exceeds her utmost power.

2 But can no sovereign balm be found?
And is no kind physician nigh
To ease the pain, and heal the wound,
Ere life and hope for ever fly?

3 There is a great physician near;
Look up, my fainting soul! and live;
See,—in his heavenly smiles appear
Such help as nature cannot give.

4 See,—in the Saviour's dying blood,
Life, health, and bliss abundant flow;
'T is only that dear sacred flood,
Can ease thy pain, and heal thy wo.

152.

7s.

Christ, our Example in Suffering.

1 GO to dark Gethsemane,
Ye that feel the tempter's power!
Your Redeemer's conflict see,
Watch with him one bitter hour;
Turn not from his griefs away,
Learn of Jesus Christ to pray.

2 Follow to the judgment-hall,
View the Lord of life arraigned;
Oh! the wormwood and the gall;
Oh! the pangs his soul sustained:
Shun not suffering, shame, nor loss;
Learn of him to bear the cross.

3 Calv'ry's mournful mountain climb;
There—adoring at his feet,
Mark that miracle of Time—
God's own sacrifice complete:
"It is finished"—hear him cry;
Learn of Jesus Christ to die.

4 Early hasten to the tomb,
Where they laid his breathless clay;
All is solitude and gloom,
Who hath taken him away?—
Christ is risen—he meets our eyes;
Saviour! teach us so to rise.

153.

L. M.

Gethsemane.

1 'T IS midnight—and, on Olive's brow,
The star is dimmed that lately shone;
'T is midnight—in the garden now
The suffering Saviour prays alone.

2 'T is midnight—and, from all removed,
Immanuel wrestles lone, with fears;
E'en the disciple that he loved
Heeds not his Master's grief and tears.

3 'T is midnight—and for others' guilt
The man of sorrows weeps in blood;
Yet he, who hath in anguish knelt,
Is not forsaken by his God.

4 'T is midnight—and, from ether-plains,
Is borne the song that angels know;
Unheard by mortals are the strains
That sweetly soothe the Saviour's wo.

154.

8s and 6s.

The Garden of Agony.

1 BEHOLD, where Cedron's waters flow,—
Behold the suffering Saviour go,
To sad Gethsemane!
His countenance is all divine,
Yet grief appears in every line.

2 He bows beneath the sins of men,
He cries to God, and cries again,
In sad Gethsemane;
He lifts his mournful eyes above—
"My Father! can this cup remove?"

3 With gentle resignation still,
He yielded to his Father's will,
In sad Gethsemane;—
"Behold me here, thine only Son,
And, Father! let thy will be done."

4 The Father heard,—and angels there
Sustained the Son of God in prayer,
In sad Gethsemane;
He drank the dreadful cup of pain,
Then rose to life and joy again.

5 When storms of sorrow round us sweep,
And scenes of anguish make us weep,
To sad Gethsemane
We 'll look, and see the Saviour there,
Then humbly bow, like him, in prayer.

155.

C. M.

Christ, dying on the Cross.

1 BEHOLD the Saviour of mankind,
Nailed to the shameful tree!
How vast the love that him inclined
To bleed and die for me.

2 Hark! how he groans, while nature shakes,
And earth's strong pillars bend!
The temple's veil asunder breaks,
The solid marbles rend.

3 'T is done! the precious ransom 's paid,
"Receive my soul!" he cries:
See—how he bows his sacred head!
He bows his head and dies!

4 But soon he 'll break death's iron-chain,
And in full glory shine;
O Lamb of God! was ever pain—
Was ever love like thine?

156.

L. M.

Christ on the Cross.

1 'T IS finished!—so the Saviour cried,
And meekly bowed his head, and died;
'T is finished!—yes, the race is run,
The battle fought, the vict'ry won.

2 'T is finished!—this his dying groan
Shall sins of every kind atone;
Millions shall be redeemed from death,
By this his last expiring breath.

3 'T is finished!—Heaven is reconciled,
And all the powers of darkness spoiled:
Peace, love, and happiness, again
Return, and dwell with sinful men.

4 'T is finished!—let the joyful sound
Be heard through all the nations round:
'T is finished!—let the echo fly, [sky.
Through heaven and hell, through earth and

157.

L. M.

Christ dying, rising, and reigning.

1 HE dies!—the friend of sinners dies!
Lo! Salem's daughters weep around!
A solemn darkness veils the skies—
A sudden trembling shakes the ground.

2 Here 's love and grief beyond degree,
The Lord of glory dies for men!
But,—lo! what sudden joys we see!
Jesus, the dead, revives again.

3 The rising God forsakes the tomb;
Up to his Father's court he flies;
Cherubic legions guard him home,
And shout him—welcome to the skies.

4 Break off your tears, ye saints! and tell
How high our great Deliverer reigns;
Sing,—how he spoiled the hosts of hell,
And led the tyrant, death, in chains

5 Say,—"Live for ever, glorious King!
Born to redeem, and strong to save!"
Then ask,—"O death! where is thy sting?
And where thy vict'ry, boasting grave?"

158.

8s, 7s and 4.

The expiring Saviour

1 HARK! the voice of love and mercy
Sounds aloud from Calvary;
See!—it rends the rocks asunder—
Shakes the earth—and veils the sky:
"It is finished!"—
Hear the dying Saviour cry.

2 "It is finished!"—Oh! what pleasure
Do these charming words afford!
Heavenly blessings, without measure,
Flow to us through Christ, the Lord:
"It is finished!"—
Saints! the dying words record.

3 Tune your harps anew, ye seraphs!
Join to sing the pleasing theme:
All in earth and heaven, uniting,
Join to praise Immanuel's name.
Hallelujah!—
Glory to the bleeding Lamb!

159.

L. M.

Salvation by the Cross.

1 HERE at thy cross, incarnate God!
I lay my soul beneath thy love,—
Beneath the droppings of thy blood,
Jesus!—nor shall it e'er remove.

2 Should worlds conspire to drive me hence,
Moveless and firm this heart should lie;

Resolved,—for that 's my last defence,—
If I must perish, here to die.

3 But speak, my Lord! and calm my fear;
Am I not safe beneath thy shade?
Thy vengeance will not strike me here,
Nor Satan dare my soul invade.

4 Yes, I 'm secure beneath thy blood.
And all my foes shall lose their aim;
Hosanna to my Saviour-God,
And my best honors to his name!

160. L. M.

Christ's Passion.

1 THE morning dawns upon the place,
Where Jesus spent the night in prayer;
Through yielding glooms behold his face:
Nor form, nor comeliness is there.

2 Brought forth to judgment, now he stands
Arraigned, condemned, at Pilate's bar;
Here, spurned by fierce prætorian bands,
There, mocked by Herod's men of war

3 He bears their buffeting and scorn,
Mock-homage of the lip, the knee—
The purple robe, the crown of thorn,—
The scourge, the nail, th' accursed tree.

4 No guile within his mouth is found,
He neither threatens nor complains;
Meek, as a lamb for slaughter bound,—
Dumb, mid his murderers he remains.

5 But hark! he prays;—'t is for his foes;
He speaks;—'t is comfort to his friends
Answers,—and paradise bestows:
He bows his head;—the conflict ends.

6 Truly this was the Son of God—
Though in a servant's mean disguise:
And, bruised beneath the Father's rod,
Not for himself,—for man he dies.

161. L. M.

A dying Saviour.

1 STRETCHED on the cross, the Saviour dies
Hark! his expiring groans arise:

See—from his hands, his feet, his side,
Fast flows the sacred crimson tide!

2 But life attends the deathful sound,
And flows from every bleeding wound:
The vital stream,—how free it flows,
To save and cleanse his rebel-foes!

3 Can I survey this scene of wo,
Where mingling grief and wonder flow,
And yet my heart unmoved remain,
Insensible to love or pain?

4 Come, dearest Lord! thy grace impart
To warm this cold, this stupid heart;
Till all its powers and passions move,
In melting grief and ardent love.

162.

L. M.

Love inscribed on the Cross.

1 WE sing the praise of him who died—
Of him who died upon the cross;
The sinner's hope let men deride,
For this we count the world but loss.

2 Inscribed upon the cross we see,
In shining letters,—"God is Love:"
He bears our sins upon the tree,
He brings us mercy from above.

3 The cross!—it takes our guilt away,
It holds the fainting spirit up;
It cheers with hope the gloomy day,
And sweetens every bitter cup.

4 It makes the coward-spirit brave.
And nerves the feeble arm for fight;
It takes its terrors from the grave,
And gilds the bed of death with light.

5 The balm of life, the cure of wo,
The measure and the pledge of love;
'T is all that sinners want below,
'T is all that angels know above.

163.

L. M. Double.

Contrition at the Cross.

1 FAST flow, my tears! the cause is great;
This tribute claims an injured friend;—

One whom I long pursued with hate,
  While he would love me to the end:
When justice frowned above my head,
And death its terrors round me spread,
He interposed, the wounds he bore,
And bade me live to die no more.

2 Fast flow, my tears! yet faster flow!
  Streams copious as yon purple tide:
Who was it gave the deadly blow?
  Who urged the hand that pierced his side
My soul! thy victim here behold,
What pangs, what agonies untold,
While justice, armed with power divine,
Pours on his head what 's due to thine!

3 Fast and yet faster flow, my tears!
  Now break this heart, and drown these eyes;—
His visage marred toward heaven he rears,
  And, pleading for his murderers, dies!
My grief no measure knows, nor end,
Till he appears the sinner's Friend,
And gives me, in some happy hour,
To feel the risen Saviour's power.

164. L. M.
Christ crucified, the Wisdom and Power of God.

1 NATURE with open volume stands,
  To spread her Maker's praise abroad;
And every labor of his hands
  Shows something worthy of a God.

2 But, in the grace that rescued man,
  His brightest form of glory shines;
Here, on the cross, 't is fairest drawn,
  In precious blood and crimson lines.

3 Oh! the sweet wonders of that cross,
  Where Christ, the Saviour, loved and died:
Her noblest life my spirit draws,
  From his dear wounds and bleeding side.

4 I would for ever speak his name,
  In sounds to mortal ears unknown;
With angels join to praise the Lamb,
  And worship at his Father's throne.

165.

L. M.

Crucifixion to the World.

1 WHEN I survey the wondrous cross,
On which the Prince of glory died,
My richest gain I count but loss,
And pour contempt on all my pride.

2 Forbid it, Lord! that I should boast,
Save in the death of Christ, my God;
All the vain things that charm me most,
I sacrifice them to his blood.

3 See,—from his head, his hands, his feet,
Sorrow and love flow mingled down:
Did e'er such love and sorrow meet,
Or thorns compose so rich a crown?

4 Were the whole realm of nature mine,
That were a present far too small;
Love, so amazing, so divine,
Demands my soul, my life, my all.

166.

L. M.

The Hidings of the Father's Face.

1 FROM Calvary a cry was heard—
A bitter and heart-rending cry!
My Saviour! every mournful word
Bespeaks thy soul's deep agony.

2 A horror of great darkness fell
On thee, thou spotless, holy One!
And all the swarming hosts of hell
Conspired to tempt God's only Son.

3 The scourge, the thorns, the deep disgrace,—
These thou could'st bear, nor once repine
But when Jehovah veiled his face,
Unutterable pangs were thine.

4 Let the dumb world its silence break!
Let pealing anthems rend the sky!
Awake, my sluggish soul! awake!
He died, that we might never die.

5 Lord! on thy cross I fix mine eye:
If e'er I lose its strong control,
Oh! let that dying, piercing cry,
Melt and reclaim my wandering soul.

167.

S. M.

Redemption completed.

1 "THE Lord is risen indeed !"—
Then is his work performed;
The mighty captive now is freed,
And death, our foe, disarmed.

2 "The Lord is risen indeed !"—
He lives to die no more;
He lives, the sinner's cause to plead,
Whose curse and shame he bore.

3 "The Lord is risen indeed !"—
Then hell has lost his prey:
With him is risen the ransomed seed,
To reign in endless day.

4 "The Lord is risen indeed !"—
Attending angels ! hear;
Up to the courts of heaven, with speed,
The joyful tidings bear.

5 Then wake your golden lyres,
And strike each cheerful chord;
Join, all ye bright, celestial choirs !
To sing our risen Lord.

168.

8s. 7s. and 4.

Christ triumphant.

1 COME, ye saints ! look here and wonder
See the place where Jesus lay;
He has burst the bands asunder—
He has borne our sins away:
Joyful tidings !—
Yes, the Lord is risen to-day.

2 Jesus triumphs !—sing ye praises;—
'T was by death he overcame:
Thus the Lord his glory raises;—
Thus he fills his foes with shame:
Sing ye praises—
Praises to the victor's name.

3 Jesus triumphs !—countless legions
Come from heaven, to meet their King
Soon, in yonder happy regions,
They shall join his praise to sing:
Songs eternal
Shall through heaven's high arches ring.

169.

7s.

Christ's Ascension.

1 HAIL the day which sees him rise
Glorious to his native skies!
Christ, awhile to mortals given,
Enters now the gates of heaven.

2 There the glorious triumph waits:—
Lift your heads, eternal gates!
Christ hath vanquished death and sin;
Take the King of glory in.

3 See,—high heaven its Lord receives;—
Yet he loves the earth he leaves:
Though returning to his throne,
Still he calls mankind his own.

4 Still for us he intercedes;
His prevailing death he pleads;
Near himself prepares our place,—
Great Forerunner of our race.

5 What though parted from our sight,
Far above yon starry height?
May our warm affections rise,
Foll'wing him beyond the skies.

170.

L. M. 6 Lines.

Our risen Lord.

1 HOW calm and beautiful the morn
That gilds the sacred tomb,
Where once the Crucified was borne,
And veiled in midnight-gloom!
Oh! weep no more the Saviour slain;
The Lord is risen—he lives again.

2 Ye mourning saints! dry every tear
For your departed Lord;
"Behold the place—he is not there,"
The tomb is all unbarred:
The gates of death were closed in vain;
The Lord is risen—he lives again.

3 Now cheerful to the house of prayer
Your early footsteps bend,
The Saviour will himself be there,
Your advocate and friend:
Once by the law your hopes were slain,
But now in Christ ye live again.

4 How tranquil now the rising day!
'T is Jesus still appears,
A risen Lord, to chase away
Your unbelieving fears:
Oh! weep no more your comforts slain,
The Lord is risen—he lives again.

5 And when the shades of evening fall,
When life's last hour draws nigh,
If Jesus shine upon the soul,
How blissful then to die:
Since he has risen who once was slain,
Ye die in Christ to live again.

171.

7s.

Resurrection and Ascension of Christ.

1 ANGELS! roll the rock away;
Death! yield up thy mighty prey;
See! the Saviour leaves the tomb,
Glowing with immortal bloom.

2 Hark! the wondering angels raise
Louder notes of joyful praise;
Let the earth's remotest bound
Echo with the blissful sound.

3 Now, ye saints! lift up your eyes,
See him high in glory rise!
Hosts of angels, on the road,
Hail him—the incarnate God.

4 Heaven unfolds its portals wide,
See the Conqueror through them ride!
King of glory! mount thy throne,—
Boundless empire is thine own.

5 Praise him, ye celestial choirs!
Tune, and sweep your golden lyres;
Raise, O earth! your noblest songs,
From ten thousand thousand tongues.

172.

L. M.

The Resurrection of Christ.

1 "COME, see the place where Jesus lay!"
For he hath left his gloomy bed;—
What angel rolled the stone away?
What spirit brought him from the dead?

2 By his omnipotence he rose,
  By his own Spirit lived again ;
To crush for ever all his foes,—
  To raise for ever ruined men.

3 They, who his image here partake,—
  Though long in dust their flesh consume,—
Shall sleep in Jesus, and awake
  To life eternal, from the tomb.

173.
7s.
The Resurrection.

1 MORNING breaks upon the tomb,
Jesus scatters all its gloom ;
Day of triumph through the skies,—
See the glorious Saviour rise !

2 Ye who are of death afraid,
Triumph in the scattered shade ;
Drive your anxious cares away ;
See the place where Jesus lay !

3 Christian ! dry your flowing tears,
Chase your unbelieving fears ;
Look on his deserted grave ;
Doubt no more his power to save.

174.
H. M.
Jesus rising and reigning.

1 YES, the Redeemer rose ;
  The Saviour left the dead ;
And o'er our hellish foes
  High raised his conquering head
In wild dismay,
  The guards around
  Fall to the ground,
And sink away.

2 Lo ! the angelic bands,
  In full assembly meet,
To wait his high commands,
  And worship at his feet :
Joyful they come,
  And wing their way,
  From realms of day,
To Jesus' tomb.

3 Then back to heaven they fly,
  The joyful news to bear:
Hark! as they soar on high,
  What music fills the air!
Their anthems say,—
  "Jesus, who bled,
  Hath left the dead;—
He rose to-day."

4 Ye mortals! catch the sound,—
  Redeemed by him from hell;
And send the echo round
  The globe, on which you dwell!
Transported, cry,—
  "Jesus, who bled,
  Hath left the dead,
No more to die."

5 All hail! triumphant Lord!
  Who sav'st us with thy blood:
Wide be thy name adored,
  Thou rising, reigning God!
With thee we rise,
  With thee we reign,
  And empires gain,
Beyond the skies.

175.

8s and 7s.

Love divine.

1 LOVE divine, all love excelling,—
  Joy of heaven, to earth come down!
Fix in us thy humble dwelling;
  All thy faithful mercies crown;
Jesus! thou art all compassion,
  Pure, unbounded love thou art;
Visit us with thy salvation,
  Enter every trembling heart.

2 Breathe,—Oh! breathe thy loving Spirit
  Into every troubled breast;
Let us all thy grace inherit,
  Let us find thy promised rest:
Take away the love of sinning,
  Take our load of guilt away;
End the work of thy beginning,—
  Bring us to eternal day.

3 Carry on thy new creation,
  Pure and holy may we be;
Let us see our whole salvation,
  Perfectly secured by thee;
Change from glory into glory,
  Till in heaven we take our place;
Till we cast our crowns before thee,
  Lost in wonder, love, and praise.

176.

H. M.

The Cross celebrated.

1 YE saints! your music bring,
  And swell the rapturous sound;
Strike every trembling string,
  Till earth and heaven resound:
The triumphs of the cross we sing,—
Awake, ye saints! each joyful string.

2 The cross—the cross alone—
  Subdued the powers of hell:
Like lightning from his throne,
  The prince of darkness fell:
The triumphs of the cross we sing,—
Awake, ye saints! each joyful string.

3 The hand of wrath is stayed,
  In its pursuit of blood;
The cross our debt has paid,
  And made our peace with God:
The triumphs of the cross we sing,—
Awake, ye saints! each joyful string.

4 The cross hath power to save,
  From all the foes that rise:
The cross hath made the grave
  A passage to the skies:
Angels and saints its power shall sing,
Till heaven's eternal arches ring.

177.

L. M.

The Resurrection of Christ.

1 WHEN I the holy grave survey,
  Where once my Saviour deigned to lie,
I see fulfilled what prophets say,
  And all the power of death defy.

2 This empty tomb shall now proclaim,
  How weak the bands of conquered death:

Sweet pledge that all who trust his name
Shall rise, and draw immortal breath.

3 Jesus, once numbered with the dead,
Unseals his eyes, to sleep no more:
And ever lives their cause to plead,
For whom the pains of death he bore.

4 Thy risen Lord, my soul! behold;
See the rich diadem he wears!
Thou too shalt bear a harp of gold,—
A crown of joy, when he appears.

5 Though in the dust I lay my head,
Yet, gracious God! thou wilt not leave
My flesh for ever with the dead,
Nor lose thy children in the grave.

178.

8s, 7s and 4.

Coronation of the King of kings.

1 LOOK, ye saints! the sight is glorious;
See the man of sorrows now,
From the fight returned victorious;—
Every knee to him shall bow:
Crown him—crown him!—
Crowns become the victor's brow.

2 Crown the Saviour, angels! crown him
Rich the trophies Jesus brings:
In the seat of power enthrone him,
While the vault of heaven rings:
Crown him—crown him!—
Crown the Saviour, King of kings.

3 Sinners in derision crowned him,—
Mocking thus the Saviour's claim:
Saints and angels! crowd around him,
Own his title, praise his name:
Crown him—crown him!—
Spread abroad the victor's fame.

4 Hark! those bursts of acclamation!
Hark! those loud triumphant chords!
Jesus takes the highest station;—
Oh! what joy the sight affords!
Crown him—crown him,—
King of kings, and Lord of lords!

179.
S. M.
Song of Moses and the Lamb.

1 AWAKE, and sing the song
Of Moses and the Lamb;
Wake, every heart and every tongue!
To praise the Saviour's name.

2 Sing of his dying love;
Sing of his rising power;
Sing—how he intercedes above
For those whose sins he bore.

3 Ye pilgrims! on the road
To Zion's city, sing!
Rejoice ye in the Lamb of God,—
In Christ, th' eternal king.

4 Soon shall we hear him say,—
"Ye blessed children! come;"
Soon will he call us hence away,
And take his wanderers home.

5 There shall each raptured tongue
His endless praise proclaim;
And sweeter voices tune the song
Of Moses and the Lamb.

180.
C. M.
Reigning with Christ.

1 THE head. that once was crowned with thorns,
Is crowned with glory now;
A royal diadem adorns
The mighty victor's brow.

2 The highest place that heaven affords
Is his, by sovereign right;
The King of kings, and Lord of lords,
He reigns in glory bright:—

3 The joy of all who dwell above,
The joy of all below,
To whom he manifests his love.
And grants his name to know.

4 To them the cross, with all its shame,
With all its grace, is given;
Their name,—an everlasting name;
Their joy,—the joy of heaven.

5 They suffer with their Lord below,
They reign with him above;
Their profit and their joy—to know
The mystery of his love.

6 The cross he bore is life and health,—
Though shame and death to him;
His people's hope, his people's wealth,
Their everlasting theme.

181.

S. M.

Christ unseen, yet beloved.

1 NOT with our mortal eyes
Have we beheld the Lord;
Yet we rejoice to hear his name,
And love him in his word.

2 On earth we want the sight
Of our Redeemer's face;
Yet, Lord! our inmost thoughts delight
To dwell upon thy grace.

3 And when we taste thy love,
Our joys divinely grow
Unspeakable, like those above,
And heaven begins below.

182.

C. M.

Access to God by Christ.

1 COME, let us lift our joyful eyes
Up to the courts above,
And smile to see our Father there,
Upon a throne of love.

2 Rich were the drops of Jesus' blood,
That calmed his frowning face,
That sprinkled o'er the burning throne,
And turned the wrath to grace.

3 Now we may bow before his feet,
And venture near the Lord;
No fiery cherub guards his seat,
Nor double-flaming sword.

4 The peaceful gates of heavenly bliss
Are opened by the Son;
High let us raise our notes of praise,
And reach th' almighty throne.

5 To thee ten thousand thanks we bring,
Great Advocate on high!
And glory to th' eternal King
Who lays his fury by.

183.

L. M.

The good Shepherd.

1 THOU! whom my soul admires above
All earthly joy, and earthly love,—
Tell me, dear Shepherd! let me know—
Where do thy sweetest pastures grow?

2 Where is the shadow of that rock,
That from the sun defends thy flock?
Fain would I feed among thy sheep,—
Among them rest, among them sleep.

3 Why should thy bride appear like one
That turns aside to paths unknown?
My constant feet would never rove,—
Would never seek another love.

4 The footsteps of thy flock I see;
Thy sweetest pastures here they be;
A wondrous feast thy love prepares,
Bought with thy wounds, and groans, and tears.

5 His dearest flesh he makes my food,
And bids me drink his richest blood:
Here to these hills my soul will come,
Till my beloved leads me home.

184.

L. M.

Worthy the Lamb.

1 WORTHY the Lamb of boundless sway,—
In earth and heaven, the Lord of all!
Let all the powers of earth obey,
And low before his footstool fall.

2 Higher—still higher, swell the strain;
Creation's voice the note prolong!
Jesus, the Lamb, shall ever reign:—
Let hallelujahs crown the song.

185.

6s and 4s.

Praise to the Redeemer.

1 COME, all ye saints of God!
Wide through the earth abroad,
Spread Jesus' name;

Tell what his love has done,
Trust in his grace alone;
Shout to his lofty throne,—
"Worthy the Lamb!"

2 Hence, gloomy doubts and fears!
Dry up your mournful tears;
Swell the glad theme;
Praise ye our gracious King,
Strike each melodious string,
Join heart and voice to sing,—
"Worthy the Lamb!'

3 Hark! how the choirs above,
Filled with the Saviour's love,
Dwell on his name!
There, too, may we be found,
With light and glory crowned,
While all the heavens resound,—
"Worthy the Lamb!"

186.

C. M.

Coronation of Christ.

1 ALL hail the power of Jesus' name!
Let angels prostrate fall;
Bring forth the royal diadem,
And crown him—Lord of all.

2 Crown him,—ye morning-stars of light!—
Who formed this floating ball;
Now hail the strength of Israel's might,
And crown him—Lord of all.

3 Ye chosen seed of Adam's race,—
Ye ransomed from the fall!
Hail him, who saves you by his grace,
And crown him—Lord of all.

4 Sinners! whose love can ne'er forget
The wormwood and the gall,—
Come, spread your trophies at his feet,
And crown him—Lord of all.

5 Let every kindred, every tribe,
On this terrestrial ball,
To him all majesty ascribe,
And crown him—Lord of all.

187.

C. M.

Our High-Priest in Heaven.

1 NOW let our cheerful eyes survey
Our great high-priest above;
And celebrate his constant care,
His sympathetic love.

2 Though raised to a superior throne,
Where angels bow around,
And high o'er all the shining train,
With matchless honors crowned;—

3 The names of all his saints he bears
Deep graven on his heart;
Nor shall the meanest Christian say,
That he hath lost his part.

4 Those characters shall fair abide,—
Our everlasting trust,—
When gems, and monuments, and crowns,
Are mouldered down to dust.

5 So, gracious Saviour! on my breast,
May thy dear name be worn,
A sacred ornament and guard,—
To endless ages borne.

188.

L. M. 6 Lines.

Our compassionate High-Priest.

1 WHEN gathering clouds around I view,
And days are dark, and friends are few,
On him I lean, who, not in vain,
Experienced every human pain;
He sees my wants, allays my fears,
And counts and treasures up my tears.

2 If aught should tempt my soul to stray
From heavenly virtue's narrow way,—
To fly the good I would pursue,
Or do the sin I would not do,—
Still he, who felt temptation's power,
Shall guard me in that dangerous hour.

3 When sorr'wing o'er some stone I bend,
Which covers all that was a friend;
And from his voice, his hand, his smile,
Divides me, for a little while,—

My Saviour sees the tears I shed,
For Jesus wept o'er Laz'rus dead.

4 And Oh! when I have safely past
Through every conflict, but the last,
Still, still unchanging, watch beside
My painful bed,—for thou hast died;
Then point to realms of cloudless day,
And wipe my latest tear away.

189.

L. M. 6 Lines.

Hope of Heaven through Christ.

1 AND art thou, gracious Master! gone
A mansion to prepare for me?
Shall I behold thee on thy throne,
And there for ever dwell with thee?
Then, let the world approve or blame,
I'll triumph in thy glorious name.

2 What transport, Lord! shall fill my heart,
When thou my worthless name shalt own!
When I shall see thee as thou art,
And know, as I myself am known!
From sin, and fear, and sorrow flee,
My soul shall find its rest in thee.

190.

7s.

Christ, our Hope.

1 CHRIST, of all my hopes the ground,—
Christ, the spring of all my joy!
Still in thee let me be found,
Still for thee my powers employ.

2 Let thy love my heart inflame;
Keep thy fear before my sight;
Be thy praise my highest aim;
Be thy smile my chief delight.

3 Fountain of o'erflowing grace!
Freely from thy fullness give:
Till I close my earthly race,
Be it "Christ for me to live!"

4 Firmly trusting in thy blood,
Nothing shall my heart confound;
Safely I shall pass the flood,
Safely reach Immanuel's ground.

5 When I touch the blessed shore,
Back the closing waves shall roll;
Death's dark stream shall never more
Part from thee my ravished soul.

6 Thus,—Oh! thus an entrance give
To the land of cloudless sky;
Having known it, "Christ to live,"
Let me know it, "gain to die."

191.

8s and 7s.

Jesus, exalted to the Throne.

1 JESUS! hail! enthroned in glory,
There for ever to abide;
All the heavenly host adore thee,
Seated at thy Father's side.

2 There for sinners thou art pleading,
There thou dost our place prepare;
Ever for us interceding,
Till in glory we appear.

3 Worship, honor, power, and blessing,
Thou art worthy to receive:
Loudest praises, without ceasing,
Meet it is for us to give.

Help, ye bright angelic spirits!
Bring your sweetest, noblest lays;
Help to sing our Saviour's merits,—
Help to chant Immanuel's praise.

192.

L. M.

Christ, the Lord of Angels.

1 GREAT God! to what a glorious height
Hast thou advanced the Lord, thy Son!
Angels, in all their robes of light,
Are made the servants of his throne.

2 Before his feet their armies wait,
And swift as flames of fire they move,
To manage his affairs of state,
In works of vengeance, or of love.

3 Now they are sent to guide our feet,
Up to the gates of thine abode,
Through all the dangers that we meet,
In travelling o'er the heavenly road.

4 Lord! when we leave this mortal ground,
And thou shalt bid us rise and come,—
Send thy beloved angels down
Safe to conduct our spirits home.

193.

L. M.

The Way to Heaven.

1 JESUS, my all, to heaven is gone,—
He whom I fix my hopes upon;
His track I see, and I 'll pursue
The narrow way, till him I view.

2 This is the way I long have sought,
And mourned because I found it not;
Till late I heard my Saviour say,—
"Come hither, soul! I am the way."

3 Lo! glad I come, and thou, blest Lamb!
Shalt take me to thee as I am;
My sinful self to thee I give—
Nothing but love shall I receive.

4 Then will I tell to sinners round,
What a dear Saviour I have found;
I 'll point to thy redeeming blood,
And say,—"Behold the way to God!"

194.

S. M.

Christ's Intercession.

1 YES, the Redeemer 's gone,
T' appear before our God;
To sprinkle o'er the flaming throne,
With his atoning blood.

2 No fiery vengeance now,—
No burning wrath comes down;
If justice calls for sinners' blood,
The Saviour shows his own.

3 Before his Father's eye
Our humble suit he moves;
The Father lays his thunder by,
And looks, and smiles, and loves.

4 Now may our joyful tongues
Our Maker's honors sing;
Jesus, the priest, receives our songs,
And bears them to the King.

5 We bow before his face,
  And sound his glories high:
Hosanna to the God of grace,
  Who lays his thunder by.

6 On earth thy mercy reigns,
  And triumphs all above:
But, Lord! how weak our mortal strains,
  To speak immortal love!

195.
L. M.
The Dominion of Christ.

1 HAIL to the Prince of life and peace,
  Who holds the keys of death and hell!
The boundless world unseen is his,
  And sovereign power becomes him well.

2 In shame and anguish once he died;—
  But now he lives for evermore:
Bow down, ye saints! around his seat,
  And, all ye angel-bands! adore.

3 Live—live for ever, glorious Lord!
  To quell thy foes—and guard thy friends;
While all thy chosen tribes rejoice,
  That thy dominion never ends.

4 Worthy thy hand to hold the keys,
  Guided by wisdom, and by love;
Worthy to rule o'er mortal life,
  O'er worlds below, and worlds above.

5 For ever reign, victorious King!
  Wide through the earth thy name be known!
And call my longing soul to sing
  Sublimer anthems near thy throne.

196.
H. M.
Our High-Priest in Heaven

1 TH' atoning work is done,—
  The victim's blood is shed;
And Jesus now is gone
  His people's cause to plead:
He stands in heaven, their great high-priest,
And bears their names upon his breast.

2 No temple made with hands
  His place of service is:

In heaven itself he stands,—
  A heavenly priesthood his:
In him the shadows of the law
Are all fulfilled, and now withdraw.

3 And though awhile he be
  Hid from the eyes of men,
His people look to see
  Their great high-priest again:
In brightest glory he will come,
And take his waiting people home.

197. C. M.
Our Great High-Priest.

1 COME, let us join our songs of praise
  To our ascended Priest;
He entered heaven, with all our names
  Engraven on his breast.

2 Below he washed our guilt away,
  By his atoning blood;
Now he appears before the throne,
  And pleads our cause with God.

3 Clothed with our nature still, he knows
  The weakness of our frame,
And how to shield us from the foes
  Whom he himself o'ercame.

4 Nor time, nor distance, e'er shall quench
  The fervors of his love;
For us he died in kindness here,
  And intercedes above.

5 Oh! may we ne'er forget his grace,
  Nor blush to bear his name;
Still may our hearts hold fast his faith –
  Our lips his praise proclaim.

HOLY SPIRIT.

198. C. M.
Breathing after the Holy Spirit.

1 COME, Holy Spirit, heavenly Dove!
  With all thy quickening powers,—

Kindle a flame of sacred love,
  In these cold hearts of ours.

2 Look—how we grovel here below,
  Fond of these trifling toys!
Our souls can neither fly nor go,
  To reach eternal joys.

3 In vain we tune our formal songs,
  In vain we strive to rise;
Hosannas languish on our tongues,
  And our devotion dies.

4 Dear Lord! and shall we ever live
  At this poor dying rate?
Our love so faint, so cold to thee,
  And thine to us so great?

5 Come, Holy Spirit, heavenly Dove!
  With all thy quickening powers;
Come, shed abroad a Saviour's love,
  And that shall kindle ours.

199

S. M.

Convicting and sanctifying Influence.

1 COME, Holy Spirit! come,
  Let thy bright beams arise;
Dispel the sorrow from our minds,
  The darkness from our eyes.

2 Convince us of our sin,—
  Then lead to Jesus' blood;
And, to our wondering view, reveal
  The secret love of God.

3 'T is thine to cleanse the heart,
  To sanctify the soul,
To pour fresh life in every part,
  And new-create the whole.

4 Revive our drooping faith;
  Our doubts and fears remove;
And kindle in our breast the flame
  Of never-dying love.

200.

7s.

Influences of the Spirit.

1 GRACIOUS Spirit! Love divine!
Let thy light within me shine:

All my guilty fears remove,
Fill me with thy heavenly love.

2 Speak thy pard'ning grace to me,
Set the burdened sinner free;
Lead me to the Lamb of God,
Wash me in his precious blood.

3 Life and peace to me impart,
Seal salvation on my heart;
Breathe thyself into my breast,—
Earnest of immortal rest.

4 Let me never from thee stray,
Keep me in the narrow way;
Fill my soul with joy divine,
Keep me, Lord! for ever thine.

201.

L. M.

The Spirit grieved.

1 THE Spirit, like a peaceful dove,
Flies from the realms of noise and strife;
Why should we vex and grieve his love,
Who seals our souls to heavenly life?

2 Tender and kind be all our thoughts,
Through all our lives let mercy run.
So God forgives our numerous faults,
For the dear sake of Christ, his Son.

202.

H. M.

Pleading the Promise of the Spirit.

1 O THOU that hearest prayer!
Attend our humble cry;
And let thy servants share
Thy blessing from on high:
We plead the promise of thy word;
Grant us thy Holy Spirit, Lord!

2 If earthly parents hear
Their children when they cry;
If they, with love sincere,
Their varied wants supply;
Much more wilt thou thy love display
And answer when thy children pray.

3 Our Heavenly Father, thou;—
We, children of thy grace:

Oh! let thy Spirit now
  Descend, and fill the place:
So shall we feel the heavenly flame,
And all unite to praise thy name.

4 Oh! send thy Spirit down
  On all the nations, Lord!
With great success to crown
  The preaching of thy word,
Till heathen lands shall own thy sway,
And cast their idol-gods away.

203. S. M.

The indwelling Influences of the Spirit.

1 'T IS God, the Spirit, leads
  In paths before unknown;
The work to be performed is ours,
  The strength is all his own.

2 Supported by his grace,
  We still pursue our way;
And hope at last to reach the prize,
  Secure in endless day.

3 'T is he that works to will,
  'T is he that works to do;
His is the power by which we act,—
  His be the glory too.

204. L. M.

Teachings of the Spirit.

1 COME, blessed Spirit! source of light,
  Whose power and grace are unconfined,
Dispel the gloomy shades of night,—
  The thicker darkness of the mind.

2 To mine illumined eyes display
  The glorious truth thy word reveals,
Cause me to run the heavenly way,
  Thy book unfold and loose the seals.

3 Thine inward teachings make me know
  The mysteries of redeeming love,
The vanity of things below,
  And excellence of things above.

4 While through this dubious maze I stray,
  Spread, like the sun, thy beams abroad,

To show the dangers of the way,
And guide my feeble steps to God.

205.

8s and 7s.

Prayer for comforting Influences.

1 HOLY GHOST! dispel our sadness,
Pierce the clouds of nature's night;
Come, thou source of joy and gladness:
Breathe thy life, and spread thy light.

2 Author of our new creation!
Bid us all thine influence prove;
Make our souls thy habitation;
Shed abroad the Saviour's love.

206.

L. M.

Prayer for spiritual Enjoyment.

1 COME, Holy Spirit! calm my mind,
And fit me to approach my God;
Remove each vain, each worldly thought,
And lead me to thy blest abode.

2 Hast thou imparted to my soul
A living spark of holy fire?
Oh! kindle now the sacred flame,
Make me to burn with pure desire.

3 A brighter faith and hope impart,
And let me now my Saviour see;
Oh! soothe and cheer my burdened heart,
And bid my spirit rest in thee.

207.

L. M.

The Sight of God and Christ in Heaven.

1 DESCEND from heaven, immortal Dove!
Stoop down, and take us on thy wings,
And mount, and bear us far above
The reach of these inferior things;—

2 Beyond—beyond this lower sky,
Up where eternal ages roll,
Where solid pleasures never die,
And fruits immortal feast the soul.

3 Oh! for a sight, a blissful sight
Of our almighty Father's throne!
There sits the Saviour, crowned with light,
Clothed in a body like our own.

4 Adoring saints around him stand,
  And thrones and powers before him fall;
The God shines gracious through the man,
  And sheds sweet glories on them all.

5 Oh! what amazing joys they feel,
  While to their golden harps they sing,
And sit on every heavenly hill,
  And spread the triumph of their King!

208.

7s.

Prayer for Light and Sanctification.

1 HOLY GHOST! with light divine,
Shine upon this heart of mine;
Chase the shades of night away,
Turn my darkness into day.

2 Holy Ghost! with power divine,
Cleanse this guilty heart of mine;
Long hath sin, without control,
Held dominion o'er my soul.

3 Holy Ghost! with joy divine,
Cheer this saddened heart of mine;
Bid my many woes depart,
Heal my wounded, bleeding heart.

4 Holy Spirit! all-divine,
Dwell within this heart of mine;
Cast down every idol-throne,
Reign supreme,—and reign alone.

209.

C. M.

Various Influences desired.

1 ETERNAL Spirit!—God of truth!
  Our contrite hearts inspire;
Kindle a flame of heavenly love,
  And feed the pure desire.

2 'T is thine to soothe the sorr'wing mind,
  With guilt and fear oppressed;
'T is thine to bid the dying live,
  And give the weary rest.

3 Subdue the power of every sin,
  Whate'er that sin may be;
That we, in singleness of heart,
  May worship only thee.

4 Then with our spirits witness bear,
That we are sons of God;
Redeemed from sin, and death, and hell,
Through Christ's atoning blood.

210.

S. M.

Prayer for the Spirit.

1 BLEST Comforter divine!
Let rays of heavenly love
Amid our gloom and darkness shine,
To guide our souls above.

2 Draw, with thy still small voice,
From every sinful way;
And bid the mourning saint rejoice,
Though earthly joys decay.

3 By thine inspiring breath,
Make every cloud of care,
And e'en the gloomy vale of death,
A smile of glory wear.

4 Oh! fill thou every heart
With love to all our race:
Great Comforter! to us impart
These blessings of thy grace.

211.

L. M.

Prayer for Light and Guidance.

1 COME, gracious Spirit, heavenly Dove!
With light and comfort from above;
Be thou our guardian, thou our guide;
O'er every thought and step preside.

2 To us the light of truth display,
And make us know and choose thy way;
Plant holy fear in every heart,
That we from God may ne'er depart.

3 Lead us to holiness—the road
That we must take to dwell with God:
Lead us to Christ, the living way,
Nor let us from his precepts stray.

4 Lead us to God, our final rest,
To be with him for ever blessed;
Lead us to heaven, its bliss to share,
And drink our fill of pleasure there.

212.
C. M.
The Sealing of the Spirit.

1 WHY should the children of a king
Go mourning all their days?—
Great Comforter! descend, and bring
Some tokens of thy grace.

2 Dost thou not dwell in all the saints,
And seal the heirs of heaven?
When wilt thou banish my complaints,
And show my sins forgiven?

3 Assure my conscience of her part
In the Redeemer's blood;
And bear thy witness with my heart,
That I am born of God.

4 Thou art the earnest of his love,
The pledge of joys to come;
And thy soft wings, celestial Dove!
Will safe convey me home.

213.
L. M.
Prayer against grieving the Spirit.

1 STAY, thou insulted Spirit! stay,
Though I have done thee such despite,
Cast not a sinner quite away,
Nor take thine everlasting flight.

2 Though I have most unfaithful been
Of all who e'er thy grace received,
Ten thousand times thy goodness seen,
Ten thousand times thy goodness grieved;—

3 Yet, Oh! the chief of sinners spare,
In honor of my great High-Priest;
Nor, in thy righteous anger, swear
I shall not see thy people's rest.

4 My weary soul, O God! release,
Uphold me with thy gracious hand;
Guide me into thy perfect peace,
And bring me to the promised land.

214.
L. M.
The Comforter.

1 SURE, the blest Comforter is nigh;
'T is he sustains my fainting heart;

Else would my hope for ever die,
  And every cheering ray depart.

2 Whene'er, to call the Saviour mine,
  With ardent wish my heart aspires,—
Can it be less than power divine,
  That animates these strong desires?

3 And, when my cheerful hope can say,—
  I love my God and taste his grace,
Lord! is it not thy blissful ray,
  That brings this dawn of sacred peace?

4 Let thy good Spirit in my heart
  For ever dwell, O God of love!
And light and heavenly peace impart—
  Sweet earnest of the joys above.

215.

C. M.

The Necessity of renewing Grace.

1 HOW helpless guilty nature lies,
  Unconscious of its load!
The heart, unchanged, can never rise
  To happiness and God.

2 Can aught, beneath a power divine,
  The stubborn will subdue?
'T is thine, eternal Spirit! thine,
  To form the heart anew.

3 'T is thine, the passions to recall,
  And upward bid them rise;
To make the scales of error fall,
  From reason's darkened eyes;—

4 To chase the shades of death away,
  And bid the sinner live;
A beam of heaven—a vital ray,
  'T is thine alone to give.

5 Oh! change these wretched hearts of ours,
  And give them life divine;
Then shall our passions and our powers,
  Almighty Lord! be thine.

216.

C. M.

The Spirit desired.

1 GREAT Father of each perfect gift!
  Behold thy servants wait;

With longing eyes, and lifted hands,
We flock around thy gate.

2 Oh! shed abroad that choicest gift,—
Thy Spirit from above,
To cheer our eyes with sacred light,
And fire our hearts with love.

3 Blest earnest of eternal joy!
Declare our sins forgiven:
And bear, with energy divine,
Our raptured thoughts to heaven.

4 Diffuse, O God! thy copious showers,
That earth its fruit may yield,
And change the barren wilderness,
To Carmel's flowery field.

217. C. M.

The Outpouring of the Spirit.

1 LET songs of praises fill the sky!
Christ, our ascended Lord,
Sends down his Spirit, from on high,
According to his word.

2 The Spirit, by his heavenly breath,
New life creates within:
He quickens sinners, from the death
Of trespasses and sin.

3 The things of Christ the Spirit takes,
And to our heart reveals:
Our bodies he his temple makes,
And our redemption seals.

4 Come, Holy Spirit! from above,
With thy celestial fire;
Come, and, with flames of zeal and love,
Our hearts and tongues inspire.

218. L. M.

The Operations of the Holy Spirit.

1 ETERNAL Spirit! we confess,
And sing the wonders of thy grace;
Thy power conveys our blessings down,
From God, the Father, and the Son.

2 Enlightened by thy heavenly ray,
Our shades and darkness turn to day:

Thine inward teachings make us know
Our danger, and our refuge too.

3 Thy power and glory work within,
And break the chains of reigning sin;
Do our imperious lusts subdue,
And form our wretched hearts anew.

4 The troubled conscience knows thy voice;
Thy cheering words awake our joys;
Thy words allay the stormy wind,
And calm the surges of the mind.

219.

C. M.

Prayer for the promised Spirit.

1 ENTHRONED on high, almighty Lord!
The Holy Ghost send down:
Fulfill in us thy faithful word,
And all thy mercies crown.

2 Though, on our heads, no tongues of fire
Their wondrous powers impart,
Grant, Saviour! what we more desire,
Thy Spirit in our heart.

3 Spirit of life, and light, and love!
Thy heavenly influence give;
Quicken our souls—born from above—
In Christ, that we may live.

4 To our benighted minds reveal
The glories of his grace,
And bring us, where no clouds conceal
The brightness of his face.

5 His love within us shed abroad,—
Life's ever-springing well,—
Till God in us, and we in God,
In love eternal dwell.

220.

C. M.

Regeneration by the Spirit.

1 NOT all the outward forms on earth,
Nor rites that God has given;
Nor will of man, nor blood, nor birth
Can raise a soul to heaven.

2 The sovereign will of God alone
Creates us heirs of grace,

Born in the image of his Son,
  A new peculiar race.

3 The Spirit, like some heavenly wind,
  Breathes on the sons of flesh;
Creates anew the carnal mind,
  And forms the man afresh.

4 Our quickened souls awake, and rise,
  From the long sleep of death:
On heavenly things we fix our eyes,
  And praise employs our breath.

TRINITY.

221.

6s and 4s.

Invocation.

1 COME, thou almighty King!
Help us thy name to sing,
  Help us to praise:
Father! all-glorious,
O'er all victorious,
Come, and reign over us,
  Ancient of days!

2 Come, thou incarnate Word!
Gird on thy mighty sword;
  Our prayer attend:
Come, and thy people bless,
And give thy word success;
Spirit of holiness!
  On us descend.

3 Come, holy Comforter!
Thy sacred witness bear,
  In this glad hour:
Thou, who almighty art,
Now rule in every heart,
And ne'er from us depart,
  Spirit of power!

4 To the great One in Three,
The highest praises be,
  Hence evermore!

His sovereign majesty
May we in glory see,
And to eternity
Love and adore.

222.
C. M.
Praise to the Godhead.

1 LET them neglect thy glory, Lord!
Who never knew thy grace;
But our loud songs shall still record
The wonders of thy praise

2 We raise our shouts, O God! to thee,
And send them to thy throne;
All glory to th' united Three,—
The undivided One.

3 'T was he—and we 'll adore his name—
That formed us by a word;
'T is he restores our ruined frame;—
Salvation to the Lord!

4 Hosanna! let the earth and skies
Repeat the joyful sound;
Rocks, hills, and vales reflect the voice,
In one eternal round.

223.
C. M.
Praise to the Trinity.

1 FATHER of glory! to thy name
Immortal praise we give,
Who dost an act of grace proclaim,
And bid us rebels live.

2 Immortal honor to the Son,
Who makes thine anger cease;—
Our lives he ransomed with his own,
And died to make our peace.

3 To thine almighty Spirit be
Immortal glory given;
Whose influence brings us near to thee,
And trains us up for heaven.

4 Let men, with their united voice,
Adore th' eternal God,
And spread his honors and their joys,
Through nations far abroad.

5 Let faith, and love, and duty join
One general song to raise;
Let saints, in earth and heaven, combine,
In harmony and praise.

224.
L. M.
Prayer to the Trinity.

1 FATHER of heaven! whose love profound
A ransom for our souls hath found,—
Before thy throne we sinners bend;
To us thy pard'ning love extend.

2 Almighty Son—incarnate Word—
Our prophet, priest, redeemer, Lord!
Before thy throne we sinners bend;
To us thy saving grace extend.

3 Eternal Spirit! by whose breath
The soul is raised from sin and death,—
Before thy throne we sinners bend,
To us thy quickening power extend.

4 Jehovah!—Father, Spirit, Son!—
Mysterious Godhead—Three in One!
Before thy throne we sinners bend;
Grace, pardon, life, to us extend.

225.
6s and 4s.
Prayer to the Triune Jehovah.

1 THOU! whose almighty word
Chaos and darkness heard,
And took their flight,—
Hear us, we humbly pray,
And where the gospel's day
Sheds not its glorious ray,—
"Let there be light!"

2 Thou! who didst come to bring,
On thy redeeming wing,
Healing and sight,—
Health to the sick in mind,
Sight to the inly blind,—
Oh! now to all mankind
"Let there be light!"

3 Spirit of truth and love,
Life-giving holy Dove!
Speed forth thy flight:

Move on the waters' face,
Bearing the lamp of grace,
And in earth's darkest place
"Let there be light!"

4 Holy, holy, holy,
Most glorious Trinity,—
Wisdom, Love, Might!
Boundless as ocean's tide
Rolling in fullest pride,
O'er the earth, far and wide—
"Let there be light!"

226. L. M.

Praise to the Father, Son and Spirit.

1 BLEST be the Father and his love,
To which celestial source we owe
Rivers of endless joy above,
And rills of comfort here below.

2 Glory to thee, great Son of God!
From whose dear wounded body rolls
A precious stream of vital blood—
Pardon and life for dying souls.

3 We give thee, sacred Spirit! praise,
Who in our hearts of sin and woe,
Mak'st living springs of grace arise,
And into boundless glory flow.

4 Thus God, the Father,—God, the Son,—
And God, the Spirit, we adore;—
That sea of life and love unknown,
Without a bottom, or a shore.

227. 7s.

Christians praising the Trinity.

1 GREAT the joy when Christians meet;
Christian fellowship, how sweet,—
When, their theme of praise the same,
They exalt Jehovah's name!

2 Sing we then eternal love;
Such as did the Father move:—
He beheld the world undone;
Loved the world, and gave his Son.

3 Sing the Son's unbounded love;—
How he left the realms above;

Took our nature and our place,—
Lived and died to save our race.

4 Sing we too the Spirit's love;—
With our stubborn hearts he strove;
Chased the mists of sin away,—
Turned our night to glorious day.

5 Great the joy, the union sweet,
When the saints in glory meet;
Where the theme is still the same;
Where they praise Jehovah's name.

228.

7s.

Communion with the Triune God.

1 IN thy presence we appear;
Lord! we love to worship here,
When, within the veil, we meet
Thee upon thy mercy-seat.

2 While thy glorious name is sung,
Touch our lips, and loose our tongue;
Then our joyful souls shall bless
Thee, the Lord, our righteousness.

3 While to thee our prayers ascend,
Let thine ear in love attend;
Hear us, for thy Spirit pleads;
Hear, for Jesus intercedes.

4 While thy word is heard with awe,
And we tremble at thy law,
Let thy gospel's wondrous love
Every doubt and fear remove.

5 While thy ministers proclaim
Peace and pardon through thy name,
In their voices, let us own
Jesus, speaking from the throne.

6 From thy house when we return,
Let our hearts within us burn;
That, at evening, we may say,—
"We have walked with God to-day."

229.

8s and 7s.

Praise to Father, Son and Spirit.

1 TO the source of every blessing,
Grateful anthems let us raise;

Holy joy, our souls possessing,
Swells the tribute of our praise.

2 Glory to th' almighty Father,
Fountain of eternal love,
Who, his wandering sheep to gather,
Sent a Saviour from above.

3 To the Son all praise be given,
Who, with love unknown before,
Left the bright abode of heaven,
And our sins and sorrows bore.

4 Equal strains of warm devotion
Let the Spirit's praise employ;
Author of each pure emotion,—
Source of wisdom, peace, and joy.

5 Thus—our joyful hearts ascending,—
Glorify Jehovah's name;
Heavenly songs with ours are blending,—
There, the theme is still the same.

230. S. M.

The Father, Son and Holy Ghost.

1 WHILE all the angel-throng
Give thanks to God on high,
Let earth repeat the joyful song,
And echo to the sky.

2 Father! in whom we live,
In whom we are and move,—
The glory, power and praise receive
Of thine eternal love.

3 Incarnate Deity!
Let all the ransomed race
Render in thanks their lives to thee,
For thy redeeming grace.

4 Spirit of holiness!
Let all thy saints adore
Thy sacred energy, and bless
Thy heart-renewing power.

5 Eternal, glorious Lord!
Let all the saints above,
Let all the sons of men, record,
And celebrate thy love.

231.

8s and 6s. Peculiar.
Hallelujah to the Triune God.

1 SING—Hallelujah! praise the Lord!
Sing with a cheerful voice;
Exalt our God with one accord,
And in his name rejoice:
Ne'er cease to sing, thou ransomed host!
To Father, Son, and Holy Ghost,
Till in the realms of endless light,
Your praises shall unite.

2 There we to all eternity,
Shall join th' angelic lays,
And sing, in perfect harmony,
To God our Saviour's praise;
He hath redeemed us by his blood,
And made us kings and priests to God:
For us—for us the Lamb was slain,—
Praise ye the Lord!—Amen.

ALARMING.

232.

7s and 6s. Peculiar.
The Alarm.

1 SINNER! stop—Oh! stop and think,
Before you farther go:
Will you sport upon the brink
Of everlasting wo?
On the verge of ruin stop;—
Now the friendly warning take;
Stay your footsteps, ere you drop
Into the burning lake.

2 Say—have you an arm like God,
That you his will oppose?
Fear you not that iron-rod
With which he breaks his foes?
Can you stand in that dread day,
Which his justice shall proclaim,
When the earth shall melt away,
Like wax before the flame?

3 Ghastly death will quickly come,
  And drag you to his bar:
Then you'll hear your awful doom,
  And sink in deep despair!
All your sins will round you crowd;
  You will mark their crimson die,
Each for vengeance crying loud,
  And then—no refuge nigh!

233. L. M.

The Sinner exhorted.

1 SINNER! Oh! why so thoughtless grown
  Why in such fearful haste to die?
Why speed thy flight to worlds unknown,—
  Regardless of thy destiny?

2 Wilt thou defy the wrath of God,
  Led on by sin's delusive dreams?
Madly despise the Saviour's blood,
  And force thy passage to the flames?

3 Sinner! Oh! lift thy thoughts above,
  And hear the Lord of life unfold
The glories of his dying love—
  For ever telling, yet untold!

234. 7s.

The Sinner warned.

1 HASTE, O sinner! to be wise,
  Stay not for the morrow's sun;
Wisdom warns thee, from the skies,
  All the paths of death to shun.

2 Haste, and mercy now implore;
  Stay not for the morrow's sun;
Thy probation may be o'er,
  Ere this evening's work is done.

3 Haste, O sinner! now return;
  Stay not for the morrow's sun;
Lest thy lamp should cease to burn,
  Ere salvation's work is done.

4 Haste, while yet thou canst be blest;
  Stay not for the morrow's sun;
Death may thy poor soul arrest,
  Ere the morrow is begun.

235

11s.

Danger of Delay.

1 DELAY not, delay not; O sinner! draw near,
The waters of life are now flowing for thee;
No price is demanded, the Saviour is here,
Redemption is purchased, salvation is free.

2 Delay not, delay not; why longer abuse
The love and compassion of Jesus, thy God?
A fountain is opened,—how canst thou refuse
To wash, and be cleansed in his pard'ning blood?

3 Delay not, delay not, O sinner! to come,
For mercy still lingers and calls thee to-day;
Her voice is not heard in the vale of the tomb,—
Her message, unheeded, will soon pass away.

4 Delay not, delay not; the Spirit of grace,
Long grieved and resisted, may take its sad flight;
And leave thee in darkness to finish thy race,—
To sink in the gloom of eternity's night.

236.

L. M.

One Thing needful.

1 WHY will ye waste, on trifling cares,
That life which God's compassion spares,
While, in the various range of thought,
The one thing needful is forgot?

2 Shall God invite you from above?
Shall Jesus urge his dying love?
Shall troubled conscience give you pain,
And all these pleas unite in vain?

3 Not so your eyes will always view
Those objects which you now pursue;
Not so will heaven and hell appear,
When death's decisive hour is near.

4 Almighty God! thy grace impart;
Fix deep conviction on each heart:
Nor let us waste, on trifling cares,
That life which thy compassion spares.

237.

C. M.

Exhortation to Repentance.

1 REPENT! the voice celestial cries,
No longer dare delay:

The soul that scorns the mandate dies,
And meets a fiery day.

2 No more the sovereign eye of God
O'erlooks the crimes of men;
His heralds now are sent abroad
To warn the world of sin.

3 O sinners! in his presence bow,
And all your guilt confess;
Accept the offered Saviour now,
Nor trifle with his grace.

4 Soon, will the awful trumpet sound,
And call you to his bar;
His mercy knows th' appointed bound,
And yields to justice there.

5 Amazing love—that yet will call,
And yet prolong our days!
Our hearts subdued by goodness fall,
And weep, and love, and praise.

238.

7s.

The Sinner meeting God.

1 SINNER! art thou still secure?
Wilt thou still refuse to pray?
Can thy heart or hand endure,
In the Lord's avenging day?

2 See,—his mighty arm is bared;
Awful terrors clothe his brow!
For his judgments stand prepared;—
Thou must either break or bow.

3 At his presence nature shakes,
Earth affrighted hastes to flee;
Solid mountains melt like wax:
What will then become of thee?

4 Who his coming may abide?
You that glory in your shame!—
Can you find a place to hide,
When the world is wrapt in flame?

239.

8s, 7s and 4.

The Voice of Mercy.

1 HEAR, O sinner! mercy hails you;
Now with sweetest voice she calls;

Bids you haste to seek the Saviour,
  Ere the hand of justice falls:
    Hear, O sinner!
  'T is the voice of mercy calls.

2 See! the storm of vengeance gathering
  O'er the path you dare to tread!
Hark! the awful thunder rolling
  Loud and louder o'er your head!
    Turn, O sinner!
  Lest the lightning strike you dead.

3 Haste, O sinner! to the Saviour;
  Seek his mercy while you may;
Soon the day of grace is over;—
  Soon your life will pass away;
    Haste, O sinner!
  You must perish if you stay.

240.

C. P. M.

Present and future Realities.

1 LO! on a narrow neck of land,
Between two boundless seas I stand,—
  Yet how insensible!
A point of time—a moment's space—
Removes me to yon heavenly place,
  Or—shuts me up in hell!

2 O God! my inmost soul convert,
And, deeply on my thoughtless heart,
  Eternal things impress;
Give me to feel their solemn weight,
And save me, ere it be too late;—
  Wake me to righteousness.

3 Before me place, in bright array,
The pomp of that tremendous day,
  When thou with clouds shalt come,
To judge the nations at thy bar;—
And tell me, Lord! shall I be there,
  To meet a joyful doom?

4 Be this my one great business here,
With holy trembling, holy fear,
  To make my calling sure?
Thine utmost counsel to fulfill,
To suffer all thy righteous will,
  And to the end endure!

5 Then, Saviour! then my soul receive,
Transported from the earth, to live
And reign with thee above:
Where faith is sweetly lost in sight,
And hope, in full supreme delight,
And everlasting love.

241. L. M.

Life, the Day of Grace and Hope.

1 LIFE is the time to serve the Lord,
The time t' insure the great reward;
And while the lamp holds out to burn,
The vilest sinner may return.

2 Life is the hour that God has given,
To 'scape from hell and fly to heaven;
The day of grace,—and mortals may
Secure the blessings of the day.

3 The living know that they must die,
But all the dead forgotten lie;
Their mem'ry and their sense are gone,
Alike unknowing and unknown.

4 Then, what my thoughts design to do,
My hands! with all your might pursue;
Since no device, nor work is found,
Nor faith, nor hope, beneath the ground.

5 There are no acts of pardon past,
In the cold grave to which we haste;
But darkness, death, and long despair,
Reign in eternal silence there.

242. C. M.

Expostulation with Sinners.

1 YE! who despise the Saviour's grace,
And scorn his gospel, here,—
How can you meet his angry face,
Or at his bar appear?

2 When every earthly hope shall fail,—
When storms of wrath are nigh,
How will your souls affrighted quail,
Beneath his burning eye!

3 Why will you madly rush on death,
And force your way to wo?

Why tempt the God, that holds your breath,
  To strike the fatal blow.

4 Turn, guilty sinners! quickly turn;
  Oh! come to Jesus now;—
Ere the fierce flames around you burn,
  To your Redeemer bow.

243. L. M.
Advice to Youth.

1 NOW, in the heat of youthful blood,
Remember your Creator, God;
Behold! the months come hastening on,
When you shall say—"My joys are gone."

2 Behold! the aged sinner goes,
Laden with guilt and heavy woes,
Down to the regions of the dead,
With endless curses on his head.

3 The dust returns to dust again;
The soul, in agonies of pain,
Ascends to God—not there to dwell,—
But hears her doom, and sinks to hell.

4 Eternal King! I fear thy name;
Teach me to know how frail I am;
And when my soul must hence remove,
Give me a mansion in thy love.

244. S. M.
Grieving the Spirit.

1 AND canst thou, sinner! slight
  The call of love divine?
Shall God, with tenderness invite,
  And gain no thought of thine?

2 Wilt thou not cease to grieve
  The Spirit from thy breast,
Till he thy wretched soul shall leave
  With all thy sins oppressed?

3 To-day, a pard'ning God
  Will hear the suppliant pray;
To-day, a Saviour's cleansing blood
  Will wash thy guilt away.

4 But, grace so dearly bought
  If yet thou wilt despise,

Thy fearful doom, with vengeance fraught,
Will fill thee with surprise.

245.

C. M.

Frailty and Sin.

1 HOW short and hasty is our life!
How vast our soul's affairs!
Yet senseless mortals vainly strive
To lavish out their years.

2 Our days run thoughtlessly along,
Without a moment's stay;
Just like a story, or a song,
We pass our lives away

3 God from on high invites us home,
But we march heedless on,
And, ever hastening to the tomb,
Stoop downward as we run.

4 How we deserve the deepest hell,
Who slight the joys above!
What chains of vengeance should we feel
Who break such cords of love!

5 Draw us, O God! with sovereign grace,
And lift our thoughts on high,
That we may end this mortal race,
And see salvation nigh.

246.

C. M.

Brevity of Life.

1 LET others boast how strong they be,
Nor death nor danger fear;
But we'll confess, O Lord! to thee,
What feeble things we are.

2 Fresh as the grass our bodies stand,
And flourish bright and gay;
A blasting wind sweeps o'er the land,
And fades the grass away.

3 Our life contains a thousand springs,
And dies, if one be gone;
Strange! that a harp of thousand strings
Should keep in tune so long.

4 But 't is our God supports our frame,—
The God who built us first;

Salvation to th' almighty Name
  That reared us from the dust.

247.

L. M.

The Road to Life and to Death.

1 BROAD is the road that leads to death,
  And thousands walk together there;
But wisdom shows a narrow path,
  With here and there a traveller.

2 "Deny thyself and take thy cross,"—
  Is the Redeemer's great command:
Nature must count her gold but dross,
  If she would gain this heavenly land.

3 The fearful soul that tires and faints,
  And walks the ways of God no more,
Is but esteemed almost a saint,
  And makes his own destruction sure.

4 Lord! let not all my hopes be vain:
  Create my heart entirely new,
Which hypocrites could ne'er attain;—
  Which false apostles never knew.

248.

S. M.

Uncertainty of Life.

1 TO-MORROW, Lord! is thine,—
  Lodged in thy sovereign hand;
And if its sun arise and shine,
  It shines by thy command.

2 The present moment flies,
  And bears our life away;
Oh! make thy servants truly wise,
  That they may live to-day.

3 Since, on this fleeting hour,
  Eternity is hung,
Awaken, by thy mighty power,
  The aged and the young.

4 One thing demands our care;—
  Be that one thing pursued;
Lest, slighted once, the season fair
  Should never be renewed.

5 To Jesus may we fly,
  Swift as the morning-light,

Lest life's young golden beams should die,
  In sudden, endless night.

CONVICTION.

249. S. M.
The Sinner arrested.

1 MY former hopes are fled,
  My terror now begins;
My guilty soul, alas! is "dead
  In trespasses and sins."

2 Ah! whither shall I fly?—
  Where seek for mercy's door?
The law proclaims destruction nigh,
  And justice armed with power.

3 When I review my ways,
  I dread th' impending doom;
While yet some friendly whisper says,—
  "Flee from the wrath to come!"

4 Oh! that I now might see
  Some glimmering from afar,—
Some beam of hope to dawn on me,
  And save me from despair.

250. 7s and 6s.
The Sinner disquieted.

1 WHY sinks my soul desponding?
  Why fill my eyes with tears?
While nature all-surrounding
  The smile of beauty wears:
Why, burdened now with sorrow,
  Is every lab'ring thought?
Each vision that I borrow,
  With gloom and sadness fraught?

2 The pleasures that deceived me
  My soul no more can charm;
Of rest they oft bereaved me,
  And filled me with alarm;
The objects, I have cherished,
  Are empty as the wind;
My earthly joys have perished;—
  What comfort shall I find?

3 If inward, still inquiring,
I turn my searching eye,
Or upward, now aspiring,
I raise my feeble cry,
No heavenly light is beaming
To cheer my troubled breast,
No ray of comfort gleaming
To give my spirit rest.

4 My soul! from this dread anguish
Is there no refuge nigh?
'T is guilt that makes thee languish,
And leaves thee thus to die:
Renounce thy sin and folly
Before the throne of grace;
And make the Lord, most holy,
Thy strength and righteousness.

251.

C. M.

Conviction by the Law.

1 LORD! how secure my conscience was,
And felt no inward dread!
I was alive without the law,
And thought my sins were dead.

2 My hopes of heaven were firm and bright;
But since the precept came,
With a convincing power and light,
I find how vile I am.

3 My guilt appeared but small before,
Till terribly I saw—
How perfect, holy, just, and pure,
Is thine eternal law.

4 Then felt my soul the heavy load,
My sins revived again:—
I have provoked a dreadful God,
And all my hopes are slain.

5 My God! I cry with every breath
For some kind power to save,—
To break the yoke of sin and death
And thus redeem the slave.

252.

L. M.

The Strivings of the Spirit.

1 SAY, sinner! hath a voice within
Oft whispered to thy secret soul,

Urged thee to leave the ways of sin,
And yield thy heart to God's control?

2 Sinner! it was a heavenly voice,—
It was the Spirit's gracious call;
It bade thee make the better choice,
And haste to seek in Christ thine all.

3 Spurn not the call to life and light;
Regard, in time, the warning kind;
That call thou may'st not always slight,
And yet the gate of mercy find.

4 God's Spirit will not always strive
With hardened, self-destroying man;
Ye, who persist his love to grieve,
May never hear his voice again.

5 Sinner! perhaps, this very day,
Thy last accepted time may be:
Oh! should'st thou grieve him now away,
Then hope may never beam on thee.

253. S. M.

Man condemned before God.

1 AH! how shall fallen man
Be just before his God?
If he contend in righteousness,
We fall beneath his rod.

2 If he our ways should mark,
With strict inquiring eyes,
Could we, for one of thousand faults,
A just excuse devise?

3 All-seeing, powerful God!
Who can with thee contend?
Or who, that tries th' unequal strife,
Shall prosper in the end?

4 The mountains, in thy wrath,
Their ancient seats forsake;
The trembling earth deserts her place,
Her rooted pillars shake.

5 Ah! how shall guilty man
Contend with such a God?
None—none can meet him, and escape
But through the Saviour's blood.

254.

S. M.

The evil Heart.

1 ASTONISHED and distressed,
I turn mine eyes within ;—
My heart with loads of guilt oppressed,
The seat of every sin.

2 What crowds of evil thoughts,
What vile affections there !
Distrust, presumption, artful guile,
Pride, envy, slavish fear !

3 Almighty King of saints !
These hateful sins subdue ;
Dispel the darkness from my mind,
And all my powers renew.

4 This done,—my cheerful voice
Shall loud hosannas raise ;
My soul shall glow with gratitude,—
My lips pronounce thy praise.

INVITING.

255.

C. M.

The Saviour's Invitation.

1 THE Saviour calls—let every ear
Attend the heavenly sound ;
Ye doubting souls ! dismiss your fear,
Hope smiles reviving round.

2 For every thirsty, longing heart,
Here streams of bounty flow,
And life, and health, and bliss impart,
To banish mortal wo.

3 Ye sinners ! come ; 't is mercy's voice :
The gracious call obey ;
Mercy invites to heavenly joys,—
And can you yet delay ?

4 Dear Saviour ! draw reluctant hearts ;
To thee let sinners fly,
And take the bliss thy love imparts,
And drink, and never die.

256.

L. M.

Rest for the weary Penitent

1 COME, weary souls! with sin distressed,
Come, and accept the promised rest;
The Saviour's gracious call obey,
And cast your gloomy fears away.

2 Here mercy's boundless ocean flows,
To cleanse your guilt and heal your woes;
Pardon and life, and endless peace,—
How rich the gift, how free the grace!

3 Lord! we accept, with thankful heart,
The hope thy gracious words impart;
We come, with trembling; yet rejoice,
And bless the kind inviting voice.

4 Dear Saviour! let thy powerful love
Confirm our faith,—our fears remove;
Oh! sweetly reign in every breast,
And guide us to eternal rest.

257.

C. M.

The Gospel-Trumpet.

1 LET every mortal ear attend,
And every heart rejoice;
The trumpet of the gospel sounds,
With an inviting voice.

2 Ho! all ye hungry, starving souls,
That feed upon the wind,
And vainly strive with earthly toils
To fill th' immortal mind!—

3 Eternal wisdom has prepared
A soul-reviving feast,
And bids your longing appetites
The rich provision taste.

4 Ho! ye that pant for living streams,
And pine away and die!
Here you may quench your raging thirst
With springs that never dry.

5 Rivers of love and mercy, here,
In a rich ocean join;
Salvation in abundance flows,
Like floods of milk and wine.

6 The happy gates of gospel-grace
Stand open night and day;—
Lord! we are come to seek supplies
And drive our wants away.

258.

L. M.

Christ's Invitation to Sinners.

1 "COME hither, all ye weary souls!
Ye heavy-laden sinners! come;
I'll give you rest from all your toils,
And raise you to my heavenly home.

2 "They shall find rest, who learn of me,—
I'm of a meek and lowly mind;
But passion rages like the sea,
And pride is restless as the wind.

3 "Blessed is the man, whose shoulders take
My yoke, and bear it with delight;
My yoke is easy to his neck,
My grace shall make the burden light."

4 Jesus! we come at thy command;
With faith, and hope, and humble zeal,
Resign our spirits, to thy hand,
To mould and guide us at thy will.

259.

L. M.

Living Waters.

1 HO! every one that thirsts! draw nigh;—
'T is God invites the fallen race;
Mercy and free salvation buy,
Buy wine, and milk, and gospel-grace.

2 Ye nothing in exchange can give,—
Leave all ye have and are behind;
Freely the gift of God receive,—
Pardon and peace in Jesus find.

3 Come to the living waters, come;
Sinners! obey your Maker's voice;
Return, ye weary wanderers! home,
And in redeeming love rejoice.

260.

C. M.

The Resolve.

1 COME, trembling sinner! in whose breast,
A thousand thoughts revolve;

Come, with your guilt and fear oppressed,
And make this last resolve:—

2 "I 'll go to Jesus, though my sin
Hath like a mountain rose;
I 'll seek his courts, and enter in,
Whatever may oppose.

3 "Prostrate I 'll fall before his throne,
And there my guilt confess;
I 'll tell him, I 'm a wretch undone,
Without his sovereign grace.

4 "Perhaps he will admit my plea,
Perhaps will hear my prayer;
But, if I perish, I will pray,
And perish only there.

5 "I can but perish if I go,
I am resolved to try;
For if I stay away, I know
I must for ever die."

261.

8s and 7s. Peculiar.

A Fountain set open.

1 COME to Calv'ry's holy mountain
Sinners, ruined by the fall!
Here a pure and healing fountain
Flows to you,—to me,—to all,—
In a full perpetual tide,
Opened when the Saviour died.

2 Come, in sorrow and contrition,
Wounded, impotent, and blind;
Here the guilty, free remission,—
Here the troubled, peace may find;
Health this fountain will restore;
He that drinks shall thirst no more:—

3 He that drinks shall live for ever,—
'T is a soul-reviving flood:
God is faithful—God will never
Break his covenant in blood;—
Signed, when our Redeemer died,
Sealed, when he was glorified.

262.

8s and 7s.

False and true Pleasure.

1 TELL us, wanderer! wildly roving
From the path that leads to peace,

Pleasure's false enchantment loving,—
  When will thy delusion cease?

2 Once, like thee, by joys surrounded,
  We could kneel at pleasure's shrine;
Then our brightest hopes were bounded,
  By delights as false as thine.

3 But those visions never blessed us,—
  Soon their fleeting day was o'er;
Then the world, that had caressed us,
  Charmed us with its smiles no more.

4 Such is pleasure's transient story;
  Lasting happiness is known
Only in the path to glory,—
  In the Saviour's love alone.

263.

L. M.

The happy Choice.

1 TO-DAY—if ye will hear his voice,
Now is the time to make your choice;
Say—will you to Mount Zion go?
Say—will you have this Christ, or no?

2 Ye wandering souls, who find no rest!
Say—will you be for ever blest?
Will you be saved from sin and hell?
Will you with Christ in glory dwell?

3 Come now, dear youth! for ruin bound,
Obey the gospel's joyful sound;
Come, go with us, and you shall prove
The joy of Christ's redeeming love.

4 Once more we ask you in his name,—
For yet his love remains the same,—
Say—will you to Mount Zion go?
Say—will you have this Christ or no?

264.

C. M.

Pardon and Sanctification in Christ.

1 HOW sad our state by nature is!
  Our sin—how deep it stains!
And Satan binds our captive minds,
  Fast in his slavish chains.

2 But there 's a voice of sovereign grace,
  Sounds from the sacred word;—

"Ho! ye despairing sinners! come,
And trust upon the Lord."

3 My soul obeys th' almighty call,
And runs to this relief;
I would believe thy promise, Lord!
Oh! help my unbelief.

4 To the dear fountain of thy blood,
Incarnate God! I fly;
Here let me wash my spotted soul,
From stains of deepest die.

5 A guilty, weak, and helpless worm,
On thy kind arms I fall:
Be thou my strength and righteousness,
My Jesus, and my all.

265.

C. M.

The Way to Zion.

1 INQUIRE, ye pilgrims! for the way
That leads to Zion's hill,
And thither set your steady face,
With a determined will.

2 Oh! come, and to his temple haste,
And seek his favor there;
Before his footstool, humbly bow,
And pour your fervent prayer.

3 Oh! come, and join your souls to God
In everlasting bands;
Accept the blessings he bestows,
With thankful hearts and hands.

266.

C. M.

Invitation to the Gospel-Feast.

1 YE wretched, hungry, starving poor!
Behold a royal feast,—
Where mercy spreads her bounteous store
For every humble guest.

2 Here Jesus stands with open arms;
He calls, he bids you, come;
Guilt holds you back, and fear alarms;
But see! there yet is room:—

3 Room in the Saviour's bleeding heart;—
There love and pity meet;

Nor will he bid the soul depart,
  That trembles at his feet.

4 Oh! come, and, with his children, taste
  The blessings of his love;
While hope attends the sweet repast
  Of nobler joys above.

5 There, with united heart and voice,
  Before th' eternal throne,
Ten thousand thousand souls rejoice,
  In songs on earth unknown.

267. C. M.

The Fountain of living Waters.

1 OH! what amazing words of grace
  Are in the gospel found,
Suited to every sinner's case
  Who hears the joyful sound!

2 Come, then, with all your wants and wounds,
  Your every burden bring;
Here love, unchanging love, abounds,—
  A deep celestial spring.

3 This spring with living water flows,
  And heavenly joy imparts;
Come, thirsty souls! your wants disclose,
  And drink, with thankful hearts.

4 Millions of sinners, vile as you,
  Have here found life and peace;
Come, then, and prove its virtues too,
  And drink, adore, and bless.

268. 7s.

Sinners urged to accept the Invitation.

1 YE! who in his courts are found,
Listening to the joyful sound,
Lost and helpless as ye are,
Sons of sorrow, sin, and care,—
Glorify the King of kings,
Take the peace the gospel brings.

2 Turn to Christ your longing eyes,
View this bleeding sacrifice;
See, in him, your sins forgiven,
Pardon, holiness, and heaven;

Glorify the King of kings,
Take the peace the gospel brings.

269.

7s.

Expostulation with Sinners.

1 SINNERS! turn, why will ye die?
God, your Maker, asks you—Why?
God, who did your being give,
Made you with himself to live,—
He the fatal cause demands,
Asks the work of his own hands,—
Why, ye thankless creatures! why,
Will ye cross his love, and die?

2 Sinners! turn, why will ye die?
God, your Saviour, asks you—Why?
He, who did your souls retrieve,
Died himself that ye might live;—
Will ye let him die in vain?
Crucify your Lord again?
Why, ye ransomed sinners! why
Will ye slight his grace, and die?

3 Sinners! turn, why will ye die?
God, the Spirit, asks you—Why?
Many a time with you he strove,
Wooed you to embrace his love
Will ye not his grace receive?
Will ye still refuse to live?
Oh! ye guilty sinners! why -
Why will ye for ever die?

270.

C. M.

Expostulation with Sinners.

1 SINNERS! the voice of God regard;
'T is Mercy speaks to-day,
He calls you by his sovereign word,
From sin's destructive way.

2 Like the rough sea that cannot rest,
You live devoid of peace:
A thousand stings within your breast,
Deprive your souls of ease.

3 Your way is dark, and leads to hell;
And will you onward go?
Can you in endless burnings dwell,
Or bear eternal wo?

4 Lo! he, who turns to God, shall live,
Through his abounding grace;
His mercy will the guilt forgive
Of those who seek his face.

5 Bow to the sceptre of his word—
Renouncing every sin:
Submit to him, your sovereign Lord,
And learn his will divine.

6 His love exceeds your highest thoughts;—
He pardons like a God;
He will forgive your numerous faults,
Through Christ's atoning blood.

271.

L. M.

Knocking at the Door.

1 BEHOLD a stranger at the door!
He gently knocks,—has knocked before;
Has waited long—is waiting still;
You treat no other friend so ill.

2 Oh! lovely attitude—he stands
With melting heart and loaded hands:
Oh! matchless kindness—and he shows
This matchless kindness to his foes!

3 But will he prove a friend indeed?
He will—the very friend you need;
The friend of sinners—yes, 't is he,
With garments dyed on Calvary.

4 Rise—touched with gratitude divine,
Turn out his enemy and thine,—
That soul-destroying monster, sin,—
And let the heavenly stranger in.

5 Admit him, ere his anger burn,—
His feet departed ne'er return;
Admit him,—or the hour 's at hand,
You 'll at his door rejected stand.

272.

8s, 7s and 4.

Invitation to Sinners.

1 COME, ye sinners! heavy-laden,
Lost and ruined by the fall,—

If you wait till you are better,
  You will never come at all:
    Sinners only,
  Christ, the Saviour, came to call.

2 Let no sense of guilt prevent you,
  Nor of fitness fondly dream;
All the fitness he requireth
  Is to feel your need of him:
    This he gives you;—
  'T is the Spirit's rising beam.

3 Agonizing in the garden,
  Lo! your Saviour prostrate lies;
On the bloody tree behold him,
  There he groans, and bleeds, and dies,
    "It is finished"—
  Heaven accepts the sacrifice.

4 Lo! th' incarnate God ascending
  Pleads the merit of his blood;
Venture on him,—venture wholly,
  Let no other trust intrude:
    None but Jesus
  Can do helpless sinners good.

5 Saints and angels, joined in concert,
  Sing the praises of the Lamb;
While the blissful seats of heaven
  Sweetly echo with his name;
    Hallelujah!—
  Sinners here may sing the same.

273.

L. M.

The Sinner entreated.

1 RETURN, O wanderer! now return,
  And seek thine injured Father's face;
Those new desires that in thee burn,
  Were kindled by reclaiming grace.

2 Return, O wanderer! now return,
  He hears thy deep repentant sigh;
He hears thy softened spirit mourn,
  When no intruding ear is nigh.

3 Return, O wanderer! now return,
  Thy Saviour bids thy spirit live;
Go to his bleeding feet, and learn
  How freely Jesus can forgive.

4 Return, O wanderer! now return,
And wipe away the falling tear;
Thy Father calls—"No longer mourn!"
'T is mercy's voice invites thee near.

274.
C. M.
The heavenly Guest.

1 AND will the Lord thus condescend
To visit sinful worms?
Thus at the door shall mercy stand,
In all her winning forms?

2 Shall Jesus for admittance plead,
His charming voice unheard?
And this vile heart, for which he bled,
Remain for ever barred?

3 'T is sin, alas! with tyrant-power,
The lodging has possessed;
And crowds of traitors bar the door,
Against the heavenly guest.

4 Lord! rise in thine all-conquering grace,
Thy mighty power display;
One beam of glory from thy face
Can drive my foes away.

5 Ye vile seducers! hence depart;
Dear Saviour! enter in;
Oh! guard the passage to my heart,
And keep out every sin.

275.
8s, 7s and 4.
Glad Tidings.

1 SINNERS! will you scorn the message
Coming from the courts above?
Mercy speaks in every passage;
Every line is full of love;
Oh! believe it,—
Every line is full of love.

2 Now, the heralds of salvation
Joyful news from heaven proclaim:—
Sinners freed from condemnation,
Through the all-atoning Lamb!
Life receiving—
Through the all-atoning Lamb.

3 Who hath their report believed?
Who received the joyful word?
Who embraced the news of pardon,
Freely offered by the Lord?
Life immortal,—
Freely offered by the Lord.

4 O ye angels! hovering round us,—
Waiting spirits! speed your way,
Hasten to the court of heaven,
Tidings bear without delay,—
Rebel-sinners—
Glad the message will obey.

276.

S. M.

The accepted Time.

1 NOW is th' accepted time,
Now is the day of grace;
O sinners! come, without delay,
And seek the Saviour's face.

2 Now is th' accepted time,
The Saviour calls to-day;
To-morrow it may be too late;—
Then why should you delay?

3 Now is th' accepted time,
The gospel bids you come;
And every promise, in his word,
Declares there yet is room.

4 Lord! draw reluctant souls,
And melt them by thy love;
Then will the angels speed their way
To bear the news above.

277.

8s and 4.

The Gospel-Trumpet.

1 HARK—hark! the gospel-trumpet sounds,—
Through the wide earth the echo bounds;
Pardon and peace by Jesus' blood!
Sinners are reconciled to God,
By grace divine.

2 Come, sinners! hear the joyful news,
Nor longer dare the grace refuse;

Mercy and justice here combine,
Goodness and truth harmonious join,
T' invite you near.

3 Ye saints in glory! strike the lyre;
Ye mortals! catch the sacred fire;
Let both the Saviour's love proclaim;—
For ever worthy is the Lamb
Of endless praise.

278.

C. M.

The Young exhorted.

1 YE hearts with youthful vigor warm!
In smiling crowds draw near;
And turn from every mortal charm,
A Saviour's voice to hear.

2 He, Lord of all the worlds on high,
Stoops to converse with you;
And lays his radiant glories by,
Your friendship to pursue.

3 The soul, that longs to see his face,
Is sure his love to gain;
And they, who early seek his grace,
Shall never seek in vain.

4 What object, Lord! my soul should move,
If once compared with thee?
What beauty should command my love,
Like what in Christ I see?

5 Away, ye false delusive toys!
Vain tempters of the mind;
'T is here I fix my lasting choice,
For here, true bliss I find.

279.

8s, 7s and 4.

Children exhorted.

1 CHILDREN! hear the melting story
Of the Lamb that once was slain;
'T is the Lord of life and glory;
Shall he plead with you in vain?
Oh! receive him,
And salvation now obtain.

2 Yield no more to sin and folly,
So displeasing in his sight;

Jesus loves the pure and holy,
They alone are his delight;
Seek his favor,
And your hearts to him unite.

3 All your sins to him confessing
Who is ready to forgive;
Seek the Saviour's richest blessing,
On his precious name believe;
He is waiting,—
Will you not his grace receive?

280.

7s.

Children invited to Christ.

1 CHILDREN! listen to the Lord,
And obey his gracious word;
Seek his face with heart and mind—
Early seek, and you shall find.

2 Sorrowful, your sins confess;
Plead his perfect righteousness;
See the Saviour's bleeding side;—
Come—you will not be denied.

3 For his worship now prepare;
Kneel to him in fervent prayer;
Serve him with a perfect heart;
Never from his ways depart.

PENITENTIAL.

281.

C. M.

Contrition.

1 O THOU! whose tender mercy hears
Contrition's humble sigh;
Whose hand, indulgent, wipes the tears
From sorrow's weeping eye;—

2 See, low before thy throne of grace,
A wretched wanderer mourn;
Hast thou not bid me seek thy face?
Hast thou not said—"Return?"

3 And shall my guilty fears prevail
To drive me from thy feet?

Oh! let not this dear refuge fail,
  This only safe retreat.

4 Oh! shine on this benighted heart,
  With beams of mercy shine;
And let thy healing voice impart
  A taste of joys divine.

282.

7s.

Repentance at the Cross of Christ.

1 HEARTS of stone! relent, relent,
  Break, by Jesus' cross subdued;
See his body, mangled, rent,
  Covered with a gore of blood!
Sinful soul! what hast thou done?
Crucified God's only Son!

2 Yes, thy sins have done the deed,
  Driven the nails that fixed him there,
Crowned with thorns his sacred head,
  Pierced him with the bloody spear,
Made his soul a sacrifice,—
While for sinful man he dies.

3 Wilt thou let him bleed in vain,—
  Still to death thy Lord pursue?
Open all his wounds again,—
  And the shameful cross renew?
No;—with all my sins I 'll part,
Break, Oh! break, my bleeding heart!

283.

L. M. 6 Lines.

Pleading in Jesus' Name.

1 FATHER of mercies, God of love!
  Oh! hear an humble suppliant's cry;
Bend from thy lofty seat above,—
  Thy throne of glorious majesty;
Oh! deign to hear my mournful voice,
And bid my drooping heart rejoice.

2 I urge no merit of my own,—
  No worth to claim thy gracious smile;
No,—when I come before thy throne,
  Dare to converse with God awhile,
Thy name, blest Jesus! is my plea,—
Dearest and sweetest name to me.

3 Father of mercies, God of love!
  Then hear thine humble suppliant's cry;
Bend from thy lofty seat above,
  Thy throne of glorious majesty;
One pard'ning word can make me whole,
And soothe the anguish of my soul.

284.

C. M.

Godly Sorrow at the Cross.

1 ALAS! and did my Saviour bleed?
  And did my Sovereign die?
Would he devote that sacred head,
  For such a worm as I?

2 Was it, for crimes that I had done,
  He groaned upon the tree?
Amazing pity!—grace unknown!—
  And love beyond degree!

3 Well might the sun in darkness hide,
  And shut his glories in,
When Christ, the mighty Maker, died,
  For man the creature's sin.

4 Thus might I hide my blushing face,
  While his dear cross appears;
Dissolve my heart in thankfulness,
  And melt mine eyes to tears.

5 But floods of tears can ne'er repay
  The debt of love I owe;
Here, Lord! I give myself away;—
  'T is all that I can do.

285.

L. M. 6 Lines.

Backslider's Return through Christ.

1 WEARY of wandering from my God,
  And now made willing to return,
I hear, and bow beneath the rod;
  To him, with penitence, I mourn:
I have an advocate above,—
A friend before the throne of love.

2 O Jesus! full of truth and grace,
  More full of grace than I of sin,—
Yet once again I seek thy face,
  Open thine arms and take me in;
Oh! freely my backslidings heal,
And love the dying sinner still.

3 Ah! give me, Lord! the tender heart,
That trembles at th' approach of sin;
A godly fear of sin impart,
Implant, and root it deep within;
That I may fear thy gracious power,
And never dare t' offend thee more.

286.

C. M.

Penitence and Hope.

1 DEAR Saviour! when my thoughts recall
The wonders of thy grace,
Low at thy feet ashamed I fall,
And hide this wretched face.

2 Oh! while I breathe to thee, my Lord!
The penitential sigh,
Confirm the kind forgiving word,
With pity in thine eye.

3 Then shall the mourner, at thy feet,
Rejoice to seek thy face;
And grateful own—how kind, how sweet,
Thy condescending grace.

287.

7s.

Confession and Entreaty.

1 SOVEREIGN Ruler, Lord of all!
Prostrate at thy feet I fall;
Hear, Oh! hear my earnest cry,
Frown not, lest I faint and die.

2 Vilest of the sons of men,—
Chief of sinners I have been;
Oft abused thee to thy face,
Trampled on thy richest grace.

3 Justly might thy righteous dart
Pierce this bleeding, broken heart;
Justly might thine angry breath
Blast me in eternal death.

4 But with thee there 's mercy found,—
Balm to heal my every wound:
Soothe, Oh! soothe the troubled breast,
Give the weary wanderer rest.

288.

C. M

Penitence.

1 PROSTRATE, dear Jesus! at thy feet,
A guilty rebel lies;
And upwards, to thy mercy-seat,
Presumes to lift his eyes.

2 Let not thy justice frown me hence;
Oh! stay the vengeful storm;
Forbid it, that Omnipotence
Should crush a feeble worm.

3 If tears of sorrow could suffice
To pay the debt I owe,
Tears should, from both my weeping eyes,
In ceaseless currents flow.

4 But no such sacrifice I plead
To expiate my guilt;
No tears, but those which thou hast shed,
No blood, but thou hast spilt.

5 Think of thy sorrows, dearest Lord!
And all my sins forgive;
Then justice will approve the word
That bids the sinner live.

289.

C. M.

Pleading for Mercy.

1 LORD! at thy feet, we sinners lie,
And knock at mercy's door;
With bleeding heart, and downcast eye,
Thy favor we implore.

2 Without thy grace, we sink oppressed,
Down to the gates of hell;
Oh! give our troubled spirits rest,
Our gloomy fears dispel.

3 'T is mercy—mercy now we plead;
Let thy compassion move;—
Mercy, that led thee once to bleed,
In tenderness and love.

4 In mercy now, for Jesus' sake,
O God! our sins forgive;
Thy grace our stubborn hearts can break,
And, breaking, bid us live.

290.

11s and 10s.

To the Mercy-Seat.

1 COME, ye disconsolate! where'er ye languish,
Come to the mercy-seat, fervently kneel:
Here bring your wounded hearts, here tell your anguish;
Earth has no sorrow that heaven cannot heal.

2 Joy of the desolate, light of the straying,
Hope of the penitent, fadeless and pure!
Here speaks the Comforter, tenderly saying,
Earth has no sorrow that heaven cannot cure.

3 Here see the bread of life; see waters flowing
Forth from the throne of God, pure from above:
Come to the feast of love; come, ever-knowing,
Earth has no sorrow, but heaven can remove.

291.

C. M.

The Friend of Sinners.

1 JESUS! thou art the sinner's friend;
As such I look to thee;
Now, in the fulness of thy love,
O Lord! remember me.

2 Remember thy pure word of grace,—
Remember Calvary;
Remember all thy dying groans,
And, then, remember me.

3 Thou wondrous Advocate with God!
I yield myself to thee;
While thou art sitting on thy throne,
Dear Lord! remember me.

4 Lord! I am guilty—I am vile,
But thy salvation 's free;
Then, in thine all-abounding grace,
Dear Lord! remember me.

5 And, when I close my eyes in death,
When creature-helps all flee,
Then, O my dear Redeemer-God!
I pray, remember me.

292.

S. M.

Repentance, in View of Christ's Compassion.

1 DID Christ o'er sinners weep?—
And shall our cheeks be dry?

Let floods of penitential grief
Burst forth from every eye.

2 The Son of God in tears
The angels wondering see!
Be thou astonished, O my soul!
He shed those tears for thee.

3 He wept—that we might weep;—
Each sin demands a tear;—
In heaven alone no sin is found,—
There is no weeping there.

293.

C. M.

The Soul casting itself on Christ.

1 APPROACH, my soul! the mercy-seat,
Where Jesus answers prayer;
There humbly fall before his feet,
For none can perish there.

2 Thy promise is my only plea,
With this I venture nigh:
Thou callest burdened souls to thee,
And such, O Lord! am I.

3 Bowed down beneath a load of sin,
By Satan sorely pressed,
By wars without and fears within,
I come to thee for rest.

4 Be thou my shield and hiding-place,
That, sheltered near thy side,
I may my fierce accuser face,
And tell him—"Thou hast died."

5 Oh! wondrous love,—to bleed and die,
To bear the cross and shame,
That guilty sinners, such as I,
Might plead thy gracious name!

294.

C. M.

In-dwelling Sin lamented.

1 WITH tears of anguish, I lament,
Before thy feet, my God!
My passion, pride, and discontent,
And vile ingratitude.

2 Sure, there was ne'er a heart so base,
So false as mine has been;

So faithless to its promises,—
  So prone to every sin.

3 How long, dear Saviour! shall I feel
  These struggles in my breast?
When wilt thou bow my stubborn will,
  And give my conscience rest?

4 Break, sovereign grace! Oh! break the charm
  And set the captive free:
Reveal, great God! thy mighty arm,
  And haste to rescue me.

295.

C. M.

Sin bewailed at the Cross.

1 OH! if my soul was formed for wo,
  How would I vent my sighs!
Repentance should, like rivers, flow
  From both my streaming eyes.

2 'T was for my sins, my dearest Lord
  Hung on the cursed tree,—
And groaned away a dying life,
  For thee, my soul!—for thee.

3 Oh! how I hate those sins of mine
  That shed the Saviour's blood;
That pierced and nailed his sacred flesh
  Fast to the fatal wood!

4 Yes, my Redeemer! they shall die;
  My heart hath so decreed;
Nor will I spare the guilty things
  That made my Saviour bleed.

5 While with a melting, broken heart,
  My murdered Lord I view,
I 'll raise revenge against my sins,
  And slay the murderers too.

296.

C. M.

Mourning at the Sepulchre.

1 YE humble souls that seek the Lord!
  Cast all your fears away;
Draw near, and, with delight, behold
  The place where Jesus lay.

2 Thus low the Lord of life was brought;—
  'T was love that brought him low;

Thus low in death the Saviour lay,
Who lived and bled for you.

3 If ye have wept at yonder cross,
And still your sorrows rise,
Stoop down and view the vanquished grave,
And wipe your weeping eyes.

4 Your Saviour lives,—for ever lives!—
Raise a triumphant strain;
No powers of hell, nor bars of death,
The conqueror could detain.

5 O'er heaven and earth he now presides,
Though once among the dead;
And to eternity shall reign
Creation's glorious Head.

6 Ye mourning souls! rejoice, while you
His empty tomb survey;
As Christ arose, so you shall rise
To realms of endless day.

297.

C. M.

Returning to Christ.

1 HOW oft, alas! this wretched heart
Has wandered from the Lord!
How oft my roving thoughts depart,—
Forgetful of his word!

2 Yet sovereign mercy calls—"Return!"
Dear Lord! and may I come?
My vile ingratitude I mourn;
Oh! take the wanderer home.

3 And canst thou—wilt thou yet forgive,
And bid my crimes remove?
And shall a pardoned rebel live
To speak thy wondrous love?

4 Almighty grace! thy healing power,
How glorious—how divine!
That can to life and bliss restore
A heart so vile as mine!

5 Thy pard'ning love—so free, so sweet—
Dear Saviour! I adore;
Oh! keep me at thy sacred feet,
And let me rove no more.

CONVERSION.

298. C. P. M.
The New-Birth.

1 AWAKED by Sinai's awful sound,
My soul in bonds of guilt I found,
And knew not where to go:
One solemn truth increased my pain,—
The sinner "must be born again,"
Or sink to endless wo.

2 I heard the law its thunders roll,
While guilt lay heavy on my soul,—
A vast oppressive load:
All creature-aid I saw was vain;—
The sinner "must be born again,"
Or drink the wrath of God.

3 The saints I heard with rapture tell—
How Jesus conquered death and hell
To bring salvation near:
Yet still I found this truth remain,—
The sinner "must be born again,"
Or sink in deep despair.

4 But while I thus in anguish lay,
The bleeding Saviour passed that way,
My bondage to remove:
The sinner, once by justice slain,
Now by his grace is born again,
And sings redeeming love.

299. L. M.
God, the Portion of the Soul.

1 FAR from thy fold, O God! my feet
Once moved in error's devious maze;
Nor found religious duties sweet,
Nor sought thy face, nor loved thy ways.

2 With tenderest voice thou bad'st me flee
The paths which thou couldst ne'er approve;
And gently drew my soul to thee,
With cords of sweet eternal love.

3 Now to thy footstool, Lord! I fly,
And low in self-abasement fall;
A vile, a helpless worm, am I
And thou, my God! art all in all.

4 Dearer—far dearer to my heart,
Than all the joys that earth can give;
From fame, from wealth, from friends I 'd part,
Beneath thy countenance to live.

300.

8s and 7s.

Taking up the Cross.

1 JESUS! I my cross have taken,
All to leave, and follow thee;
Naked, poor, despised, forsaken,
Thou, from hence, my all shalt be;
Perish every fond ambition,—
All I 've sought, or hoped, or known!
Yet how rich is my condition,—
God and heaven are still my own!

2 Let the world despise and leave me;
They have left my Saviour, too;
Human hearts and looks deceive me:—
Thou art not, like them, untrue;
Oh! while thou dost smile upon me,
God of wisdom, love and might!
Foes may hate, and friends disown me;—
Show thy face, and all is bright.

3 Perish, earthly fame and treasure!
Come, disaster, scorn, and pain!
In thy service, pain is pleasure;
With thy favor, life is gain:
Oh! 't is not in grief to harm me,
While thy love is left to me;
Oh! 't were not in joy to charm me—
Were that joy unmixed with thee.

301.

8s, 7s and 4.

The Surrender.

1 WELCOME, welcome, dear Redeemer!
Welcome to this heart of mine;
Lord! I make a full surrender,
Every power and thought be thine;
Thine entirely,—
Through eternal ages thine.

2 Known to all to be thy mansion,
  Earth and hell will disappear;
Or in vain attempt possession,
  When they find the Lord is near:—
Shout, O Zion!
  Shout, ye saints! the Lord is here.

302.

7s.

Love to the Saints.

1 PEOPLE of the living God!
  I have sought the world around,
Paths of sin and sorrow trod,
  Peace and comfort no where found:
Now to you my spirit turns,—
  Turns, a fugitive unblest;
Brethren! where your altar burns,
  Oh! receive me into rest.

2 Lonely, I no longer roam,
  Like the cloud, the wind, the wave;
Where you dwell, shall be my home,
  Where you die, shall be my grave:
Mine the God whom you adore,
  Your Redeemer shall be mine;
Earth can fill my soul no more,—
  Every idol I resign.

303.

C. M.

Subdued by the Cross.

1 IN evil, long I took delight,
  Unawed by shame or fear,
Till a new object struck my sight,
  And stopped my wild career.

2 I saw one hanging on a tree,
  In agonies and blood;
He fixed his languid eyes on me,
  As near his cross I stood.

3 Oh! never, till my latest breath,
  Shall I forget that look;
It seemed to charge me with his death,
  Though not a word he spoke.

4 My conscience felt and owned the guilt,
  It plunged me in despair;

I saw, my sins his blood had spilt,
And helped to nail him there.

5 A second look he gave, that said,
"I freely all forgive;
This blood is for thy ransom paid,—
I die that thou may'st live."

6 Thus, while his death my sin displays,
In all its blackest hue,—
Such is the mystery of grace,—
It seals my pardon too.

304.

8s and 7s.

Redemption.

1 SWEET the moments, rich in blessing
Which before the cross I spend!
Life, and health, and peace possessing
From the sinner's dying friend.

2 Here I 'll sit, for ever viewing
Mercy streaming in his blood;—
Precious drops! my soul bedewing,
Plead and claim my peace with God

3 Here it is I find my heaven,
While upon the cross I gaze;
Love I much?—I 've much forgiven,—
I 'm a miracle of grace.

4 Love and grief my heart dividing,
Gazing here I 'd spend my breath;
Constant still in faith abiding,—
Life deriving from his death.

5 Lord! in ceaseless contemplation,
Fix my heart and eyes on thine,
Till I taste thy whole salvation,
Where, unveiled, thy glories shine.

305.

L. M.

Parting with carnal Joys.

1 I SEND the joys of earth away,—
Away, ye tempters of the mind!
False as the smooth, deceitful sea,
And empty as the whistling wind.

2 Your streams were floating me along
Down to the gulf of black despair:

And, while I listened to your song,
Your streams had e'en conveyed me there.

3 Lord! I adore thy matchless grace,
That warned me of that dark abyss;
That drew me from those treacherous seas,
And bade me seek superior bliss.

4 Now to the shining realms above,
I stretch my hands, and glance mine eyes;
Oh! for the pinions of a dove,
To bear me to the upper skies.

5 There, from the bosom of my God,
Oceans of endless pleasure roll;
There would I fix my last abode,
And drown the sorrows of my soul.

306.

S. M.

Rejoicing.

1 NOW let our voices join
To raise a sacred song;
Ye pilgrims! in Jehovah's ways,
With music pass along.

2 See—flowers of paradise,
In rich profusion, spring;
The sun of glory gilds the path,
And dear companions sing.

3 See—Salem's golden spires,
In beauteous prospect, rise;
And brighter crowns than mortals wear,
Which sparkle through the skies.

4 All honor to his name,
Who marks the shining way,—
To him who leads the pilgrims on
To realms of endless day.

307.

C. M.

Salvation welcomed.

1 SALVATION! Oh! the joyful sound;
'T is pleasure to our ears;—
A sovereign balm for every wound,
A cordial for our fears.

2 Buried in sorrow and in sin,
At hell's dark door we lay;

But we arise, by grace divine,
  To see a heavenly day.

3 Salvation!—let the echo fly
  The spacious earth around;
While all the armies of the sky
  Conspire to raise the sound.

308.

7s.

Darkness turned to Light.

1 BOUNDLESS glory, Lord! be thine,
Thou hast made the darkness shine;
Thou hast sent a cheering ray;
Thou hast turned our night to day.

2 Darkness long involved us round,
Till we knew the joyful sound;
Then our darkness fled away,—
Chased by truth's effulgent ray.

3 They are blessed, and none beside,—
They, who in the truth abide;
Clear, the light that marks their way—
Leading to eternal day.

4 Guide us, Saviour! through the road,
Till we reach the saints' abode;
Till we see thee throned above,
As thou art,—the God of love.

309.

C. M.

Returning to Zion.

1 SING, all ye ransomed of the Lord!
  Your great Deliverer sing:
Ye pilgrims! now, for Zion bound,
  Be joyful in your King.

2 See the fair way his hand hath made;—
  How peaceful and how plain!
The simplest traveler need not err,
  Nor seek the path in vain.

3 A hand divine shall lead you on,
  Through all the blissful road;
Till to the sacred mount you rise,
  And see your smiling God.

4 Bright garlands of immortal joy
  Shall bloom on every head;

While sorrow, sighing, and distress,
Like shadows, all are fled.

5 March on, in your Redeemer's strength;
Pursue his footsteps still;
With joyful hope, still fix your eye
On Zion's heavenly hill.

310.

S. M.

Submission to Christ.

1 JESUS! I come to thee,
A sinner doomed to die;
My only refuge is thy cross,—
Here at thy feet I lie.

2 Can mercy reach my case,
And all my sins remove?
Break, O my God! this heart of stone,
And melt it by thy love.

3 Too long my soul has gone,
Far from my God, astray;
I 've sported on the brink of hell,
In sin's delusive way.

4 But, Lord! my heart is fixed,—
I hope in thee alone;
Break off the chains of sin and death,
And bind me to thy throne.

5 Thy blood can cleanse my heart,
Thy hand can wipe my tears;—
Oh! send thy blessed Spirit down,
To banish all my fears.

6 Then shall my soul arise,
From sin and Satan free;
Redeemed from hell and every foe,
I 'll trust alone in thee.

311.

C. M.

Self-Dedication.

1 WELCOME, O Saviour! to my heart;
Possess thine humble throne;
Bid every rival hence depart,
And claim me for thine own.

2 The world and Satan I forsake,—
To thee, I all resign;

My longing heart, O Jesus! take,
And fill with love divine.

3 Oh! may I never turn aside,
Nor from thy bosom flee;
Let nothing here my heart divide,—
I give it all to thee.

312. C. M.
Prayer for the Spirit of Adoption.

1 SPIRIT of holiness! look down,
Our fainting hearts to cheer;
And, when we tremble at thy frown,
Oh! bring thy comforts near.

2 The terrors thy convictions wrought,
Oh! let thy grace remove;
And may the souls, which thou hast taught
To weep, now learn to love.

3 Now let thy saving mercy heal
The wounds it made before;
Now on our hearts impress thy seal,
That we may doubt no more.

4 Complete the work thou hast begun,
And make our darkness light,—
That we a glorious race may run,
Till faith be lost in sight.

5 Then, as our wandering eyes discern
The Lord's unclouded face,
In fitter language, we shall learn
To sing triumphant grace.

313. C. M.
Old Things passed away.

1 LET earthly minds the world pursue,
It has no charms for me;
Once I admired its trifles too,
But grace hath set me free.

2 Its joys can now no longer please,
Nor e'en content afford:
Far from my heart be joys like these,
For I have seen the Lord.

3 As by the light of opening day,
The stars are all concealed;

So earthly pleasures fade away,
  When Jesus is revealed.

4 Creatures no more divide my choice,
  I bid them all depart;
His name, his love, his gracious voice,
  Have fixed my roving heart.

5 But may I hope that thou wilt own
  A worthless worm like me?
Dear Lord! I would be thine alone,
  And wholly live to thee.

314.

C. M.

The full Purpose.

1 IN all my Lord's appointed ways,
  My journey I 'll pursue;
Hinder me not,—ye much-loved saints!
  For I must go with you.

2 Through floods and flames, if Jesus leads,
  I 'll follow where he goes;
Hinder me not!—shall be my cry,
  Though earth and hell oppose.

3 Through duty, and through trials too,
  I 'll go at his command;
Hinder me not, for I am bound
  To my Immanuel's land.

4 And when my Saviour calls me home,
  Still this my cry shall be,—
Hinder me not,—come, welcome, death!
  I 'll gladly go with thee.

315.

8s and 7s.

Redeeming Love.

1 COME, thou Fount of every blessing!
  Tune my heart to grateful lays;
Streams of mercy, never-ceasing,
  Call for songs of loudest praise.

2 Teach me some melodious measure,
  Sung by raptured saints above;
Fill my soul with sacred pleasure,
  While I sing redeeming love.

3 Jesus sought me when a stranger,
  Wandering from the fold of God;

He to save my soul from danger,
  Interposed his precious blood.

4 Oh! to grace how great a debtor,
  Daily I 'm constrained to be!
Let thy grace, Lord! like a fetter,
  Bind my wandering heart to thee.

5 Prone to wander,—Lord! I feel it;
  Prone to leave the God I love;
Here 's my heart, Oh! take and seal it,—
  Seal it from thy courts above.

316.

C. M.

Joy over the Penitent.

1 OH! how divine, how sweet the joy,
  When but one sinner turns,
And with an humble, broken heart,
  His sin and error mourns!

2 Pleased with the news, the saints below
  In songs, their tongues employ;
Beyond the skies the tidings go,
  And heaven is filled with joy.

3 Well-pleased, the Father sees and hears
  The conscious sinner's moan;
Jesus receives him in his arms,
  And claims him for his own.

4 Nor angels can their joys contain,
  But kindle with new fire:
"The sinner lost is found!" they sing,
  And strike the sounding lyre.

317.

L. M.

Joy in Heaven for a repenting Sinner.

1 WHO can describe the joys that rise,
Through all the courts of Paradise,
To see a prodigal return,—
To see an heir of glory born?

2 With joy the Father doth approve
The fruit of his eternal love;
The Son with joy looks down, and sees
The purchase of his agonies.

3 The Spirit takes delight to view
The holy soul he formed anew;

And saints and angels join to sing
The growing empire of their king.

318.
S. M.
The Song of the Saved on Earth.

1 FROM Egypt's bondage come,
Where death and darkness reign,
We seek a new, a better home,
Where we our rest shall gain.

2 To Canaan's sacred bound,
We haste with songs of joy,
Where peace and liberty are found,
And sweets that never cloy.

3 There sin and sorrow cease,
And every conflict 's o'er:
There we shall dwell in endless peace,
Nor thirst nor hunger more.

4 There, in celestial strains,
Enraptured myriads sing;
And love in every bosom reigns,—
For God himself is king.

5 We hope to join the throng,
And soon their pleasures share:—
To sing the everlasting song,
With all the ransomed there.

6 How sweet the prospect is!
It cheers the pilgrim's breast;
We 're journeying through the wilderness,
To our eternal rest.

319.
L. M.
A Youth, seeking heavenly Wisdom.

1 I ASK not wealth, nor pomp, nor power,
Nor fleeting pleasures of an hour:
My soul aspires to nobler things
Than all the pride and state of kings.

2 One thing I ask;—Lord! wilt thou hear,
And grant my soul a gift so dear?—
Wisdom, descending from above,
The sweetest token of thy love:—

3 Wisdom, betimes to know the Lord,
To fear his name, and keep his word;

To lead my feet in paths of truth,
And guide and guard my wandering youth.

4 Then shouldst thou grant a length of days,
My life shall still proclaim thy praise;
Or early death my soul convey
To realms of everlasting day.

320.

H. M.

Renouncing the World.

1 COME, my fond fluttering heart!
Come, struggle to be free;
Thou and the world must part,
However hard it be:
My trembling spirit owns it just,
But cleaves yet closer to the dust.

2 Ye tempting sweets! forbear;
Ye dearest idols! fall;
My love ye must not share,
Jesus shall have it all:
'T is bitter pain,—'t is cruel smart,—
But, ah! thou must consent, my heart!

3 Ye fair enchanting throng!
Ye golden dreams! farewell!
Earth has prevailed too long,
And now I break the spell:
Farewell, ye joys of early years!—
Jesus! forgive these parting tears.

4 In Gilead there is balm,
A kind Physician there,
My fevered mind to calm,
And bid me not despair:
Aid me, dear Saviour! set me free;
My all I would resign to thee.

5 Oh! may I feel thy worth,
And let no idol dare,—
No vanity of earth,
With thee, my Lord! compare:
Now bid all worldly joys depart,
And reign supremely in my heart.

CHRISTIAN.

321.

7s.

Rejoicing in Jesus.

1 NOW begin the heavenly theme,
Sing aloud in Jesus' name;
Ye, who his salvation prove,
Triumph in redeeming love.

2 Ye, who see the Father's grace
Beaming in the Saviour's face,
As to Canaan on ye move,
Praise, and bless redeeming love.

3 Mourning souls! dry up your tears;
Banish all your sinful fears;
See your guilt and curse remove,—
Cancelled by redeeming love.

4 Welcome all, by sin oppressed,—
Welcome to his sacred rest!
Nothing brought him from above,—
Nothing but redeeming love.

5 Hither, then, your music bring;
Strike aloud each joyful string;
Mortals! join the hosts above,—
Join to praise redeeming love.

6 When his Spirit leads us home,
When we to his glory come,
We shall all the fulness prove
Of the Lord's redeeming love.

322.

8s and 7s.

Joyful Hope.

1 KNOW, my soul: thy full salvation;
Rise o'er sin, and fear and care,
Joy to find, in every station,
Something still to do or bear:
Think, what spirit dwells within thee;
Think, what Father's smiles are thine;
Think, what Jesus did to win thee;—
Child of heaven! canst thou repine?

2 Haste thee on from grace to glory,
  Armed with faith, and winged with prayer
Heaven's eternal day 's before thee,
  God's own hand shall guide thee there:
Soon shall close thine earthly mission,
  Soon shall pass thy pilgrim-days;
Hope shall change to glad fruition,—
  Faith to sight, and prayer to praise.

323. S. M.

Salvation by Grace.

1 GRACE!—'t is a charming sound,—
  Harmonious to the ear;
Heaven with the echo shall resound,
  And all the earth shall hear.

2 Grace first contrived the way
  To save rebellious man;
And all the steps that grace display,
  Which drew the wondrous plan.

3 Grace led my roving feet
  To tread the heavenly road;
And new supplies each hour I meet,
  While pressing on to God.

4 Grace all the work shall crown,
  Through everlasting days;
It lays in heaven the topmost stone,
  And well deserves the praise.

324. C. M.

Filial Obedience.

1 GRACE, like an uncorrupted seed,
  Abides and reigns within;
Immortal principles forbid
  The sons of God to sin.

2 Not by the terrors of a slave,
  Do they perform his will;
But, with the noblest powers they have,
  His sweet commands fulfill.

3 They find access, at every hour,
  To God, within the veil;
Hence they derive a quickening power,
  And joys that never fail.

4 Oh! happy souls!—Oh! glorious state
Of overflowing grace,—
To dwell so near their Father's seat,
And see his lovely face.

5 Lord! I address thy heavenly throne;
Call me a child of thine;
Send down the Spirit of thy Son
To form my heart divine.

6 There shed thy choicest love abroad,
And make my comforts strong;
Then shall I say,—"My Father, God!"
With an unwavering tongue.

325. C. M.

Faith encouraged by ancient Examples.

1 RISE, O my soul! pursue the path,
By ancient worthies trod;
Aspiring, view those holy men,
Who lived and walked with God.

2 Though dead, they speak in reason's ear,
And in example live;
Their faith, and hope, and mighty deeds,
Still fresh instruction give.

3 'T was through the Lamb's most precious blood,
They conquered every foe;
And to his power and matchless grace,
Their crowns of life they owe.

4 Lord! may I ever keep in view
The patterns thou hast given;
And ne'er forsake the blessed road,
That led them safe to heaven.

326. L. M.

Salvation through Christ.

1 NOW, to the power of God supreme
Be everlasting honors given;
He saves from hell,—we bless his name,—
He calls our wandering feet to heaven.

2 Not for our duties, or deserts,
But of his own abounding grace,
He works salvation in our hearts,
And forms a people for his praise.

3 'T was his own purpose that begun
  To rescue rebels, doomed to die;
He gave us grace in Christ, his Son,
  Before he spread the starry sky.

4 Jesus, the Lord, appears at last,
  And makes his Father's counsels known;
Declares the great transaction past,
  And brings immortal blessings down.

5 He dies,—and, in that dreadful night,
  Did all the powers of hell destroy;
Rising—he brought our heaven to light,
  And took possession of the joy.

327.

C. M.

The Hope of Heaven.

1 WHEN I can read my title, clear,
  To mansions in the skies,
I bid farewell to every fear,
  And wipe my weeping eyes.

2 Should earth against my soul engage,
  And hell's fierce darts be hurled:
Then I can smile at Satan's rage,
  And face a frowning world.

3 Let cares, like a wild deluge, come,
  And storms of sorrow fall;
May I but safely reach my home,
  My God, my heaven, my all;—

4 There shall I bathe my weary soul,
  In seas of heavenly rest;
And not a wave of trouble roll,
  Across my peaceful breast.

328.

7s and 6s. Peculiar.

Pilgrim's Song.

1 RISE, my soul! and stretch thy wings,
  Thy better portion trace;
Rise from transitory things,
  Toward heaven, thy native place:
Sun, and moon, and stars decay,
  Time shall soon this earth remove;
Rise, my soul! and haste away,
  To seats prepared above.

2 Rivers to the ocean run,
  Nor stay in all their course;
Fire ascending seeks the sun,—
  Both speed them to their source;
So a soul, that 's born of God,
  Pants to view his glorious face;
Upward tends to his abode,
  To rest in his embrace.

3 Cease, ye pilgrims! cease to mourn,
  Press onward to the prize;
Soon the Saviour will return,
  Triumphant in the skies:
Yet a season,—and you know,
  Happy entrance will be given;
All our sorrows left below,
  And earth exchanged for heaven.

329. C. M.

Salvation by Grace.

1 LORD! we confess our numerous faults;
  How great our guilt has been!
Foolish and vain were all our thoughts,
  And all our lives were sin.

2 But, O my soul! for ever praise,
  For ever love his name,
Who turns thy feet from dangerous ways
  Of folly, sin, and shame.

3 'T is not by works of righteousness
  Which our own hands have done;
But we are saved by sovereign grace,
  Abounding through his Son

4 'T is from the mercy of our God,
  That all our hopes begin;
'T is by the water, and the blood,
  Our souls are washed from sin.

5 'T is through the purchase of his death
  Who hung upon the tree,
The Spirit is sent down, to breathe
  On such dry bones as we.

6 Raised from the dead, we live anew;
  And, justified by grace,
We shall appear in glory too,
  And see our Father's face.

330.

S. M.

Heavenly Joy on Earth

1 COME, ye who love the Lord!
And let your joys be known:
Join in a song of sweet accord,
And thus surround the throne.

2 Let those refuse to sing,
Who never knew our God;
But children of the heavenly King
May speak their joys abroad.

3 The men of grace have found
Glory begun below;
Celestial fruits on earthly ground
From faith and hope may grow.

4 The hill of Zion yields
A thousand sacred sweets,
Before we reach the heavenly fields,
Or walk the golden streets.

5 Then let our songs abound,
And every tear be dry;
We 're marching through Immanuel's ground,
To fairer worlds on high.

331.

C. M.

Redemption and Protection.

1 ARISE, my soul! my joyful powers!
And triumph in my God;
Awake, my voice! and loud proclaim
His glorious grace abroad.

2 He raised me from the deeps of sin,—
The opening gates of hell;
And fixed my standing more secure,
That 't was before I fell.

3 The arms of everlasting love,
Beneath my soul he placed;
And on the rock of ages set
My slippery footsteps fast.

4 The city of my blest abode
Is walled around with grace;
Salvation for a bulwark stands,
To shield the sacred place.

5 Arise, my soul! awake, my voice!
And tunes of pleasure sing;
Loud hallelujahs shall address
My Saviour and my King.

332.

C. M.

Pleasures unseen.

1 OH! could our thoughts and wishes fly,
Above these gloomy shades,
To those bright worlds, beyond the sky,
Which sorrow ne'er invades!—

2 There, joys, unseen by mortal eyes,
Or reason's feeble ray,
In ever-blooming prospects rise,
Unconscious of decay.

3 Lord! send a beam of light divine,
To guide our upward aim;
With one reviving touch of thine,
Our languid hearts inflame.

4 Oh! then, on faith's sublimest wing,
Our ardent hope shall rise
To those bright scenes, where pleasures spring,
Immortal, in the skies.

333.

C. M.

The Robe of Righteousness.

1 AWAKE, my heart! arise, my tongue!
Prepare a tuneful voice;
In God, the life of all my joys,
Aloud will I rejoice.

2 'T is he adorned my naked soul,
And made salvation mine;
Upon a poor polluted worm,
He makes his graces shine.

3 And, lest the shadow of a spot
Should on my soul be found,
He took the robe the Saviour wrought,
And cast it all around.

4 How far the heavenly robe exceeds
What earthly princes wear!
These ornaments—how bright they shine!
How white the garments are!

5 Strangely, my soul! art thou arrayed
By the great sacred Three!
In sweetest harmony of praise,
Let all thy powers agree.

334.

L. M.

The Christian Race.

1 AWAKE, our souls! away, our fears!
Let every trembling thought be gone;
Awake—and run the heavenly race,
And put a cheerful courage on.

2 True,—'t is a strait and thorny road,
And mortal spirits tire and faint;
But they forget the mighty God,
Who feeds the strength of every saint;—

3 The mighty God, whose matchless power
Is ever new, and ever young,
And firm endures while endless years
Their everlasting circles run.

4 From thee, the overflowing spring,
Our souls shall drink a full supply;
While such as trust their native strength,
Shall melt away, and droop, and die.

5 Swift as an eagle cuts the air,
We'll mount aloft to thine abode;
On wings of love, our souls shall fly,
Nor tire amid the heavenly road.

335.

C. M.

The Christian Race.

1 AWAKE, my soul! stretch every nerve,
And press with vigor on;
A heavenly race demands thy zeal,
And an immortal crown.

2 'T is God's all-animating voice,
That calls thee from on high;
'T is he, whose hand presents the prize
To thine aspiring eye.

3 A cloud of witnesses around
Hold thee in full survey;
Forget the steps already trod,
And onward urge thy way.

4 Blest Saviour! introduced by thee,
  Our race have we begun:
And, crowned with vict'ry, at thy feet,
  We 'll lay our trophies down.

336.

7s.

Rejoicing in Hope.

1 CHILDREN of the heavenly King!
As ye journey, sweetly sing;
Sing your Saviour's worthy praise,
Glorious in his works and ways.

2 Ye are travelling home to God,
In the way the fathers trod;
They are happy now, and ye
Soon their happiness shall see.

3 Shout, ye little flock! and blest;
You on Jesus' throne shall rest;
There, your seat is now prepared,—
There, your kingdom and reward.

4 Fear not, brethren! joyful stand
On the borders of your land;
Jesus Christ, your Father's Son,
Bids you undismayed go on.

5 Lord! submissive make us go,
Gladly leaving all below;
Only thou our leader be,
And we still will follow thee.

337.

L. M.

The Christian Warfare.

1 STAND up, my soul! shake off thy fears,
  And gird the gospel-armor on;
March to the gates of endless joy,
  Where Jesus, thy great Captain 's gone,

2 Hell and thy sins resist thy course,—
  But hell and sin are vanquished foes;
Thy Jesus nailed them to the cross,
  And sung the triumph, when he rose.

3 Then, let my soul march boldly on,
  Press forward to the heavenly gate;
There, peace and joy eternal reign,
  And glittering robes for conquerors wait.

4 There shall I wear a starry crown,
And triumph in almighty grace;
While all the armies of the skies
Join in my glorious leader's praise.

338.

C. M.
Holy Love.

1 HAPPY the heart where graces reign,
Where love inspires the breast;
Love is the brightest of the train,
And strengthens all the rest.

2 Knowledge,—alas! 't is all in vain,
And all in vain our fear;
Our stubborn sins will fight and reign,
If love be absent there.

3 This is the grace that lives and sings,
When faith and hope shall cease;
'T is this shall strike our joyful strings,
In the sweet realms of bliss.

4 Before we quite forsake our clay,
Or leave this dark abode,
The wings of love bear us away
To see our smiling God.

339.

L. M.
Love to God and Man.

1 HAD I the tongues of Greeks and Jews,
And nobler speech than angels use,—
If love be absent, I am found
Like tinkling brass—an empty sound.

2 Were I inspired to preach, and tell
All that is done in heaven and hell,—
Or could my faith the world remove,
Still—I am nothing without love.

3 Should I distribute all my store
To feed the hungry—clothe the poor;
Or give my body to the flame,
To gain a martyr's glorious name;—

4 If love to God, and love to men,
Be absent, all my hopes are vain:
Nor tongues, nor gifts, nor fiery zeal,
The work of love can e'er fulfill.

340.

L. M.

Who on earth are blessed.

1 BLEST are the humble souls, that see
Their emptiness and poverty;
Treasures of grace to them are given,
And crowns of joy laid up in heaven.

2 Blest are the men of broken heart,
Who mourn for sin with inward smart;
The blood of Christ divinely flows—
A healing balm for all their woes.

3 Blest are the meek, who stand afar
From rage and passion, noise and war;
God will secure their happy state,
And plead their cause against the great.

4 Blest are the souls, that thirst for grace,—
Hunger and long for righteousness;
They shall be well-supplied, and fed,
With living streams and living bread.

341.

L. M.

Who on earth are blessed.

1 BLEST are the men, whose hearts do move
And melt with sympathy and love;
From Christ, the Lord, shall they obtain
Like sympathy and love again.

2 Blest are the pure, whose hearts are clear
From the defiling power of sin;
With endless pleasure, they shall see
A God of spotless purity.

3 Blest are the men of peaceful life,
Who quench the coals of growing strife;
They shall be called the heirs of bliss,—
The sons of God, the God of peace.

4 Blest are the sufferers, who partake
Of pain and shame, for Jesus' sake;
Their souls shall triumph in the Lord,—
Glory and joy are their reward.

342.

C. M.

Brotherly Love.

1 HOW sweet and heavenly is the sight,
When those who love the Lord

In one another's peace delight,
And so fulfill his word!

2 Oh! may we feel each brother's sigh,
And with him bear a part;
May sorrows flow from eye to eye,
And joy from heart to heart.

3 Let love, in one delightful stream,
Through every bosom flow;
Let union sweet, and dear esteem,
In every action, glow.

4 Love is the golden chain that binds
The happy souls above;
And he 's an heir of heaven who finds
His bosom glow with love.

343.

7s.

Christian Union and Love.

1 JESUS, Lord! we look to thee,
Let us in thy name agree;
Show thyself the Prince of peace,
Bid all strife for ever cease.

2 Make us one in heart and mind,
Courteous, pitiful, and kind,
Lowly, meek, in thought and word,
Wholly like our blessed Lord.

3 Let us each for others care,
Each his brother's burden bear,
To thy church a pattern give,
Showing how believers live.

4 Let us, then, with joy, remove
To thy family above;
On the wings of angels fly,—
Showing how believers die.

344.

S. M.

Christian Union.

1 BLEST be the tie, that binds
Our hearts, in christian love;
The fellowship of kindred minds
Is like to that above.

2 Before our Father's throne,
We pour our ardent prayers;

Our fears, our hopes, our aims are one,—
Our comforts and our cares.

3 We share our mutual woes,
Our mutual burdens bear;
And often, for each other, flows
The sympathizing tear.

4 When we asunder part,
It gives us inward pain;
But we shall still be joined in heart,
And hope to meet again.

5 This glorious hope revives
Our courage, by the way;
While each, in expectation, lives,
And long to see the day.

6 From sorrow, toil, and pain,
And sin, we shall be free;
And perfect love and friendship reign,
Through all eternity.

345.

S. M.

All, one in Christ.

1 LET party-names no more
The christian world o'erspread:
Gentile and Jew, and bond and free,
Are one, in Christ, their head.

2 Among the saints on earth,
Let mutual love abound;—
Heirs of the same inheritance,
With mutual blessings crowned.

3 Thus will the church below
Resemble that above;
Where streams of endless pleasure flow,
And every heart is love.

346.

7s.

Parting of Christians.

1 FOR a season called to part,
Let us now ourselves commend,
To the gracious eye and heart
Of our ever-present friend.

2 Jesus! hear our humble prayer;
Tender shepherd of thy sheep!

Let thy mercy and thy care
All our souls in safety keep.

3 In thy strength, may we be strong,
Sweeten every cross and pain;
Grant, that, if we live, ere-long
We may meet in peace again.

4 Then, if thou thy help afford,
Joyful songs to thee shall rise,
And our souls shall praise the Lord,
Who regards our humble cries.

347. C. M.

Love to our Neighbor.

1 FATHER of mercies! send thy grace,
All-powerful from above,
To form, in our obedient souls,
The image of thy love.

2 Oh! may our sympathizing breasts
That generous pleasure know,
Kindly to share in others' joy,
And weep for others' wo.

3 When the most helpless sons of grief,
In low distress, are laid,
Soft be our hearts their pains to feel,
And swift our hands to aid.

4 So Jesus looked on dying men,
When throned above the skies;
And mid th' embraces of thy love,
He felt compassion rise.

5 On wings of love the Saviour flew,
To raise us from the ground;
And gave his own most precious blood,
A balm for every wound.

348. C. M.

Compassion and Charity.

1 BLEST is the man, whose softening heart
Feels all another's pain;
To whom the supplicating eye
Is never raised in vain;—

2 Whose breast expands with generous warmth,
A brother's woes to feel,

And bleeds in pity o'er the wound
He wants the power to heal.

3 He spreads his kind supporting arms
To every child of grief;
His secret bounty largely flows,
And brings unasked relief.

4 To gentle offices of love,
His feet are never slow;
He views, through mercy's melting eye,
A brother in a foe.

5 He, from the bosom of his God,
Shall present peace receive;
And, when he kneels before the throne,
His trembling soul shall live.

349. C. M.

For benevolent Societies.

1 BRIGHT Source of everlasting love!
To thee our souls we raise;
And to thy sovereign bounty rear
A monument of praise.

2 Thy mercy gilds the path of life,
With every cheering ray:
Kindly restrains the rising tear,
Or wipes that tear away.

3 When sunk in guilt, our souls approached
The borders of despair,
Thy grace, through Jesus' blood, proclaimed
A free salvation near.

4 What shall we render, bounteous Lord!
For all the grace we see?
Alas! the goodness, worms can yield,
Extendeth not to thee.

5 To tents of wo, to beds of pain,
Our cheerful feet repair;
And, with the gifts thy hand bestows,
Relieve the mourners there.

6 The widow's heart shall sing for joy,
The orphan shall be fed;
The hungering soul, we 'll gladly point
To Christ, the living bread.

350.

C. M.

Charitable Appropriations.

1 JESUS, our Lord! how rich thy grace!
Thy bounties—how complete!
How shall we count the wondrous sum,
Or pay the mighty debt?

2 High on a throne of radiant light,
Dost thou exalted shine;
What can our poverty bestow,
Since all the world is thine.

3 But thou hast brethren here below,
The children of thy grace,
Whose humble names thou wilt confess,
Before thy Father's face.

4 In them may'st thou be clothed and fed,
Be visited and cheered;
And, in their accents of distress,
The Saviour's voice be heard.

5 Whate'er our willing hands can give,
Lord! at thy feet we lay;
Grace will the humble gift receive,
And grace at length repay.

351.

S. M.

Supports of Religion.

1 WHEN gloomy doubts and fears
The trembling heart invade,
And all the face of nature wears
A universal shade;—

2 Religion can assuage
The tempest of the soul;
And every fear gives up its rage
At her divine control.

3 Through life's bewildered way,
Her hand unerring leads;
And o'er the path, her heavenly ray
A cheering lustre sheds.

4 When reason, tired and blind,
Sinks helpless and afraid;
Thou blest supporter of the mind!
How powerful is thine aid!

5 Oh ! let me feel thy power
And find thy sweet relief,
To cheer my every gloomy hour,
And calm my every grief.

352.

C. M.

Contrition and Prayer.

1 OH ! for that tenderness of heart,
That bows before the Lord ;
That owns how just and good thou art,
And trembles at thy word.

2 Oh ! for those humble, contrite tears,
Which from repentance flow ;
That sense of guilt, which, trembling, fears
The long-suspended blow !

3 Saviour ! to me, in pity give,
For sin, the deep distress ;
The pledge thou wilt, at last, receive,
And bid me die in peace.

4 Oh ! fill my soul with faith and love,
And strength to do thy will ;
Raise my desires and hopes above,—
Thyself to me reveal.

353.

8s, 7s and 4.

Hope encouraged.

1 O MY soul ! what means this sadness ?
Wherefore art thou thus cast down ?
Let thy grief be turned to gladness,
Bid thy restless fear begone ;
Look to Jesus,
And rejoice in his dear name.

2 Though ten thousand ills beset thee,
Though thy heart is stained with sin,
Jesus lives, he 'll ne'er forget thee,
He will make thee pure within ;
He is faithful
To perform his gracious word.

3 Though distresses now attend thee,
And thou tread'st the thorny road ;
His right hand shall still defend thee ;
Soon he 'll bring thee home to God ;
Thou shalt praise him,—
Praise the great Redeemer's name.

4 Oh! that I could now adore him,
Like the heavenly host above,
Who for ever bow before him,
And unceasing sing his love!
Happy spirits!
When shall I your chorus join?

354.
C. M.
Strength from Heaven.

1 WHENCE do our mournful thoughts arise?
And where 's our courage fled?
Have restless sin, and raging hell,
Struck all our comforts dead?

2 Have we forgot th' almighty name,
That formed the earth and sea?
And can an all-creating arm
Grow weary, or decay?

3 Treasures of everlasting might
In our Jehovah dwell;
He gives the conquest to the weak,
And treads their foes to hell.

4 Mere mortal powers shall fade and die,
And youthful vigor cease;
But we, that wait upon the Lord,
Shall feel our strength increase.

5 The saints shall mount on eagles' wings,
And taste the promised bliss,
Till their unwearied feet arrive,
Where perfect pleasure is.

355.
H. M.
Spiritual Desertion.

1 WHERE is my Saviour now,
Whose smiles I once possessed?
Till he return, I bow,
By heaviest grief oppressed:
My days of happiness have gone,
And I am left to weep alone.

2 Where can the mourner go,
And tell his tale of grief?
Ah! who can soothe his wo,
And give him sweet relief?

Earth cannot heal the wounded breast,
Nor give the troubled sinner rest.

3 Jesus! thy smiles impart;
My dearest Lord! return,
And ease my wounded heart,
And bid me cease to mourn:
Then shall this night of sorrow flee,
And peace and heaven be found in thee.

356.

L. M.

Asking divine Consolation.

1 SWEET peace of conscience, heavenly guest!
Come, fix thy mansion in my breast,
Dispel my doubts, my fears control,
And heal the anguish of my soul.

2 Come, smiling hope! and joy sincere!
Come, make your constant dwelling here;
Still let your presence cheer my heart,
Nor sin compel you to depart.

3 Thou God of hope and peace divine!
Oh! make these sacred pleasures mine;
Forgive my sins, my fears remove,
And send the tokens of thy love.

4 Then should mine eyes, without a tear,
See death with all its terrors near;
My heart should then in death rejoice,
And raptures tune my faltering voice.

357.

C. M.

Beatific Vision of Christ.

1 FROM thee, my God! my joys shall rise,
And run eternal rounds,
Beyond the limits of the skies,
And all created bounds.

2 The holy triumphs of my soul
Shall death itself out-brave,
Leave dull mortality behind,
And fly beyond the grave.

3 There, where my blessed Jesus reigns,
In heaven's unmeasured space,
I 'll spend a long eternity
In pleasure, and in praise.

4 Blest Jesus! every smile of thine
Shall fresh endearments bring,
And thousand tastes of new delight
From all thy graces spring.

5 Haste, my Beloved! fetch my soul
Up to thy blest abode;
Fly—for my spirit longs to see
My Saviour, and my God.

358.

C. M.

Heaven on Earth.

1 WHILE through this changing world we roam,
From infancy to age,
Heaven is the christian pilgrim's home,
His rest at every stage.

2 Thither, his raptured thought ascends,
Eternal joys to share;
There his adoring spirit bends,
While here, he kneels in prayer.

3 From earth his freed affections rise,
To fix on things above,
Where all his hope of glory lies,—
Where all is perfect love.

4 There too may we our treasure place,
There let our hearts be found;
That still, where sin abounded, grace
May more and more abound.

5 Henceforth, our conversation be,
With Christ before the throne;
Ere long we, eye to eye, shall see,
And know as we are known.

359.

C. P. M.

Worldliness lamented.

1 THE mind was formed, to mount sublime
Beyond the narrow bounds of time,
To everlasting things;
But earthly vapors dim her sight,
And hang, with cold oppressive weight,
Upon her drooping wings.

2 Bright scenes of bliss,—unclouded skies,
Invite my soul;—Oh! could I rise,
Nor leave a thought below,

I 'd bid farewell to anxious care,
And say, to every tempting snare,—
Heaven calls, and I must go :—

3 Heaven calls,—and can I yet delay?
Can aught on earth engage my stay?
Ah! wretched lingering heart!
Come, Lord! with strength, and life, and light,
Assist and guide my upward flight,
And bid the world depart.

360.

8s.

Backsliders invited to return.

1 RETURN to the guide of thy youth,—
Thy Maker, thy Father, thy Friend!
Behold him prepared to receive
The child who has dared to offend:
Return—the Redeemer invites;
Full oft he hath sought thee before;
But, lo! with unspeakable grace,
He deigns to entreat thee once more.

2 Return,—and enjoyments are thine,
Too vast for the heart to conceive;—
Enjoyments which only belong
To those who repent and believe;
A love which for ever expands;
Unceasing composure of heart;
A crown of unfading delight;
A kingdom which cannot depart.

361.

C. M.

God, the Author of Mercies and Afflictions.

1 NAKED, as from the earth we came,
And rose to life at first,
We to the earth return again,
And mingle with the dust.

2 The dear delights we here enjoy,
And fondly call our own,
Are only favors borrowed now,
To be repaid anon.

3 'T is God, who lifts our comforts high,
Or sinks them in the grave;
He gives, and—blessed be his name!—
He takes but what he gave.

4 Peace, all our angry passions! then;
Let each rebellious sigh
Be silent, at his sovereign will,
And every murmur die.

5 If smiling mercy crown our lives,
Its praises shall be spread;
And we 'll adore the justice too,
That strikes our comforts dead.

362.

8s and 7s.
Eternity.

1 IN this world of sin and sorrow,
Compassed round with every care,
From eternity we borrow
Hope that banishes despair.

2 Thee, triumphant God and Saviour!
In the glass of faith we see,
Oh! assist each faint endeavor,
Raise our earth-born souls to thee.

3 Bring that awful scene, before us,
Of the last tremendous day,
When to life thou wilt restore us;—
Lingering ages! haste away.

4 Then this vile and sinful nature
Incorruption shall put on;
Life-renewing, glorious Saviour!
Let thy gracious will be done.

363.

S. M.
Trust in God.

1 YOUR harps, ye trembling saints'
Down from the willows take:
Loud to the praise of love divine,
Bid every string awake.

2 Though in a foreign land,
We are not far from home;
And nearer to our house above,
We every moment come.

3 His grace will, to the end,
Stronger and brighter shine;
Nor present things—nor things to come
Shall quench this spark divine.

4 When we in darkness walk,
Nor feel the heavenly flame;
Then will we trust our gracious God,
And rest upon his name.

5 Soon shall our doubts and fears
Subside at his control;
His loving-kindness shall break through
The midnight of the soul.

6 Blest is the man, O God!
That stays himself on thee:—
Who waits for thy salvation, Lord!
Shall thy salvation see.

364.

8s, 7s and 4.

The Gladness of the Righteous.

1 FAR from us be grief and sadness;
Farther still unhallowed mirth:
Zion's sons may sing, with gladness,
Theirs are joys of heavenly birth:
Jesus owns them,—
Jesus, Lord of heaven and earth.

2 All the worlding's mirth is madness,
All his labor fruitless toil:
'T is the saints that taste of gladness,
Though the world their choice revile:
Sweet their portion;—
Life is in the Saviour's smile.

3 Worlds would seem as nothing to us,
Balanced with a Saviour's love:
Since the Lord in mercy drew us—
Drew our souls to things above,
Earthly objects
Can no longer greatly move.

4 Once the world was all our treasure;
Then the world our hearts possessed;
Now we taste sublimer pleasure,
Since the Lord has made us blest;
We can witness,—
Jesus gives his people rest.

365.

8s and 7s.
Pilgrim.

1 GENTLY, Lord! Oh! gently lead us,
Through this lonely vale of tears;
Through the changes thou 'st decreed us
Till our last great change appears:
When temptation's darts assail us,
When in devious paths we stray,
Let thy goodness never fail us,
Lead us in thy perfect way.

2 In the hour of pain and anguish,
In the hour when death draws near,
Suffer not our hearts to languish,—
Suffer not our souls to fear:
And, when mortal life is ended,
Bid us on thy bosom rest,
Till, by angel-bands attended,
We awake among the blest.

366.

7s and 6s. Peculiar.
Pleading by the Cross.

1 LAMB of God! whose bleeding love
We now recall to mind;—
Send the answer from above,
And let us mercy find:
Think on us who think on thee;
Every burdened soul release;
Oh! remember Calvary,
And bid us go in peace.

2 Let thy blood, by faith applied,
The sinner's pardon seal;
Speak us freely-justified,
And all our sickness heal:
By thy passion on the tree,
Let our griefs and troubles cease;
Oh! remember Calvary,
And bid us go in peace.

3 Can we ever hence depart
Till thou our wants relieve?
Write forgiveness on our heart,
And all thine image give:
Still our souls shall cry to thee,
Till renewed by holiness,—
Oh! remember Calvary,
And bid us go in peace.

367.

C. M.

Asking Mercy in Affliction.

1 O THOU whose mercy guides my way!
Though now it seems severe,
Forbid my unbelief to say
There is no mercy here.

2 Oh! grant me to desire the pain
That comes in kindness down,
More than the world's alluring gain
Succeeded by a frown.

3 Then, though thou bend my spirit low,
Love only shall I see;
The very hand, that strikes the blow,
Was wounded once for me.

368.

C. M.

Confidence in God's Government.

1 SINCE all the varying scenes of time
God's watchful eye surveys,
Oh! who so wise to choose our lot,
Or to appoint our ways?

2 Good, when he gives—supremely good;
Nor less, when he denies;
E'en crosses, from his sovereign hand,
Are blessings in disguise.

3 Why should we doubt a Father's love,
So constant and so kind?
To his unerring gracious will
Be every wish resigned.

4 In thy fair book of life divine,
My God! inscribe my name;
There let it fill some humble place
Beneath my Lord, the Lamb!

369.

11s.

Relying on the Promises.

1 HOW firm a foundation, ye saints of the Lord!
Is laid for your faith in his excellent word!
What more can he say, than to you he hath said?—
You, who unto Jesus for refuge have fled.

2 Fear not, I am with thee, Oh! be not dismayed,
I—I am thy God, and will still give thee aid;
I'll strengthen thee, help thee, and cause thee to stand,
Upheld by my righteous, omnipotent hand.

3 When through the deep waters I cause thee to go,
The rivers of sorrow shall not thee o'erflow;
For I will be with thee thy troubles to bless,
And sanctify to thee thy deepest distress.

4 When thro' fiery trials thy path-way shall lie,
My grace all-sufficient shall be thy supply;
The flame shall not hurt thee,—I only design
Thy dross to consume, and thy gold to refine.

5 E'en down to old age, all my people shall prove
My sovereign, eternal, unchangeable love;
And when hoary hairs shall their temples adorn,
Like lambs they shall still, in my bosom, be borne.

6 The soul that on Jesus hath leaned for repose,
I will not, I cannot, desert to his foes;
That soul, tho' all hell should endeavor to shake,
I'll never,—no, never,—no, never forsake.

370. C. M.

Complaining of spiritual Sloth.

1 MY drowsy powers! why sleep ye so?
Awake, my sluggish soul!
Nothing has half thy work to do,
Yet nothing 's half so dull.

2 The little ants, for one poor grain,
Labor, and tug, and strive;
Yet we, who have a heaven t' obtain,—
How negligent we live!—

3 We, for whose sake all nature stands,
And stars their courses move;—
We, for whose guard the angel-bands
Come flying from above;—

4 We, for whom God, the Son, came down,
And labored for our good;—
How careless to secure that crown
He purchased with his blood!

5 Lord! shall we lie so sluggish still,
And never act our parts?
Come, holy Dove! from th' heavenly hill,
And sit and warm our hearts.

6 Then shall our active spirits move,—
Upward our souls shall rise:
With hands of faith, and wings of love,
We'll fly and take the prize.

371.

7s and 6s.

Desire for Heaven.

1 FROM every earthly pleasure,
From every transient joy,
From every mortal treasure
That soon will fade and die;—
No longer these desiring,
Upward our wishes tend,
To nobler bliss aspiring,
And joys that never end.

2 From every piercing sorrow
That heaves our breast to-day,
Or threatens us to-morrow,
Hope turns our eyes away;
On wings of faith ascending,
We see the land of light,
And feel our sorrows ending,
In infinite delight.

3 'T is true we are but strangers
And pilgrims here below,
And countless snares and dangers
Surround the path we go:
Though painful and distressing,
Yet there's a rest above;
And onward still we're pressing,
To reach that land of love.

372.

7s.

In Darkness.

1 ONCE I thought my mountain strong,
Firmly fixed, no more to move;
Then my Saviour was my song,
Then my soul was filled with love:
Those were happy, golden days,
Sweetly spent in prayer and praise.

2 Little, then, myself I knew,
Little thought of Satan's power;
Now I feel my sins renew,
Now I feel the stormy hour;
Sin has put my joys to flight,—
Sin has turned my day to night.

3 Saviour! shine, and cheer my soul,
Bid my dying hopes revive,

Make my wounded spirit whole,
  Far away, the tempter drive;
Speak the word and set me free,—
  Let me live alone to thee.

373.
L. M.
Inconstant Heart lamented.

1 AH ! wretched, vile, ungrateful heart !
That can from Jesus thus depart;
Thus, fond of trifles, vainly rove,
Forgetful of a Saviour's love.

2 In vain I charge my thoughts to stay,
And chide earth's vanities away:
There 's naught beneath a power divine,
That can this roving heart confine.

3 Jesus ! to thee I would return,
And, at thy feet repenting, mourn:
There let me view thy pard'ning love,
And never from thy sight remove.

4 Oh ! let thy love, with sweet control,
Bind all the passions of my soul;
Bid every earthly charm depart,
And dwell for ever in my heart.

374.
L. M.
Secret Self-Examination.

1 RETURN, my roving heart ! return,
  And chase those shadowy forms no more;
Now seek, in solitude, to mourn,
  And thy forsaken God implore.

2 O thou great God ! whose piercing eye
  Distinctly marks each deep recess;—
In these sequestered hours draw nigh,
  And with thy presence fill the place.

3 Through all the windings of my heart,
  My search let heavenly wisdom guide,
And still its radiant beams impart,
  Till all be cleansed and purified.

4 Oh ! with the visits of thy love,
  Vouchsafe my inmost soul to cheer;
Till every grace shall join to prove,
  That God has fixed his dwelling here.

375.

C. M.

The Pilgrimage of the Saints.

1 LORD! what a wretched land is this,
That yields us no supply,—
No cheering fruits, no wholesome trees,
Nor streams of living joy!

2 Long nights and darkness dwell below,
With scarce a twinkling ray:
But the bright world, to which we go
Is everlasting day.

3 Our journey is a thorny maze,
But we march upward still,—
Forget these troubles of the ways,
And reach at Zion's hill.

4 See the kind angels, at the gates,
Inviting us to come!
There Jesus, the forerunner, waits
To welcome travelers home.

5 There, on a green and flowery mount,
Our weary souls shall sit,
And, with transporting joys, recount
The labors of our feet.

6 Eternal glory to the King,
Who brought us safely through,
Our tongues shall never cease to sing,
And endless praise renew.

376.

C. M.

Filial Submission.

1 AND can my heart aspire so high,
To say—"My Father, God?"
Lord! at thy feet I fain would lie,
And learn to kiss the rod.

2 I would submit to all thy will,
For thou art good and wise;
Let each rebellious thought be still,
Nor one faint murmur rise.

3 Thy love can cheer the darkest gloom,
And bid me wait serene;
Till hopes and joys immortal bloom,
And brighten all the scene.

4 "My Father, God!" permit my heart
To plead her humble claim,
And ask the bliss those words impart,
In my Redeemer's name.

377.

C. M.

Unfruitfulness.

1 LONG have I sat beneath the sound
Of thy salvation, Lord!
But still, how weak my faith is found
And knowledge of thy word!

2 Oft I frequent thy holy place,
And hear almost in vain;
How small a portion of thy grace
My mem'ry can retain!

3 How cold and feeble is my love!
How negligent my fear!
How low my hope of joys above!
How few affections there!

4 Great God! thy sovereign power impart
To give thy word success;
Write thy salvation in my heart,
And make me learn thy grace.

5 Show my forgetful feet the way,
That leads to joys on high;
There knowledge grows without decay,
And love shall never die.

378.

S. M.

Ingratitude to divine Goodness.

1 IS this the kind return?
Are these the thanks we owe?
Thus to abuse eternal love,
Whence all our blessings flow!

2 To what a stubborn frame
Hath sin reduced our mind!
What strange, rebellious wretches we,
And God as strangely kind!

3 Turn, turn us, mighty God!
And mould our souls afresh;
Break, sovereign grace! these hearts of stone,
And give us hearts of flesh.

4 Let past ingratitude
Provoke our weeping eyes;
And hourly, as new mercies fall,
Let hourly thanks arise.

379. C. M.

Repentance in View of divine Patience.

1 AND are we, wretches, yet alive?
And do we yet rebel?
'T is boundless—'t is amazing love,—
That bears us up from hell!

2 The burden of our weighty guilt
Would sink us down to flames;
And threatening vengeance rolls above
To crush our feeble frames.

3 Almighty goodness cries—"Forbear!"—
And straight the thunder stays;
And dare we now provoke his wrath,
And weary out his grace?

4 Lord! we have long abused thy love,—
Too long indulged our sin;
Our aching hearts e'en bleed to see
What rebels we have been.

5 No more, ye lusts! shall ye command;
No more will we obey:
Stretch out, O God! thy conquering hand,
And drive thy foes away.

380. C. M.

Backslidings and Returns.

1 WHY is my heart so far from thee,
My God! my chief delight?
Why are my thoughts no more, by day,—
With thee, no more by night?

2 Why should my foolish passions rove?
Where can such sweetness be,
As I have tasted in thy love,—
As I have found in thee?

3 When my forgetful soul renews
The savor of thy grace,
My heart presumes, I cannot lose
The relish all my days.

4 But ere one fleeting hour is past,
The flattering world employs
Some sensual bait, to seize my taste,
And to pollute my joys.

5 Wretch that I am, to wander thus,
In chase of false delight!
Let me be fastened to thy cross,
Rather than lose thy sight.

6 Make haste, my days! to reach the goal,
And bring my heart to rest
On the dear centre of my soul,—
My God, my Saviour's breast.

381.

C. M.

Watchfulness and Prayer.

1 ALAS! what hourly dangers rise,
What snares beset my way!
To heaven, Oh! let me lift mine eyes,
And, hourly, watch and pray.

2 How oft my mournful thoughts complain,
And melt in flowing tears!
I strive against my foes in vain,—
I sink amid my fears.

3 O Lord! increase my faith and hope,
When foes and fears prevail;
And bear my fainting spirit up,
Or soon my strength will fail.

4 Oh! keep me in thy heavenly way,
And bid the tempter flee;
And never, never let me stray
From happiness and thee.

382.

L. M.

Hardness of Heart lamented.

1 OH! for a glance of heavenly day,
To chase the shades of night away;
To melt, with beams of love divine,
This unrelenting heart of mine.

2 The rocks can rend, the earth can quake,
The ocean roar, the mountain shake;
All nature feels, and gives the sign;
But not this stubborn heart of mine.

3 Dear Lord! the sorrows, thou hast felt,
Might cause a heart of stone to melt;
Yet, I can read each sacred line,
And nothing melt this heart of mine.

4 But power supreme the soul can move,
And purify, and melt to love;
Come, Holy Spirit! Power divine!
Oh! come, subdue this heart of mine.

383.

S. M.

Dead to Sin by the Cross of Christ.

1 SHALL we go on to sin,
Because thy grace abounds?
Or crucify the Lord again,
And open all his wounds?

2 Forbid it, mighty God!
Nor let it e'er be said,
That we, whose sins are crucified,
Should raise them from the dead.

3 We will be slaves no more,
Since Christ has made us free,
Has nailed our tyrants to the cross,
And bought our liberty.

384.

L. M.

Faith, our Guide.

1 'T IS by the faith of joys to come,
We walk through deserts dark as night;
Till we arrive at heaven, our home,
Faith is our guide, and faith our light.

2 The want of sight she well supplies;
She makes the pearly gates appear;
Far into distant worlds she pries,
And brings eternal glories near.

3 Cheerful we tread the desert through,
While faith inspires a heavenly ray;
Though lions roar, and tempests blow,
And rocks and dangers fill the way.

4 So Abr'am, by divine command,
Left his own home to walk with God;
His faith beheld the promised land,
And fired his zeal along the road.

385.

C. M.

Faith of Things unseen.

1 FAITH is the brightest evidence
Of things beyond our sight;
Breaks through the clouds of flesh and sense,
And dwells in heavenly light.

2 It sets times past, in present view,
Brings distant prospects home—
Of things a thousand years ago,
Or thousand years to come.

3 By faith, we know the worlds were made
By God's almighty word:
Abr'am, to unknown countries led,
By faith, obeyed the Lord.

4 He sought a city fair and high,
Built by th' eternal hands;
And faith assures us, though we die,
That heavenly building stands.

386.

C. M.

The Power of Faith.

1 FAITH adds new charms to earthly bliss,
And saves me from its snares;
Its aid, in every duty, brings,
And softens all my cares.

2 The wounded conscience knows its power,
The healing balm to give;
That balm the saddest heart can cheer,
And make the dying live.

3 Wide it unveils celestial worlds,
Where deathless pleasures reign;
And bids me seek my portion there,
Nor bids me seek in vain.

4 It shows the precious promise, sealed
With the Redeemer's blood;
And helps my feeble hope to rest
Upon a faithful God.

5 There—there unshaken would I rest,
Till this vile body dies;
And then, on faith's triumphant wings,
To endless glory rise.

387.

C. M.

Justification; or, Law and Grace.

1 VAIN are the hopes, the sons of men
On their own works have built;—
Their hearts, by nature, all unclean,
And all their actions, guilt.

2 Let Jew and Gentile stop their mouths,
Without a murm'ring word;
And the whole race of Adam stand
Guilty before the Lord.

3 In vain we ask God's righteous law
To justify us now;
Since to convince, and to condemn,
Is all the law can do.

4 Jesus! how glorious is thy grace!—
When in thy name we trust,
Our faith receives a righteousness
That makes the sinner just.

388.

L. M.

The Value of Christ and his Righteousness.

1 NO more,—my God! I boast no more,
Of all the duties I have done;
I quit the hopes I held before,
To trust the merits of thy Son.

2 Now, for the love I bear his name,
What was my gain, I count my loss;
My former pride I call my shame,
And nail my glory to his cross.

3 Yes,—and I must, and will, esteem
All things but loss for Jesus' sake;
Oh! may my soul be found in him,
And of his righteousness partake.

4 The best obedience of my hands
Dares not appear before thy throne;
But faith can answer thy demands,
By pleading what my Lord has done.

389.

C. M.

Retirement.

1 FAR from the world, O Lord! I flee,—
From strife and tumult far;

From scenes, where Satan wages still
His most successful war.

2 The calm retreat, the silent shade,
With prayer and praise agree;
And seem, by thy sweet bounty, made
For those who follow thee.

3 There, if thy Spirit touch the soul,
And grace her mean abode,
Oh! with what peace, and joy, and love,
She then communes with God.

4 There, like the nightingale, she pours
Her solitary lays;
Nor asks a witness of her song,
Nor thirsts for human praise.

5 Author and guardian of my life,—
Sweet source of light divine,—
And—all harmonious names in one—
Blest Saviour!—thou art mine.

6 What thanks I owe thee, and what love!
And praise, an endless store,
Shall echo through the realms above,
When time shall be no more.

390.

7s.

Privileges of Adoption.

1 BLESSED are the sons of God;
They are bought with Jesus' blood;
They are ransomed from the grave;—
Life eternal they shall have:
With them numbered may we be,
Here, and in eternity.

2 They are justified by grace;
They enjoy the Saviour's peace;
All their sins are washed away;
They shall stand in God's great day:
With them numbered may we be,
Here, and in eternity.

3 They produce the fruits of grace,
In the works of righteousness;
They are harmless, meek and mild,
Holy, blameless, undefiled:

With them numbered may we be,
Here, and in eternity.

4 They are lights upon the earth,—
Children of a heavenly birth,—
One with God, with Jesus one;
Glory is in them begun:
With them numbered may we be,
Here, and in eternity,

391. C. M.

Hope of Heaven through Christ.

1 BLEST be the everlasting God.
The Father of our Lord;
Be his abounding mercy praised,—
His majesty adored.

2 When from the dead he raised his Son,
And called him to the sky,
He gave our souls a lively hope,
That they should never die.

3 What though our inbred sins require
Our flesh to see the dust;
Yet, as the Lord, our Saviour, rose,
So all his followers must.

4 There 's an inheritance divine,
Reserved against that day;
'T is uncorrupted, undefiled,
And cannot waste away.

5 Saints, by the power of God, are kept
Till the salvation come;
We walk by faith, as strangers here,
Till Christ shall call us home.

392. S. M.

Adoption.

1 BEHOLD! what wondrous grace
The Father has bestowed,
On sinners of a mortal race,
To call them sons of God.

2 'T is no surprising thing,
That we should be unknown;
The Jewish world knew not their king,—
God's everlasting Son.

3 Nor doth it yet appear
How great we must be made:

But when we see our Saviour here,
We shall be like our head.

4 A hope, so much divine,
May trials well endure;
May purge our souls from sense and sin,
As Christ, the Lord, is pure.

5 If, in my Father's love,
I share a filial part,
Send down thy Spirit, like a dove,
To rest upon my heart.

6 We would no longer lie,
Like slaves, beneath the throne;
Our faith shall—"Abba, Father!"—cry
And thou the kindred own.

393.

C. M.

The Fearful encouraged.

1 YE trembling souls! dismiss your fears,
Be mercy all your theme;
Mercy—which, like a river, flows,
In one perpetual stream.

2 Fear not the powers of earth and hell;—
Those powers will God restrain;
His arm shall all their rage repel,
And make their efforts vain.

3 Fear not the want of outward good;
For his he will provide,
Grant them supplies of daily food,
And all they need beside.

4 Fear not that he will e'er forsake,
Or leave his work undone;
He 's faithful to his promises,
And faithful to his Son.

5 Fear not the terrors of the grave,
Nor death's tremendous sting;
He will, from endless wrath, preserve—
To endless glory bring.

394.

C. M.

Saints in the Hands of Christ.

1 FIRM as the earth, thy gospel stands,
My Lord, my hope, my trust!

If I am found in Jesus' hands,
My soul can ne'er be lost.

2 His honor is engaged to save
The meanest of his sheep;
All, whom his heavenly Father gave,
His hands securely keep.

3 Nor death, nor hell shall e'er remove
His fav'rites from his breast;
In the dear bosom of his love,
They must for ever rest.

395. L. M.

Hope in the Covenant.

1 HOW oft have sin and Satan strove
To rend my soul from thee, my God!
But everlasting is thy love,
And Jesus seals it with his blood.

2 The oath and promise of the Lord
Join to confirm the wondrous grace;
Eternal power performs the word,
And fills all heaven with endless praise.

3 Amid temptations, sharp and long,
My soul to this dear refuge flies;
Hope is my anchor, firm and strong,
While tempests blow, and billows rise.

4 The gospel bears my spirit up;
A faithful and unchanging God
Lays the foundation for my hope,
In oaths, and promises, and blood.

396. L. M.

Security of the Saints.

1 WHO shall the Lord's elect condemn?—
'T is God, who justifies their souls;
And mercy, like a mighty stream,
O'er all their sins divinely rolls.

2 Who shall adjudge the saints to hell?—
'T is Christ, who suffered in their stead,
And, the salvation to fulfill,
Behold him, rising from the dead!

3 He lives!—he lives, and reigns above,
For ever interceding there;

Who shall divide us from his love?—
Or what shall tempt us to despair?

4 Not all that men on earth can do,
Nor powers on high, nor powers below,
Shall cause his mercy to remove,
Or wean our hearts from Christ, our love,

397.

8s, 7s and 4.

God, the Pilgrim's Guide

1 GUIDE me, O thou great Jehovah!
Pilgrim through this barren land;
I am weak, but thou art mighty;
Hold me with thy powerful hand:
Bread of heaven!
Feed me till I want no more.

2 Open, Lord! the crystal fountain,
Whence the healing waters flow;
Let the fiery cloudy pillar
Lead me all my journey through:
Strong deliverer!
Be thou still my strength and shield.

3 When I tread the verge of Jordan,
Bid my anxious fears subside;
Death of death, and hell's destruction!
Land me safe on Canaan's side:
Songs of praises—
I will ever give to thee.

398.

C M.

Joys departed.

1 SWEET was the time, when first I felt
The Saviour's pard'ning blood,
Applied to cleanse my soul from guilt,
And bring me home to God.

2 Soon as the morn the light revealed,
His praises tuned my tongue;
And, when the evening-shade prevailed,
His love was all my song.

3 In prayer, my soul drew near the Lord,
And saw his glory shine;
And when I read his holy word,
I called each promise mine.

4 But now, when evening-shade prevails,
My soul in darkness mourns;

And, when the morn the light reveals,
No light to me returns.

5 Rise, Saviour!—help me to prevail,
And make my soul thy care;
I know thy mercy cannot fail,—
Let me that mercy share.

399.

C. M.

Seeking God.

1 OH! that I knew the secret place,
Where I might find my God;
I 'd spread my wants before his face,
And pour my woes abroad.

2 I 'd tell him how my sins arise,—
What sorrows I sustain;
How grace decays, and comfort dies,
And leave my heart in pain.

3 He knows what arguments I 'd take
To wrestle with my God;
I 'd plead for his own mercy's sake,
And for my Saviour's blood.

4 My God will pity my complaints,
And heal my broken bones;
He takes the meaning of his saints,—
The language of their groans.

5 Arise, my soul! from deep distress,
And banish every fear;
He calls thee, to his throne of grace
To spread thy sorrows there.

400.

C. M.

Walking with God.

1 OH! for a closer walk with God,
A calm and heavenly frame,—
A light to shine upon the road
That leads me to the Lamb!

2 Where is the blessedness I knew,
When first I saw the Lord?
Where is the soul-refreshing view
Of Jesus, and his word?

3 What peaceful hours I once enjoyed!
How sweet their mem'ry still!

But they have left an aching void,
  The world can never fill.

4 Return, O holy Dove! return,
  Sweet messenger of rest!
I hate the sins that made thee mourn,
  And drove thee from my breast.

5 The dearest idol I have known,—
  Whate'er that idol be,—
Help me to tear it from thy throne,
  And worship only thee.

6 So shall my walk be close with God,
  Calm and serene my frame;
So purer light shall mark the road
  That leads me to the Lamb.

401.

7s.

Love to Christ.

1 HARK! my soul! it is the Lord;
'T is thy Saviour—hear his word;
Jesus speaks, and speaks to thee,—
"Say, poor sinner! lovest thou me?

2 "I delivered thee, when bound,
And, when bleeding, healed thy wound;
Sought thee wandering, set thee right,
Turned thy darkness into light.

3 "Can a woman's tender care
Cease towards the child she bare?
Yes, she may forgetful be,
Yet will I remember thee.

4 "Mine is an unchanging love,
Higher than the heights above;
Deeper than the depths beneath—
Free and faithful—strong as death.

5 "Thou shalt see my glory soon,
When the work of grace is done;
Partner of my throne shalt be;—
Say, poor sinner! lovest thou me?"

6 Lord! it is my chief complaint,
That my love is weak and faint;
Yet I love thee, and adore,—
Oh! for grace to love thee more.

402.

C. M.

Love to Christ.

1 DO not I love thee, O my Lord?
  Behold my heart, and see;
And turn each hateful idol out,
  That dares to rival thee.

2 Do not I love thee, from my soul?
  Then let me nothing love:
Dead be my heart to every joy
  Which thou dost not approve.

3 Is not thy name melodious still
  To mine attentive ear?
Doth not each pulse with pleasure beat
  My Saviour's voice to hear?

4 Hast thou a lamb in all thy flock,
  I would disdain to feed?
Hast thou a foe, before whose face,
  I fear thy cause to plead?

5 Would not my heart pour forth its blood
  In honor of thy name,
And challenge the cold hand of death
  To damp th' immortal flame?

6 Thou knowest I love thee, dearest Lord!
  But Oh! I long to soar,
Far from the sphere of mortal joys,
  That I may love thee more.

403.

S. M.

Christian Watchfulness.

1 A CHARGE to keep I have,
  A God to glorify;
A never-dying soul to save,
  And fit it for the sky:—

2 To serve the present age,
  My calling to fulfill,—
Oh! may it all my powers engage
  To do my Master's will.

3 Arm me with jealous care,
  As in thy sight to live;
And Oh! thy servant, Lord! prepare
  A strict account to give.

4 Help me to watch and pray,
  And on thyself rely,—

Assured, if I my trust betray,
  I shall for ever die.

404.

C. M.

Seeking a Rest.

1 WE seek a rest beyond the skies,
  In everlasting day;
Through floods and flames the passage lies,
  But Jesus guards the way.

2 The swelling flood, and raging flame,
  Hear and obey his word;
Then let us triumph in his name,—
  Our Saviour is the Lord.

405.

C. M. Double.

Sinai and Zion.

1 NOT to the terrors of the Lord,
  The tempest, fire, and smoke;—
Not to the thunder of that word,
  Which God on Sinai spoke;—
But we are come to Zion's hill,
  The city of our God,
Where milder words declare his will,
  And spread his love abroad.

2 Behold th' innumerable host
  Of angels clothed in light!
Behold the spirits of the just,
  Whose faith is turned to sight!
Behold the blest assembly there,
  Whose names are writ in heaven!
And God, the judge of all, declares
  Their every sin forgiven.

3 The saints on earth, and all the dead,
  But one communion make;
All join in Christ, their living head,
  And of his grace partake:
In such society as this
  My weary soul would rest:
The man who dwells where Jesus is,
  Must be for ever blest.

406.

S. M.

The vigilant Servant.

1 YE servants of the Lord!
  Each in his office wait;

With joy obey his heavenly word,
  And watch before his gate.

2 Let all your lamps be bright,
  And trim the golden flame;
Gird up your loins, as in his sight,
  For awful is his name.

3 Watch—'t is your Lord's command;
  And while we speak, he 's near:
Mark the first signal of his hand,
  And ready all appear.

4 Oh! happy servant he,
  In such a posture found!
He shall his Lord with rapture see,
  And be with honor crowned.

407. S. M.

Watching and Praying.

1 MY soul! be on thy guard,
  Ten thousand foes arise;
And hosts of sins are pressing hard,
  To draw thee from the skies.

2 Oh! watch, and fight, and pray;—
  The battle ne'er give o'er;
Renew it boldly every day,
  And help divine implore.

3 Ne'er think the vict'ry won,
  Nor lay thine armor down;
Thine arduous work will not be done,
  Till thou obtain thy crown.

408. C. M.

Desiring the Presence of God.

1 HEAR, gracious God! my humble moan,
  To thee I breathe my sighs;
When will the mournful night be gone,
  And when my joys arise?

2 My God! Oh! could I make the claim,—
  My Father and my friend,—
And call thee mine, by every name,
  On which thy saints depend:—

3 By every name of power and love,
  I would thy grace entreat;
Nor should my humble hopes remove,
  Nor leave thy mercy-seat.

4 Yet, though my soul in darkness mourns,
Thy word is all my stay;
Here I would rest till light returns;—
Thy presence makes my day.

5 Speak, Lord! and bid celestial peace
Relieve my aching heart;
Oh! smile and bid my sorrows cease,
And all the gloom depart.

6 Then, shall my drooping spirit rise
And bless the healing rays;
And change these deep, complaining sighs.
To songs of sacred praise.

409. C. M.

Submission.

1 O LORD! my best desires fulfill,
And help me to resign
Life, health, and comfort to thy will,
And make thy pleasure mine.

2 Why should I shrink at thy command.
Thy love forbids my fears;
Why tremble at the gracious hand,
That wipes away my tears?

3 No,—let me rather freely yield
What most I prize, to thee;
Thou never hast a good withheld,
Nor wilt withhold from me.

4 Thy favor, all my journey through,
Shall be my rich supply;
What more I want, or think I do,
Let wisdom still deny.

410. S. M.

Restoration to Health.

1 KINDLY the Lord appeared
In nature's trying hour;
His love my sinking spirit cheered;—
I felt his strengthening power.

2 He found me on the bed
Of languishing and pain;
And bade me lean on him my head,
Nor seek his aid in vain

3 I saw his mighty arm
Stretched o'er the rolling wave;
He snatched my life from threatening harm,
And showed his power to save.

4 How, then, can I refuse
The glad and grateful strain?
The Lord my wasted strength renews,
And makes me well again.

5 Oh! may my future days
My gratitude display;
Nor speak alone, but live thy praise,
Through each revolving day.

411.

C. M.

Sickness and Recovery.

1 MY God! thy service well demands
The remnant of my days;
Why was this fleeting breath renewed,
But to renew thy praise?

2 Thine arms of everlasting love
Did this weak frame sustain,
When life was hovering o'er the grave,
And nature sunk with pain.

3 Calmly I bowed my fainting head,
On thy dear faithful breast;
Pleased to obey my Father's call
To his eternal rest.

4 Into thy hands, my Saviour-God!
Did I my soul resign,
In firm reliance on that truth
Which made salvation mine.

5 Back from the borders of the grave,
At thy command I come;
Nor will I ask a speedier flight
To my celestial home.

6 Where thou appointest mine abode,
There would I choose to be;
For, in thy presence death is life,
And earth is heaven with thee.

412.

7s.

The Mind that was in Christ.

1 FATHER of eternal grace!
Glorify thyself in me;

Meekly beaming in my face,
May the world thine image see.

2 Happy only in thy love,
Poor, unfriended, or unknown;
Fix my thoughts on things above,—
Stay my heart on thee alone.

3 Humble, holy, all-resigned
To thy will:—thy will be done!
Give me, Lord! the perfect mind
Of thy well-beloved Son.

4 Counting gain and glory loss,
May I tread the path he trod;
Die with Jesus on the cross,—
Rise with him, to thee, my God!

413.
L. M.
Holiness and Grace.

1 SO let our lips and lives express
The holy gospel, we profess;
So let our works and virtues shine,
To prove the doctrine all-divine.

2 Thus shall we best proclaim abroad
The honors of our Saviour-God;
When his salvation reigns within,
And grace subdues the power of sin.

3 Religion bears our spirits up,
While we expect that blessed hope,—
The bright appearance of the Lord;—
And faith stands leaning on his word.

414.
C. M.
Hope in Affliction.

1 WHEN musing sorrow weeps the past,
And mourns the present pain,
How sweet to think of peace at last,
And feel that death is gain!

2 'T is not that murm'ring thoughts arise,
And dread a Father's will;
'T is not that meek submission flies,
And would not suffer still;—

3 It is that heaven-taught faith surveys
The path to realms of light,
And longs her eagle-plumes to raise,
And lose herself in sight.

4 It is that hope with ardor glows
To see him face to face,
Whose dying love no language knows
Sufficient art to trace.

5 It is that harrassed conscience feels
The pangs of struggling sin;
Sees, though afar, the hand that heals
And ends her war within.

6 Oh! let me wing my hallowed flight,
From earth-born wo and care,
And soar beyond these realms of night,
My Saviour's bliss to share.

415. C. L. M.

Faith struggling in Darkness.

1 OH! let my trembling soul be still,
While darkness veils the sky;
And wait thy wise, thy holy will,
Wrapt yet in mystery:
I cannot, Lord! thy purpose see,
But all is well since ruled by thee.

2 Thus trusting in thy love, I tread
The path of duty on:
What though some cherished joys are fled,
Some flattering dreams are gone?
Yet purer, brighter joys remain;
Why should my spirit then complain?

416. C. M.

Presence of God in Afflictions.

1 THY gracious presence, O my God!
Can soothe my inward pains:
With this, beneath affliction's load,
My heart no more complains.

2 This can my every care control,
And gild each scene with light;
This is the sunshine of the soul;
Without it, all is night.

3 My Lord! my Life! Oh! cheer my heart,
With thy reviving ray;
Oh! bid these mournful shades depart,
And bring the dawn of day.

4 Oh! happy scenes of pure delight,
Where thy full beams arise:

Unclouded beauty to the sight,—
Sweet rapture and surprise!

5 Lord! shall these breathings of my heart
Aspire, in vain, to thee?
Confirm my hope, that, where thou art,
I shall for ever be.

6 Then shall my cheerful spirit sing
The darkest hours away,
And rise, on faith's expanding wing,
To everlasting day.

417. L. M.

Submission to the Will of God.

1 WAIT, O my soul! thy Maker's will;
Tumultuous passions! all be still!
Nor let a murm'ring thought arise,—
His ways are just,—his counsels wise.

2 He in the thickest darkness dwells,
Performs his work,—the cause conceals
But, though his methods are unknown,
Judgment and truth support his throne

3 Wait then, my soul! submissive wait,—
Prostrate before his awful seat:
Mid all the terrors of his rod,
Still trust a wise and gracious God.

418. C. M.

The christian Soldier.

1 AM I a soldier of the cross,—
A foll'wer of the Lamb?
And shall I fear to own his cause,
Or blush to speak his name?

2 Are there no foes for me to face?
Must I not stem the flood?
Is this vile world a friend to grace
To help me on to God?

3 Sure I must fight, if I would reign;
Increase my courage, Lord!
I'll bear the toil—endure the pain,—
Supported by thy word.

4 Thy saints, in all this glorious war,
Shall conquer, though they die;

They see the triumph from afar,
  And seize it with their eye.

5 When that illustrious day shall rise,
  And all thine armies shine,
In robes of vict'ry, through the skies,—
  The glory shall be thine.

419.

C. M.

Christian Assurance.

1 I'M not ashamed to own my Lord,
  Or to defend his cause;
Maintain the honor of his word,—
  The glory of his cross.

2 Jesus, my God!—I know his name,
  His name is all my trust;
Nor will he put my soul to shame,
  Nor let my hope be lost.

3 Firm as his throne, his promise stands,
  And he can well secure
What I've committed to his hands,
  Till the decisive hour.

4 Then will he own my worthless name,
  Before his Father's face,
And, in the New-Jerusalem,
  Appoint my soul a place.

420.

7s.

The three Mounts.

1 WHEN on Sinai's top I see
God descend, in majesty,
To proclaim his holy law,—
All my spirit sinks with awe.

2 When in ecstacy sublime,
Tabor's glorious steep I climb,
At the too-transporting light,
Darkness rushes o'er my sight.

3 When on Calvary I rest,
God, in flesh made manifest,
Shines in my Redeemer's face,
Full of beauty, truth, and grace.

4 Here, I would for ever stay,
Weep and gaze my soul away;

Thou art heaven on earth to me,—
Lovely, mournful Calvary!

421.

8s and 7s.

Hope in God encouraged.

1 WHY, when storms around you gather,
Should your trembling spirit sink?
Look to God, your heavenly Father,
And of his sweet promise think.

2 Fancy will be often painting
Scenes, in dark and fearful shade:
Yet why should thy soul be fainting,
Of prospective woes afraid?

3 Cease that dark anticipation!
Still let love and faith abound;
For the day of tribulation,
Strength sufficient will be found.

4 God is love, and will not leave you,
When you most his kindness need;
God is true—nor can deceive you,—
Though your faith be weak indeed.

422.

8s.

The Promise of God sure.

1 HOW sweet on thy bosom to rest,
When nature's affliction is near!
The soul that can trust thee is blest,—
Thy smiles bring deliverance from fear:
The Lord has, in kindness, declared,
That those who will trust in his name,
Shall in the sharp conflict be spared,
His mercy and love to proclaim.

2 This promise shall be, to my soul,
A messenger sent from the skies,—
An anchor when billows shall roll,—
A refuge when tempests arise:
O Saviour! the promise fulfill,
Its comfort impart to my mind,
Then calmly I 'll bow to thy will,—
To the cup of affliction resigned.

423.

C. P. M.

Resignation.

1 O LORD! in sorrow I resign,
And bow to that dear hand of thine,—
While yet the rod appears;
That hand can wipe these streaming eyes,
Or, into smiles of glad surprise,
Transform these falling tears.

2 My sole possession is thy love;
On earth beneath, in heaven above,
I have no other store:
And though, with fervor, now I pray,
And importune thee night and day—
I cannot ask for more.

424.

C. L. M.

Submission in Trials.

1 WHEN I can trust my all with God,
In trial's fearful hour,—
Bow all resigned beneath his rod,
And bless his sparing power;—
A joy springs up amid distress,—
A fountain in the wilderness.

2 Oh! to be brought to Jesus' feet,
Though trials fix me there,
Is still a privilege most sweet;
For he will hear my prayer;
Though sighs and tears its language be,
The Lord is nigh to answer me.

3 Then, blessed be the hand that gave,
Still blessed when it takes;
Blessed be he who smites to save,
Who heals the heart he breaks:
Perfect and true are all his ways,
Whom heaven adores and death obeys.

425.

C. M.

Depending on Grace.

1 AMAZING grace!—how sweet the sound,
That saved a wretch like me!
I once was lost, but now am found,—
Was blind, but now I see.

2 'T was grace that taught my heart to fear.
And grace my fears relieved;
How precious did that grace appear,
The hour I first believed!

3 Through many dangers, toils and snares,
I have already come;
'T is grace hath brought me safe thus far,
And grace will lead me home.

4 Yea—when this flesh and heart shall fail,
And mortal life shall cease;
I shall possess, within the vail,
A life of joy and peace.

5 The earth shall soon dissolve like snow,
The sun forbear to shine;
But God, who called me here below,
Will be for ever mine.

426.

C. M.

Submission in Trials.

1 MY times of sorrow and of joy,
Great God! are in thy hand;
My choicest comforts come from thee,
And go at thy command.

2 If thou should'st take them all away,
Yet would I not repine;
Before they were possessed by me,
They were entirely thine.

3 Nor would I drop a murm'ring word,
Though the whole world were gone,
But seek enduring happiness,
In thee, and thee alone.

PRAYER.

427.

C. M.

Habitual Devotion.

1 WHILE thee I seek, protecting Power!
Be my vain wishes stilled;
And may this consecrated hour
With better hopes be filled.

2 Thy love the power of thought bestowed;
  To thee my thoughts would soar;
Thy mercy o'er my life has flowed,—
  That mercy I adore.

3 In each event of life, how clear
  Thy ruling hand I see!
Each blessing to my soul more dear,
  Because conferred by thee.

4 In every joy that crowns my days,
  In every pain I bear,
My heart shall find delight in praise,
  Or seek relief in prayer.

5 When gladness wings my favored hour,
  Thy love my breast shall fill;
Resigned, when storms of sorrow lower,
  My soul shall meet thy will.

6 My lifted eye, without a tear,
  The gathering storm shall see;
My steadfast heart shall know no fear,—
  That heart shall rest on thee.

428.

7s.

A Blessing humbly requested.

1 LORD! we come before thee now;
At thy feet we humbly bow;
Oh! do not our suit disdain;—
Shall we seek thee, Lord! in vain?

2 Lord! on thee our souls depend,
In compassion, now descend;
Fill our hearts with thy rich grace;
Tune our lips to sing thy praise.

3 In thine own appointed way,
Now we seek thee, here we stay;
Lord! we know not how to go,
Till a blessing thou bestow.

4 Send some message, from thy word,
That may joy and peace afford;
Let thy Spirit now impart
Full salvation to each heart.

5 Comfort those who weep and mourn;
Let the time of joy return;

Those, who are cast down, lift up;
Make them strong in faith and hope.

6 Grant, that all may seek and find
Thee, a God supremely kind:
Heal the sick, the captive free—
Let us all rejoice in thee.

429.

L. M.

Forgiveness sought.

1 FORGIVE us, Lord! to thee we cry,
Forgive us through thy matchless grace!
On thee alone our souls rely,
Be thou our strength and righteousness.

2 Forgive thou us, as we forgive
The ills we suffer from our foes;
Restore us, Lord! and bid us live;
Oh! let us in thine arms repose.

3 Forgive us, for our guilt is great,
Our wretched souls no merit claim;
For sovereign mercy still we wait,
And ask but in the Saviour's name.

4 Forgive us,—O thou bleeding Lamb!
Thou risen—thou exalted Lord!
Thou great High-Priest! our souls redeem,
And speak the pardon-sealing word.

430.

C. M.

The God of Bethel.

1 O GOD of Bethel! by whose hand
Thy people still are fed,
Who, through this weary pilgrimage,
Hast all our fathers led:—

2 Our vows, our prayers, we now present,
Before thy throne of grace:
God of our fathers! be the God
Of their succeeding race.

3 Through each perplexing path of life,
Our wandering footsteps guide;
Give us each day our daily bread,
And raiment fit provide.

4 Oh! spread thy covering wings around,
Till all our wanderings cease,
And at our Father's loved abode,
Our souls arrive in peace.

5 Such blessings, from thy gracious hand,
Our humble prayers implore;
And thou shalt be our chosen God,—
Our portion evermore.

431.

7s.

Christ's Presence invoked.

1 LIGHT of life!—seraphic fire!—
Love divine!—thyself impart;
Every fainting soul inspire;
Shine in every drooping heart.

2 Every mourning sinner cheer;
Scatter all our guilty gloom:
Saviour—Son of God! appear;
To thy living temples come.

3 Come, in this accepted hour,
Bring thy heavenly kingdom in:
Fill us with thy glorious power—
Rooting out the love of sin.

4 Nothing more can we require,
We will covet nothing less;
Be thou all our heart's desire,—
All our joy and all our peace.

432.

C. M.

The Nature of Prayer.

1 PRAYER is the soul's sincere desire,
Uttered or unexpressed;
The motion of a hidden fire
That trembles in the breast.

2 Prayer is the burden of a sigh,
The falling of a tear,
The upward glancing of an eye,—
When none but God is near.

3 Prayer is the simplest form of speech
That infant lips can try;—
Prayer, the sublimest strains that reach
The Majesty on high.

4 Prayer is the Christian's vital breath,
The Christian's native air;
His watchword at the gates of death,—
He enters heaven with prayer.

5 Prayer is the contrite sinner's voice,
Returning from his ways;
While angels, in their songs, rejoice,
And cry,—"Behold he prays!"

6 O Thou! by whom we come to God,
The life, the truth, the way,—
The path of prayer thyself hast trod:—
Lord! teach us how to pray.

433.

7s.

Sin bewailed.

1 COME, my soul! thy suit prepare,
Jesus loves to answer prayer;
He himself has bid thee pray;
Rise, and ask without delay.

2 With my burden I begin;—
Lord! remove this load of sin;
Let thy blood, for sinners spilt,
Set my conscience free from guilt.

3 Lord! I come to thee for rest,
Take possession of my breast;
There, thy sovereign right maintain,
And, without a rival, reign.

4 While I am a pilgrim here,
Let thy love my spirit cheer;
Be my guide, my guard, my friend;—
Lead me to my journey's end.

5 Shew me what I have to do,
Every hour my strength renew;
Let me live a life of faith,
Let me die thy people's death.

434.

C. M.

Prayer for needed Grace.

1 FATHER! whate'er of earthly bliss,
Thy sovereign will denies,
Accepted, at thy throne of grace,
Let this petition rise:—

2 "Give us a calm, a thankful heart,
From every murmur free;
The blessings of thy grace impart,
And make us live to thee.

3 "Let the sweet hope, that we are thine,
Our life and death attend;
Thy presence through our journey shine,
And crown our journey's end."

435.

C. M.

Seeking God.

1 AUTHOR of good! to thee we turn;
Thine ever-wakeful eye
Alone can all our wants discern,—
Thy hand alone supply.

2 Oh! let thy love within us dwell,
Thy fear our footsteps guide;
That love shall vainer loves expel,—
That fear, all fears beside.

3 Not what we wish—but what we want,
Let mercy still supply;
The good we ask not, Father! grant;
The ill we ask—deny.

436.

C. M.

Prayer for Wisdom.

1 ALMIGHTY God! in humble prayer,
To thee our souls we lift;
Do thou our waiting minds prepare
For thy most needful gift.

2 We ask not golden streams of wealth,
Along our path to flow;
We ask not undecaying health,
Nor length of years below:—

3 We ask not honors, which an hour
May bring and take away;
We ask not pleasure, pomp, and power,
Lest we should go astray:—

4 We ask for wisdom;—Lord! impart
The knowledge how to live:
A wise and understanding heart,
To all thy servants give;—

5 The young—remember thee in youth,
Before the evil days!
The old—be guided by thy truth,
In wisdom's pleasant ways!

437.
C. M.
Prayer for Sincerity.

1 LORD! when we bend before thy throne,
And our confessions pour,
Oh! may we feel the sins we own,
And hate what we deplore.

2 Our contrite spirits pitying see;—
True penitence impart;
And let a healing ray, from thee,
Beam hope on every heart.

3 When we disclose our wants in prayer,
Oh! let our wills resign;
And not a thought our bosom share,
Which is not wholly thine.

4 Let faith each meek petition fill,
And waft it to the skies;
And teach our hearts—'t is goodness still
That grants it, or denies.

438.
S. M.
Christ will hear Prayer.

1 JESUS, who knows full well
The heart of every saint,
Invites us, all our griefs to tell,
To pray, and never faint.

2 He bows his gracious ear,—
We never plead in vain;
Then let us wait till he appear,
And pray, and pray again.

3 Jesus, the Lord, will hear
His chosen when they cry;
Yes, though he may a while forbear,
He 'll help them from on high.

4 Then let us earnest cry,
And never faint in prayer,
He sees, he hears, and, from on high,
Will make our cause his care.

439.
L. M.
The Presence of Christ implored.

1 WHERE two or three, with sweet accord,
Obedient to their sovereign Lord,
Meet to recount his acts of grace,
And offer solemn prayer and praise;—

2 There will the gracious Saviour be,
To bless the little company;—
There, to unveil his smiling face,
And bid his glories fill the place.

3 We meet at thy command, O Lord!
Relying on thy faithful word;
Now send the Spirit from above,
And fill our hearts with heavenly love.

440.
L. M.
The Lord's Prayer.

1 FATHER, adored in worlds above!
Thy glorious name be hallowed still;
Thy kingdom come, with power and love;
And earth, like heaven, obey thy will.

2 Lord! make our daily wants thy care,
Forgive the sins that we forsake;
Oh! let us in thy kindness share,
As fellow-men of ours partake.

3 Evils beset us every hour;—
Thy kind protection we implore:
Thine is the kingdom, thine the power,—
Be thine the glory evermore.

441.
S. M.
The Lord's Prayer.

1 OUR heavenly Father! hear
The prayer we offer now;—
"Thy name be hallowed far and near;
To thee all nations bow!

2 "Thy kingdom come:—Thy will
On earth be done in love,
As saints and seraphim fulfill
Thy perfect law above.

3 "Our daily bread supply,
While, by thy word, we live:

The guilt of our iniquity
  Forgive, as we forgive.

4 "From dark temptation's power,—
  From Satan's wiles defend:
Deliver, in the evil hour,
  And guide us to the end.

5 "Thine, then, for ever be
  Glory and power divine:
The sceptre, throne, and majesty
  Of heaven and earth are thine."

3 Thus humbly taught to pray,
  By thy beloved Son,
Through him we come to thee, and say,—
  "All for his sake be done!"

442. S. M.

Coming boldly to the Throne of Grace.

1 BEHOLD the throne of grace!
  The promise calls us near;
There Jesus shows a smiling face,
  And waits to answer prayer.

2 That rich atoning blood,
  Which sprinkled round we see,
Provides for those who come to God
  An all-prevailing plea.

3 Thine image, Lord! bestow,
  Thy presence and thy love;
We ask to serve thee here below
  And reign with thee above.

4 Teach us to live by faith,
  Conform our will to thine;
Let us victorious be in death,
  And, then, in glory shine.

5 If thou these blessings give,
  And wilt our portion be,
All worldly joys we 'll cheerful leave,
  And find our heaven in thee.

443. 7s.

Pleading with God.

1 LORD! I cannot let thee go,
Till a blessing thou bestow;

Do not turn away thy face,
Mine 's an urgent, pressing case.

2 Once, a sinner near despair
Sought thy mercy-seat by prayer;
Mercy heard and set him free,—
Lord! that mercy came to me.

3 Many days have passed since then,
Many changes I have seen;
Yet have been upheld till now;—
Who could hold me up but thou?

4 Thou hast helped in every need—
This emboldens me to plead;
After so much mercy past,
Canst thou let me sink at last?

5 No—I must maintain my hold;
'T is thy goodness makes me bold;
I can no denial take,
Since I plead for Jesus' sake.

REVIVAL.

444. L. M.
The Sun of Righteousness.

1 O SUN of righteousness! arise,
With gentle beams on Zion shine;
Dispel the darkness from our eyes,
And souls awake to life divine.

2 On all around, let grace descend,
Like heavenly dew, or copious showers;
That we may call our God our friend,—
That we may hail salvation ours.

445. S. M.
Prayer for a Revival.

1 O LORD! thy work revive
In Zion's gloomy hour;
And let our dying graces live,
By thy restoring power.

2 Oh! let thy chosen few
Awake to earnest prayer;

Their solemn vows again renew,
  And walk in filial fear.

3 Thy Spirit then will speak,
  Through lips of humble clay,
Till hearts of adamant shall break,—
  Till rebels shall obey.

4 Now lend thy gracious ear,
  Now listen to our cry;
Oh! come, and bring salvation near;—
  Our souls on thee rely.

446.

L. M.

Weeping over Sinners.

1 ARISE, my tenderest thoughts! arise;
Dissolve in grief, my streaming eyes!
And thou, my heart! with anguish feel
Those evils which thou canst not heal.

2 See human nature sunk in shame;
See scandal poured on Jesus' name;
The Father wounded, through the Son,
The world abused,—the soul undone!

3 See the short course of vain delight,
Closing in everlasting night,
In flames that no abatement know,
Though bitter tears for ever flow!

4 My God! I feel the mournful scene,
And yearn with grief o'er dying men;
While fain my pity would reclaim
Souls that may perish in the flame.

5 But feeble my compassion proves,
And can but weep, where most it loves;
Thine own all-saving arm employ,
And turn these drops of grief to joy.

447.

H. M.

The Jubilee proclaimed.

1 BLOW ye the trumpet!—blow,—
  The gladly solemn sound!
Let all the nations know,
  To earth's remotest bound,—
The year of jubilee is come;
Return, ye ransomed sinners! home.

2 Exalt the Lamb of God,—
  The sin-atoning Lamb;
Redemption by his blood,
  Through all the world proclaim:
The year of jubilee is come;
Return, ye ransomed sinners! home.

3 Ye slaves of sin and hell!
  Your liberty receive:
And safe in Jesus dwell,
  And blest in Jesus live:
The year of jubilee is come;
Return, ye ransomed sinners! home.

4 The gospel-trumpet hear,
  The news of pard'ning grace:
Ye happy souls! draw near,
  Behold your Saviour's face:
The year of jubilee is come;
Return, ye ransomed sinners! home.

5 Jesus, our great High-Priest,
  Has full atonement made:
Ye weary spirits! rest,
  Ye mourning souls! be glad.
The year of jubilee is come;
Return, ye ransomed sinners! home.

448. L. M.

Hope in Times of Darkness.

1 WHILE I to grief my soul gave way,
  To see the work of God decline,
Methought I heard the Saviour say,—
  "Dismiss thy fears, the ark is mine.

2 "Though for a time I hid my face,
  Rely upon my love and power;
Still wrestle at the throne of grace,
  And wait for a reviving hour.

3 "Take down thy long-neglected harp,
  I 've seen thy tears and heard thy prayer;
The winter-season has been sharp,
  But spring shall all its wastes repair."

4 Lord! I obey,—my hopes revive;
  Come, join with me, ye saints! and sing:
Our foes in vain against us strive,
  For God will help and triumph bring.

449.

L. M.

The Vision of dry Bones.

1 LOOK down, O Lord! with pitying eye,
See Adam's race in ruin lie;
Sin spreads its trophies o'er the ground,
And scatters slaughtered heaps around.

2 And can these dead awake and live?
And can these perished bones revive?
That, mighty God! to thee is known;
That wondrous work is all thine own.

3 Thy ministers are sent in vain,
To prophesy upon the slain,
In vain they call, in vain they cry,—
Till thine almighty aid is nigh.

4 But if thy Spirit deign to breathe,
Life spreads through all the realms of death,
Dry bones obey thy powerful voice,—
They move, they waken, they rejoice.

5 So when thy trumpet's awful sound
Shall shake the heavens and rend the ground,
Dead saints shall from their tombs arise,
And spring to life beyond the skies.

450.

H. M.

Rejoicing in a Revival.

1 O ZION! tune thy voice,
And raise thy hands on high;
Tell all the earth thy joys,
And boast salvation nigh;
Cheerful in God
Arise and shine,
While rays divine
Stream all abroad.

2 He gilds thy mourning face
With beams that cannot fade;
His all-resplendent grace
He pours around thy head;
The nations round,
Thy form shall view,
With lustre new,
Divinely crowned.

3 In honour to his name,
Reflect that sacred light;
And loud that grace proclaim,
Which makes thy darkness bright;
Pursue his praise,
Till sovereign love,
In worlds above,
The glory raise.

4 There, on his holy hill,
A brighter sun shall rise,
And, with his radiance, fill
Those fairer, purer skies;
While, round his throne,
Ten thousand stars,
In nobler spheres,
His influence own.

451.

8s and 7s.

Prayer for a Revival.

1 SAVIOUR! visit thy plantation;
Grant us, Lord! a gracious rain:
All will come to desolation,
Unless thou return again.

2 Keep no longer at a distance;—
Shine upon us from on high,
Lest, for want of thine assistance,
Every plant should droop and die.

3 Let our mutual love be fervent,
Make us prevalent in prayers;
Let each one, esteemed thy servant,
Shun the world's enticing snares.

4 Break the tempter's fatal power;
Turn the stony heart to flesh;
And begin, from this good hour,
To revive thy work afresh.

452.

8s and 7s.

Future Peace and Glory of Zion.

1 HEAR what God, the Lord, hath spoken;—
"O my people! faint and few,
Comfortless, afflicted, broken,—
Fair abodes I build for you:
Scenes of heart-felt tribulation
Shall no more perplex your ways:

You shall name your walls—Salvation,—
And your gates shall all be praise."

2 There, like streams that feed the garden,
Pleasures, without end, shall flow;
For the Lord, your faith rewarding,
All his bounty shall bestow:
Still, in undisturbed possession,
Peace and righteousness shall reign;
Never shall you feel oppression—
Hear the voice of war again.

3 Ye, no more your suns declining,
Waning moons no more shall see;
But, your griefs for ever ending,
Find eternal noon in me:
God will rise, and, shining o'er you,
Change to day the gloom of night;
He, the Lord, will be your glory,—
God your everlasting light.

453.

7s.

Winning Souls.

1 WOULD you win a soul to God?
Tell him of a Saviour's blood,
Once for dying sinners spilt,
To atone for all their guilt.

2 Tell him how the streams did glide,
From his hands, his feet, his side,—
How his head, with thorns, was crowned,
And his heart in sorrow drowned:—

3 How he yielded up his breath,
How he agonized in death,
How he lives to intercede,—
Christ, our advocate and head.

4 Tell him,—it was sovereign grace
Led thee first to seek his face;
Made thee choose the better part,
Wrought salvation in thy heart.

5 Tell him of that liberty
Wherewith Jesus makes us free;
Sweetly speak of sins forgiven,
Earnest of the joys of heaven.

454.

8s, 7s and 4.

Fountain of Life.

1 SEE, from Zion's sacred mountain,
Streams of living water flow!
God has opened there a fountain
That supplies the plains below:
They are blessed,
Who its sovereign virtues know.

2 Through ten thousand channels, flowing,
Streams of mercy find their way;
Life, and health, and joy bestowing,
Making all around look gay:
O ye nations!
Hail the long-expected day.

3 Gladdened by the flowing treasure,
All-enriching as it goes;
Lo, the desert smiles with pleasure,—
Buds and blossoms as the rose:
Every object
Sings for joy where'er it flows.

4 Trees of life, the banks adorning,
Yield their fruit to all around;
Those who eat are saved from mourning,
Pleasure comes, and hopes abound;
Fair their portion!—
Endless life, with glory crowned.

ORDINANCES.

455.

C. M.

Christ receiving Children.

1 SEE Israel's gentle Shepherd stand,
With all-engaging charms!
Hark! how he calls the tender lambs,
And folds them in his arms!

2 "Permit them to approach," he cries,
"Nor scorn their humble name;
For 't was to bless such souls as these,
The Lord of angels came."

3 We bring them, Lord! in thankful hands,
And yield them up to thee;
Joyful that we ourselves are thine,—
Thine let our offspring be.

4 Ye little flock! with pleasure hear,—
Ye children! seek his face;
And fly, with transports, to receive
The blessings of his grace.

5 If orphans they are left behind,
Thy guardian care we trust;—
That care shall heal our bleeding hearts
If weeping o'er their dust.

456.

L. M.

Infant Baptism.

1 O LORD! encouraged by thy grace,
We bring our infant to thy throne;
Give it within thy heart a place,
Let it be thine, and thine alone.

2 Wash it from every stain of guilt,
And let this child be sanctified;
Lord! thou canst cleanse it, if thou wilt,
And all its native evils hide.

3 We ask not, for it, earthly bliss,
Or earthly honors, wealth or fame:
The sum of our request is this—
That it may love and fear thy name.

4 This infant, we by faith commit
To thy kind love and guardian care;
We lay it at the Saviour's feet,
He will not let it perish there.

457.

C. M.

The promise to Abraham.

1 HOW large the promise—how divine,
To Abra'm and his seed!
"I 'll be a God to thee and thine,
Supplying all their need."

2 The words of his extensive love,
From age to age, endure;
The angel of the covenant proves,
And seals the blessings sure.

3 Jesus the ancient faith confirms,
To our forefathers given;
He takes young children in his arms,
And calls them heirs of heaven.

4 Our God,—how faithful are his ways!
His love endures the same;
Nor, from the promise of his grace,
Blots out the children's name.

458. S. M.

Christ blessing Children.

1 THE Saviour kindly calls
Our children to his breast;
He holds them in his gracious arms;—
Himself declares them blest.

2 "Let them approach," he cries,
"Nor scorn their humble claim;
The heirs of heaven are such as these,—
For such as these I came."

3 With joy we bring them, Lord!
Devoting them to thee,
Imploring, that, as we are thine,
Thine may our offspring be.

459. C. M.

The Saviour blessing Children.

1 WHEN Jesus left the throne of God,
He chose an humble birth;
A man of grief, like, us he trod
A lonely path on earth.

2 Like him, may we be found below,
In wisdom's paths of peace;
Like him, in grace and knowledge, grow,
As years and strength increase.

3 Sweet were his words, and kind his look,
When mothers round him pressed;
Their infants, in his arms, he took,
And on his bosom blessed.

4 When Jesus into Salem rode,
The children sang around;
For joy, they plucked the palms, and strewed
Their garments on the ground.

5 "Hosanna!"—our glad voices raise—
"Hosanna to our King!"
Could we forget our Saviour's praise,
The stones themselves would sing.

460. C. M.
Infants, living or dying, in the Arms of Christ.

1 THY life I read, my dearest Lord!
With transport all-divine;
Thine image trace, in every word,
Thy love, in every line.

2 With joy, I see a thousand charms,
Spread o'er thy lovely face;
While infants in thy tender arms,
Receive the smiling grace.

3 "I take these little lambs," said he,
"And lay them on my breast;
Protection they shall find in me—
In me, be ever blest.

4 "Death may the bands of life unloose,
But can 't dissolve my love;
Millions of infant souls compose
The family above.

5 "Their feeble frames my power shall raise,
And mould with heavenly skill;
I 'll give them tongues to sing my praise,
And hands to do my will."

6 His words, ye happy parents! hear,
And shout, with joys divine,
Dear Saviour! all we have and are
Shall be for ever thine.

461. S. M.
The Spirit in Baptism.

1 GREAT God! now condescend
To bless our rising race;
Soon may their willing spirits bend,
The subjects of thy grace.

2 Oh! what a pure delight
Their happiness to see!
Our warmest wishes all unite,
To lead their souls to thee.

3 Now bless, thou God of love!
This ordinance divine;
Send thy good Spirit from above,
And make these children thine.

462.
L. M.
Baptism of the Holy Ghost.

1 COME, Holy Ghost! come from on high!
Baptizer of our spirits thou!
The sacramental seal apply,
And witness with the water now.

2 Exert thy gracious power divine,
And sprinkle thou th' atoning blood;
May Father, Son, and Spirit, join
To seal this child, a child of God.

463.
L. M.
The Baptism of a Household.

1 UNITED prayers ascend to thee,
Eternal Parent of mankind!
Smile on this waiting family;
Thy blessing let thy servants find.

2 Let the dear pledges of their love,
Like tender plants, around them grow:
Thy present grace, and joys above,
Upon their little ones bestow.

3 Receive, at their believing hand,
The charge which they devote as thine
Obedient to their Lord's command;
And seal, with power, the rite divine.

4 To every member of their house,
Thy grace impart, thy love extend;
Grant every good that time allows,
With heavenly joys that never end.

464.
S. M.
Prayer for the Sanctification of Children.

1 O GOD of Abra'm! hear
The parents' humble cry;
In covenant-mercy now appear,
While in the dust we lie.

2 These children of our love,
In mercy thou hast given,

That we through grace may faithful prove,
In training them for heaven.

3 Oh! grant thy Spirit, Lord!
Their hearts to sanctify;
Remember now thy gracious word;—
Our hopes on thee rely.

4 Draw forth the melting tear,
The penitential sigh;
Inspire their hearts with faith sincere,
And fix their hopes on high.

5 These children now are thine,—
We give them back to thee;
Oh! lead them by thy grace divine,
Along the heavenly way.

465.

C. M.

The Condescension of Christ

1 BEHOLD what condescending love
Jesus on earth displays!
To babes and sucklings, he extends
The riches of his grace!

2 He still the ancient promise keeps,
To our forefathers given;
Young children in his arms he takes,
And calls them heirs of heaven.

3 Forbid them not, whom Jesus calls,
Nor dare the claim resist,
Since his own lips to us declare
Of such will heaven consist.

4 With flowing tears, and thankful hearts,
We give them up to thee;
Receive them, Lord! into thine arms,—
Thine may they ever be.

466.

L. M.

Entering into Covenant.

1 OH! happy day, that fixed my choice
On thee, my Saviour, and my God!
Well may this glowing heart rejoice,
And tell its raptures all abroad.

2 Oh! happy bond, that seals my vows
To him who merits all my love!

Let cheerful anthems fill the house,
While to his altar now I move.—

3 'T is done—the great transaction 's done;—
I am my Lord's, and he is mine;
He drew me, and I followed on,
Rejoiced to own the call divine.

4 Now rest, my long-divided heart!
Fixed on this blissful centre, rest;
Here have I found a nobler part,
Here heavenly pleasures fill my breast.

5 High Heaven, that hears the solemn vow,
That vow renewed, shall daily hear;
Till, in life's latest hour, I bow,
And bless in death a bond so dear.

467. L. M.

A Welcome to christian Fellowship.

1 COME in, thou blessed of the Lord!
Oh! come in Jesus' precious name;
We welcome thee, with one accord,
And trust the Saviour does the same.

2 Those joys which earth cannot afford,
We 'll seek in fellowship to prove,
Joined in one spirit to our Lord,
Together bound by mutual love.

3 And, while we pass this vale of tears,
We 'll make our joys and sorrows known;
We 'll share each other's hopes and fears,
And count a brother's cares our own.

4 Once more, our welcome we repeat;
Receive assurance of our love;
Oh! may we all together meet,
Around the throne of God above.

468. L. M.

Entire Consecration.

1 NOW I resolve, with all my heart,
With all my powers, to serve the Lord;
Nor from his ways will I depart,
Whose service is a rich reward.

2 Oh! be his service all my joy!—
Around let my example shine,

Till others love the blest employ,
  And join in labors so divine.

3 Be this the purpose of my soul,
  My solemn, my determined choice,
To yield to his supreme control,
  And, in his kind commands, rejoice.

4 Oh! may I never faint nor tire,
  Nor wandering leave his sacred ways;
Great God! accept my soul's desire,
  And give me strength to live thy praise

469. L. M.

Self-Dedication to God.

1 LORD! I am thine, entirely thine,
Purchased and saved by blood divine;
With full consent thine I would be,
And own thy sovereign right in me.

2 Grant me, in mercy, now a place,
Among the children of thy grace,—
A wretched sinner, lost to God,
But ransomed by Immanuel's blood.

3 Thee, my new master, now I call,
And consecrate to thee my all;
Lord! let me live and die to thee,—
Be thine through all eternity.

470. C. M.

The Young entering into Covenant.

1 COME, let us join our souls to God,
  In everlasting bands;
And seize the blessings he bestows,
  With eager hearts and hands.

2 Come, let us to his temple haste,
  And seek his favor there;
Before his footstool humbly bow,
  And pour our fervent prayer.

3 Come, let us seal, without delay
  The covenant of his grace;
Nor shall the years of distant life
  Its mem'ry o'er efface.

4 Thus may our young companions haste
  To seek their fathers' God;

Nor e'er forsake the happy path
Their fathers' feet have trod.

471.

C. M.

Public Profession.

1 YE men and angels ! witness now,
Before the Lord we speak ;
To him we make our solemn vow,
A vow we dare not break ;—

2 That, long as life itself shall last,
Ourselves to Christ we yield ;
Nor, from his cause will we depart,
Nor ever quit the field.

3 We trust not in our native strength,
But on his grace rely ;
May he, with our returning wants,
A needful aid supply.

4 Oh ! guide our doubtful feet aright,
And keep us in thy ways ;
And, while we turn our vows to prayers,
Turn thou our prayers to praise.

472.

L. M.

On receiving new Memoers.

1 KINDRED in Christ ! for his dear sake,
A hearty welcome here receive ;
May we together now partake
The joys which only he can give.

2 May he, by whose kind care, we meet,
Send his good Spirit from above ;
Make our communications sweet,
And cause our hearts to burn with love.

3 Forgotten be each worldly theme,
When Christians see each other thus ;
We only wish to speak of him,
Who lived, and died, and reigns, for us.

4 We 'll talk of all he did and said,
And suffered for us, here below ;—
The path he marked for us to tread,
And what he 's doing for us now.

5 Thus,—as the moments pass away,—
We 'll love, and wonder, and adore ;

And hasten on the glorious day,
  When we shall meet to part no more.

473.

L. M.

The Lord's Supper instituted.

1 'T WAS on that dark—that doleful night,
  When powers of earth and hell arose
Against the Son of God's delight,
  And friends betrayed him to his foes :—

2 Before the mournful scene began,
  He took the bread, and blessed and brake
What love through all his actions ran!
  What wondrous words of grace he spake!

3 "This is my body, broke for sin;
  Receive and eat the living food:"—
Then took the cup and blessed the wine,—
  "'T is the new covenant in my blood."

4 "Do this," he cried, "till time shall end,
  In mem'ry of your dying friend;
Meet, at my table, and record
  The love of your departed Lord."

5 Jesus! thy feast we celebrate;
  We show thy death, we sing thy name—
Till thou return, and we shall eat
  The marriage-supper of the Lamb.

474.

C. M.

The new Covenant sealed.

1 THE promise of my Father's love
  Shall stand for ever good:
He said—and gave his soul to death,
  And sealed the grace with blood.

2 To this dear covenant of thy word
  I set my worthless name;
I seal th' engagement to my Lord,
  And make my humble claim.

3 I call that legacy my own,
  Which Jesus did bequeath;
'T was purchased with a dying groan,
  And ratified in death.

4 The light and strength, the pard'ning grace
  And glory shall be mine:

My life and soul—my heart and flesh,—
And all my powers are thine.

475.

7s.

Sacramental Emblems.

1 BREAD of heaven! on thee I feed,
For thy flesh is meat indeed;
Ever may my soul be fed,
With the true and living bread;
Day by day, with strength supplied,
Through the life of him that died.

2 Vine of heaven! thy blood supplies
This blest cup of sacrifice;
'T is thy wounds, my healing give;
To thy cross I look and live:
Thou, my life! Oh! let me be
Rooted, grafted, built on thee

476.

L. M.

The Memorials of Grace.

1 JESUS is gone above the skies,
Where our weak senses reach him not;
And carnal objects court our eyes,
To thrust our Saviour from our thought.

2 He knows what wandering hearts we have,
Apt to forget his lovely face;
And, to refresh our minds, he gave
These kind memorials of his grace.

3 Let sinful sweets be all forgot,
And earth grow less in our esteem;
Christ and his love fill every thought,
And faith and hope be fixed on him.

4 While he is absent from our sight,
'T is to prepare our souls a place,
That we may dwell in heavenly light,
And live for ever near his face.

477.

S. M.

Communion with Christ and with Saints.

1 JESUS invites his saints
To meet around his board;
Here pardoned rebels sit, and hold
Communion with their Lord.

2 This holy bread and wine
Maintain our fainting breath,
By union with our living Lord,
And interest in his death.

3 Our heavenly Father calls
Christ and his members one;
We the young children of his love
And he the first-born Son.

4 Let all our powers be joined,
His glorious name to raise:
Pleasure and love fill every mind,
And every voice be praise.

478.
L. M.
Not ashamed of Christ.

1 AT thy command, our dearest Lord.
Here we attend thy dying feast;
Thy blood, like wine, adorns thy board,
And thine own flesh feeds every guest.

2 Our faith adores thy bleeding love,
And trusts for life in one who died;
We hope for heavenly crowns above,
From a Redeemer crucified.

3 Let the vain world pronounce it shame,
And cast their scandals on thy cause;
We come to boast our Saviour's name,
And make our triumphs in his cross.

4 With joy we tell the scoffing age,
He that was dead has left his tomb;
He lives above their utmost rage,
And we are waiting till he come.

479.
C. M.
The Love of Christ.

1 HOW condescending and how kind
Was God's eternal Son!
Our misery reached his heavenly mind,
And pity brought him down.

2 He sunk beneath our heavy woes,
To raise us to his throne;
There 's ne'er a gift his hand bestows,
But cost his heart a groan.

3 This was compassion, like a God,
That when the Saviour knew—
The price of pardon was his blood,
His pity ne'er withdrew.

4 Now, though he reigns exalted high,
His love is still as great;
Well he remembers Calvary,
Nor lets his saints forget.

5 Here let our hearts begin to melt,
While we his death record,
And, with our joy for pardoned guilt,
Mourn that we pierced the Lord.

480. L. M.

The Day of Espousals.

1 JESUS, thou everlasting King!
Accept the tribute that we bring;
Accept the well-deserved renown,
And wear our praises as thy crown.

2 Let every act of worship be,
Like our espousals, Lord! to thee;—
Like the dear hour, when, from above
We first received thy pledge of love.

3 The gladness of that happy day—
Our hearts would wish it long to stay;
Nor let our faith forsake its hold,
Nor comfort sink, nor love grow cold.

4 Each foll'wing minute as it flies,
Increase thy praise, improve our joys;
Till we are raised to sing thy name,
At the great supper of the Lamb.

481. C. M.

Humble Communion with Christ.

1 LORD! at thy table, we behold
The wonders of thy grace;
But most of all admire, that we
Should find a welcome-place.

2 We, who were all defiled with sin,
And rebels to our God;—
We, who have crucified thy Son,
And trampled on his blood;—

3 What strange, surprising grace is this,
That we, so lost, have room?
Jesus our weary souls invites,
And freely bids us come.

4 Ye saints below, and hosts above!
Join all your sacred powers;
No theme is like redeeming love,—
No Saviour is like ours.

482.

C. M.

The triumphal Feast.

1 COME, let us lift our voices high,—
High as our joys arise,
And join the songs above the sky,
Where pleasure never dies.

2 Jesus, our God, invites us here,
To this triumphal feast:
And brings immortal blessings down
For each redeemed guest.

3 Victorious God! what can we pay
For favors so divine?
We would devote our hearts away,
To be for ever thine.

4 We give thee, Lord! our highest praise—
The tribute of our tongues;
But themes, so infinite as these,
Exceed our noblest songs.

483.

C. M.

The Gospel-Feast.

1 HOW sweet and awful is the place,
With Christ within the doors—
While everlasting love displays
The choicest of her stores!

2 While all our hearts, and all our songs,
Join to admire the feast;
Each of us cry, with thankful tongues,—
"Lord! why was I a guest?

3 "Why was I made to hear thy voice,
And enter while there 's room—
When thousands make a wretched choice,
And rather starve than come?"

4 'T was the same love that spread the feast,
That sweetly forced us in;
Else we had still refused to taste,
And perished in our sin.

5 Pity the nations, O our God!
Constrain the earth to come;
Send thy victorious word abroad,
And bring the strangers home.

6 We long to see thy churches full,
That all the chosen race
May, with one voice, and heart, and soul,
Sing thy redeeming grace.

484.

C. M.

Remembering Christ.

1 IF human kindness meets return,
And owns the grateful tie;
If tender thoughts within us burn,
To feel a friend is nigh;—

2 Oh! shall not warmer accents tell
The gratitude we owe
To him, who died, our fears to quell—
Our more than orphan's wo!

3 While yet his anguished soul surveyed
Those pangs he would not flee,
What love his latest words displayed,—
"Meet and remember me!"

4 Remember thee—thy death, thy shame,
Our sinful hearts to share!—
O mem'ry! leave no other name
But his recorded there.

485.

L. M.

The Presence of Christ desired.

1 FAR from my thoughts, vain world! be gone,
Let my religious hours alone:
Fain would mine eyes my Saviour see;—
I wait a visit, Lord! from thee.

2 My heart grows warm with holy fire,
And kindles with a pure desire;
Come, my dear Jesus! from above,
And feed my soul with heavenly love.

3 Blest Saviour! what delicious fare—
How sweet thine entertainments are!
Never did angels taste above
Redeeming grace and dying love.

4 Hail, great Immanuel, all-divine!
In thee thy Father's glories shine:
Thou brightest, sweetest, fairest one,
That eyes have seen, or angels known!

486. C. M.

Remembering Christ.

1 ACCORDING to thy gracious word,—
In meek humility,—
This will I do, my dying Lord!
I will remember thee.

2 Thy body, broken for my sake,
My bread from heaven shall be;
Thy testamental cup I take,
And thus remember thee.

3 Gethsemane can I forget?
Or there thy conflict see,—
Thine agony and bloody sweat,—
And not remember thee?

4 When to the cross I turn mine eyes,
And rest on Calvary,
O Lamb of God, my sacrifice!
I must remember thee:—

5 Remember thee, and all thy pains,
And all thy love to me!—
Yea, while a breath, a pulse remains,
Will I remember thee.

6 And when these failing lips grow dumb,
And mind and mem'ry flee;
When, in thy kingdom, thou shalt come—
Jesus! remember me.

SABBATH.

487.

7s.

The Sabbath in the Sanctuary.

1 SAFELY through another week,
God has brought us on our way;—
Let us now a blessing seek,
Waiting in his courts to-day:
Day of all the week the best,
Emblem of eternal rest.

2 While we seek supplies of grace,
Through the dear Redeemer's name,
Show thy reconciled face,
Take away our sin and shame;
From our worldly cares set free,
May we rest, this day, in thee.

3 Here we come thy name to praise;
Let us feel thy presence near:
May thy glory meet our eyes,
While we in thy house appear:
Here afford us, Lord! a taste
Of our everlasting feast.

4 May the gospel's joyful sound
Conquer sinners—comfort saints
Make the fruits of grace abound,
Bring relief from all complaints:
Thus let all our Sabbaths prove
Till we join the church above.

488.

S. M.

The Lord's Day and public Worship.

1 WELCOME—sweet day of rest,
That saw the Lord arise!
Welcome to this reviving breast,
And these rejoicing eyes.

2 The king himself comes near,
And feasts his saints to-day;
Here we may sit, and see him here,
And love, and praise, and pray

3 One day, amidst the place
Where my dear God hath been,

Is sweeter than ten thousand days,
Of pleasurable sin.

4 My willing soul would stay,
In such a frame as this,—
And sit and sing herself away
To everlasting bliss.

489.

H. M.
Sabbath-Morning.

1 WELCOME—delightful morn,
Thou day of sacred rest!
I hail thy kind return;—
Lord! make these moments blest;
From the low train of mortal toys,
I soar to reach immortal joys.

2 Now may the king descend,
And fill his throne of grace;
Thy sceptre, Lord! extend,
While saints address thy face:
Let sinners feel thy quickening word,
And learn to know and fear the Lord.

3 Descend, celestial Dove!
With all thy quickening powers;
Disclose a Saviour's love,
And bless the sacred hours;
Then shall my soul new life obtain,
Nor Sabbaths be bestowed in vain.

490.

C. M.
Dawn of the Sabbath.

1 AGAIN, the Lord of life and light
Awakes the kindling ray,
Dispels the darkness of the night,
And pours increasing day.

2 Oh! what a night was that which wrapt
A sinful world in gloom!
Oh! what a sun, which broke this day,
Triumphant from the tomb!

3 This day be grateful homage paid,
And loud hosannas sung;
Let gladness dwell in every heart,
And praise on every tongue.

4 Ten thousand thousand lips shall join
To hail this welcome morn,
Which scatters blessings, from its wings,
To nations yet unborn.

491.
H. M
Morning of the Lord's Day.

1 AWAKE, ye saints! awake,
And hail this sacred day;
In loftiest songs of praise
Your joyful homage pay:
Come, bless the day that God hath blessed,—
The type of heaven's eternal rest.

2 On this auspicious morn
The Lord of life arose,
And burst the bars of death,
And vanquished all our foes;
And now he pleads our cause above,
And reaps the fruit of all his love.

3 All hail! triumphant Lord!
Heaven with hosannas rings;
And earth, in humbler strains,
Thy praise responsive sings;—
"Worthy the Lamb that once was slain,
Through endless years, to live and reign!"

4 Great King! gird on thy sword,
Ascend thy conquering car;
While justice, power and love
Maintain the glorious war:
This day let sinners own thy sway,
And rebels cast their arms away.

492.
L. M.
The Morning of the Lord's Day.

1 HAIL! morning known among the blest,—
Morning of hope, and joy, and love,—
Of heavenly peace, and holy rest,
Pledge of the endless rest above!

2 Blest be the Father of our Lord,
Who, from the dead, hath brought his Son;
Hope to the lost was then restored,
And everlasting glory won.

3 Scarce morning-twilight had begun
To chase the shades of night away,
When Christ arose—unsetting sun—
The dawn of joy's eternal day.

4 Mercy looked down, with smiling eye,
When our Immanuel left the dead;
Faith marked his bright ascent on high,
And hope, with gladness, raised her head.

5 Descend, O Spirit of the Lord!
Thy fire to every bosom bring;
Then shall our ardent hearts accord,
And teach our lips God's praise to sing.

493. C. M.

The Resurrection-Morn.

1 BLEST morning! whose young dawning rays
Beheld our rising God;
That saw him triumph o'er the dust,
And leave his dark abode.

2 In the cold prison of a tomb,
The great Redeemer lay,
Till the revolving skies had brought
The third, th' appointed day.

3 Hell and the grave unite their force
To hold our God in vain:
The sleeping Conqueror arose,
And burst their feeble chain.

4 To thy great name, almighty Lord!
These sacred hours we pay;
And loud hosannas shall proclaim
The triumph of the day.

5 Salvation, and immortal praise,
To our victorious King!
Let heaven and earth, and rocks and seas,
With glad hosannas ring.

494. L. M.

The Rest of the Sabbath.

1 ANOTHER six days' work is done,
Another Sabbath is begun;
Return, my soul! enjoy thy rest,
Improve the day thy God hath blessed.

2 Oh! that our thoughts and thanks may rise,
As grateful incense to the skies;
And draw, from heaven, that sweet repose
Which none, but he that feels it, knows.

3 This heavenly calm, within the breast,
Is the dear pledge of glorious rest—
Which for the church of God remains,—
The end of cares, the end of pains.

4 In holy duties let the day,—
In holy pleasures, pass away;
How sweet a Sabbath thus to spend,
In hope of one that ne'er shall end!

495. L. M.

The earthly and heavenly Sabbath.

1 THINE earthly Sabbaths, Lord! we love,
But there 's a nobler rest above;
To that our longing souls aspire,
With cheerful hope and strong desire.

2 No more fatigue, no more distress,
Nor sin, nor death shall reach the place;
No groans shall mingle with the songs
That warble from immortal tongues.

3 No rude alarms of raging foes,
No cares to break the long repose,
No midnight-shade, no clouded sun,
But sacred, high, eternal noon.

4 Soon shall that glorious day begin,
Beyond this world of death and sin;
Soon shall our voices join the song
Of the triumphant, holy throng.

496. 7s.

The holy Day of Rest.

1 WELCOME—sacred day of rest!
Sweet repose from worldly care;—
Day above all days the best,
When our souls for heaven prepare;—
Day when our Redeemer rose,
Victor o'er the hosts of hell:
Thus he vanquished all our foes;—
Let our lips his glory tell.

2 Gracious Lord! we love this day,
When we hear thy holy word;
When we sing thy praise, and pray;—
Earth can no such joys afford:
But a better rest remains,
Heavenly Sabbaths,—happier days
Rest from sin, and rest from pains,—
Endless joys, and endless praise.

497.
C. M.
A Sabbath in the House of God.

1 HERE cares and angry passions cease,
For saints together meet
To spend an hour of prayer and peace,
At their Redeemer's feet.

2 No sculptured wonders meet the sight,—
Nor pictured saints appear,
Nor storied window's gorgeous light,
For God himself is here.

3 And here are comrades in the war
With Satan and with sin,
Who now in God's own favor share,
And soon their heaven will win.

4 Glory to God! who deigns to bless
This consecrated day,
Unfolds his wondrous promises,
And makes it sweet to pray.

5 Glory to God! who deigns to hear
The humblest sigh we raise,
And answers every heart-felt prayer,
And hears our hymn of praise.

498.
C. M.
The first Day of the Week.

1 AND now another week begins,
This day we call the Lord's;
This day he rose, who bore our sins,—
For so his word records.

2 Hark, how the angels sweetly sing!—
Their voices fill the sky;
They hail their great victorious king,
And welcome him on high.

3 We 'll catch the note of lofty praise;
May we their rapture feel;
Our thankful song with theirs we 'll raise,
And emulate their zeal.

4 Come, then, ye saints! and grateful sing
Of Christ, our risen Lord,—
Of Christ, the everlasting king,—
Of Christ, th' incarnate word.

5 Hail, mighty Saviour! thee we hail!
High on thy throne above;
Till heart and flesh together fail,
We 'll sing thy matchless love.

499. C. M.

The first Sabbath.

1 HOW bright a day was that, which saw
Creation's work complete!
All nature owned her Maker's law,
And worshiped at his feet.

2 The world, arranged by power divine,
In perfect order stood;
And, resting from his great design,
God saw that all was good.

3 Not such a Sabbath now appears,
For sin has ruined all;
No longer man with pleasure hears
A gracious Father's call.

4 Yet, Lord! bring back the reign of peace,
Let brighter days begin;
And teach vain creatures how to cease
From folly and from sin.

5 Let sinners be again made thine,
Though once with vengeance cursed;
And let a second Sabbath shine,
As glorious as the first.

500. C. M.

The Resurrection of Christ.

1 THE Lord of Sabbath let us praise,
In concert with the blest:
And joyful, in harmonious lays,
Employ this day of rest.

2 Lord! may we still remember thee,
And more in knowledge grow;
Oh! may we more of glory see,
While waiting here below.

3 On this blest day, a brighter scene
Of glory was displayed,
By God, th' eternal word, than when
This universe was made.

4 He rises, who our souls hath bought
With blood, and grief, and pain:
'T was great—to speak the world from nought,—
'T was greater—to redeem.

501.

L. M.

The Lord's Day.

1 THIS day the Lord hath called his own;—
Oh! let us then his praise declare,
Fix our desires on him alone,
And seek his face, with fervent prayer.

2 Lord! in thy love, would we rejoice,
That bids the burdened soul be free;
And, with united heart and voice,
Devote these sacred hours to thee.

3 Now let the world's delusive things
No more our groveling thoughts employ,
But faith be taught to stretch her wings,
In search of heaven's unfailing joy.

4 Oh! let these earthly Sabbaths, Lord!
Be to our lasting welfare blest;
The purest comfort here afford,
And fit us for eternal rest.

502.

10s.

The Sabbath, a holy Rest.

1 AGAIN the day returns of holy rest,
Which, when he made the world, Jehovah blest;
When, like his own, he bade our labours cease,
And all be piety, and all be peace.

2 Let us devote this consecrated day
To learn his will, and all we learn obey;
So shall he hear when fervently we raise
Our supplications, and our songs of praise.

3 Father in heaven! in whom our hopes confide,
Whose power defends us, and whose precepts guide;
In life our guardian, and in death our friend,—
Glory supreme be thine, till time shall end.

503.

C. M.

The Sacrifice of the Heart.

1 WHEN, as returns this solemn day,
  Man comes to meet his God,
What rites—what honors shall he pay?
  How spread his praise abroad?

2 From marble-domes and gilded spires
  Shall clouds of incense rise?
And gems, and gold, and garlands deck
  The costly sacrifice?

3 Vain, sinful man!—creation's Lord
  Thine offerings well may spare;
But give thy heart—and thou shalt find,
  That God will hear thy prayer.

504.

7s and 6s.

Sabbath-Contemplations.

1 LORD of the vast creation,
  Support of worlds unknown,
Desire of every nation!—
  Behold us at thy throne;
We come for mercy crying,
  Through thine atoning blood;
And on thy grace relying,
  We seek each promised good.

2 We bless the condescension
  That brought thee down to earth;
Of which the seers made mention,
  Who prophesied thy birth:
We celebrate the glory,
  That marked thy wondrous way
And own the joyful story,
  That claims this hallowed day.

3 Oh! when shall thy salvation
  Be known through every land,
And men, in every station,
  Obey thy great command?

44

In God's own Son believing,
  From sin may they be free;
And gospel-grace receiving,
  Find life and peace in thee.

505. L. M.
The Close of the Sabbath.

1 ANOTHER day has passed along,
  And we are nearer to the tomb,—
Nearer to join the heavenly song,
  Or hear the last eternal doom.

2 Sweet is the light of Sabbath-eve,
  And soft the sunbeams lingering there:
For these blest hours, the world I leave,
  Wafted on wings of faith and prayer.

3 The time how lovely and how still;
  Peace shines and smiles on all below,—
The plain, the stream, the wood, the hill,—
  All fair with evening's setting glow.

4 Season of rest! the tranquil soul
  Feels the sweet calm, and melts to love,—
And while these sacred moments roll,
  Faith sees a smiling heaven above.

5 Nor will our days of toil be long,
  Our pilgrimage will soon be trod;
And we shall join the ceaseless song,—
  The endless Sabbath of our God.

506. C. M.
Evening of the Lord's Day.

1 FREQUENT the day of God returns,
  To shed its quickening beams;
And yet how slow devotion burns!
  How languid are its flames!

2 Accept our faint attempts to love,
  Our frailties, Lord! forgive;
We would be like thy saints above,
  And praise thee while we live.

3 Increase, O Lord! our faith and hope,
  And fit us to ascend,
Where the assembly ne'er breaks up,
  The Sabbath ne'er shall end:—

4 Where we shall breathe in heavenly air,
With heavenly lustre shine,
Before the throne of God appear,
And feast on love divine:—

5 Where we, in high seraphic strains,
Shall all our powers employ;
Delighted range th' ethereal plains,
And take our fill of joy.

507. C. M.

Lord's Day-Evening.

1 WHEN, O dear Jesus! when shall I
Behold thee all-serene;
Blest in perp'etual Sabbath-day,
Without a veil between?

2 Assist me while I wander here
Amidst a world of cares;
Incline my heart to pray with love,
And then accept my prayers.

3 Spare me, my God! Oh! spare the soul
That gives itself to thee;
Take all that I possess below,
And give thyself to me.

4 Thy Spirit, O my Father! give
To be my guide and friend,
To light my path to ceaseless joys—
Where Sabbaths never end.

SANCTUARY.

508. S. M.

The Mercy-Seat.

1 HOW charming is the place,
Where my Redeemer-God
Unveils the glories of his face,
And sheds his love abroad!

2 Not the fair palaces,
To which the great resort,
Are once to be compared with this,
Where Jesus holds his court.

3 Here, on the mercy-seat,
With radiant glory crowned,
Our joyful eyes behold thee sit,
And smile on all around.

4 To thee, our prayers and cries
Each humble soul presents:
Oh! listen to our broken sighs,
And grant us all our wants.

5 Give us, O Lord! a place,
Within thy blest abode,
Among the children of thy grace,—
The servants of our God.

509.

C. M.

The Glory of Zion.

1 HOW honorable is the place,
Where we adoring stand;
Zion!—the glory of the earth,
And beauty of the land.

2 Bulwarks of mighty grace defend
The city where we dwell;
The walls, of strong salvation made,
Defy th' assaults of hell.

3 Lift up the everlasting gates,
The doors wide open fling;
Enter, ye nations that obey
The statutes of our king!

4 Here shall you taste unmingled joys,
And live in perfect peace,—
You that have known Jehovah's name,
And ventured on his grace!

5 Trust in the Lord, for ever trust,
And banish all your fears:
Strength, in the Lord Jehovah, dwells,
Eternal as his years.

510.

L. M.

The Church, the Palace of God.

1 HAPPY the church, thou sacred place,
The seat of thy Creator's grace!
Thy holy courts are his abode,
Thou earthly palace of our God!

2 Thy walls are strength,—and at thy gates
A guard of heavenly warriors waits;
Nor shall thy deep foundation move,
Fixed on his counsels and his love.

3 Thy foes in vain designs engage—
Against thy throne in vain they rage,
Like rising waves, with angry roar,
That dash and die upon the shore.

4 God is our shield, and God our sun;
Swift as the fleeting moments run,
On us he sheds new beams of grace,
And we reflect his brightest praise.

511.

H. M.

The House of Prayer.

1 GREAT Father of mankind!
We bless that wondrous grace,
Which could for Gentiles find,
Within thy courts, a place:
How kind the care
Our God displays,
For us to raise
A house of prayer!

2 Though once estranged afar,
We now approach the throne,
For Jesus brings us near,
And makes our cause his own;
Strangers no more,
To thee we come;
We find our home,
And rest secure.

3 To thee our souls we join,
And love thy sacred name:
No more our own, but thine.
We triumph in thy claim:
Our Father-King!
Thy covenant-grace
Our souls embrace,
Thy titles sing.

4 Let all the nations throng
To worship in thy house;
And thou attend the song,
And smile upon their vows,

Indulgent still,
Till earth conspire
To join the choir,
On Zion's hill.

512.

7s.

The House of Prayer and Praise.

1 LORD of hosts! to thee we raise,
Here, a house of prayer and praise;
Thou thy people's heart prepare,
Here to meet for praise and prayer.

2 Let the living here be fed,
With thy word, the heavenly bread;
Here, in hope of glory blest,
May the dead be laid to rest.

3 Here, to thee a temple stand,
While the sea shall girt the land;
Here, reveal thy mercy sure,
While the sun and moon endure.

4 Hallelujah!—earth and sky
To the joyful sound reply:
Hallelujah!—hence ascend
Prayer and praise, till time shall end.

513.

L. M.

On opening a House of Worship.

1 HERE, in thy name, eternal God!
We build this earthly house for thee;
Oh! make it now thy fixed abode,
And keep it, Lord! from error free.

2 When here thy people seek thy face,
And dying sinners pray to live;
Hear thou, in heaven, thy dwelling-place,
And when thou hearest, Lord! forgive.

3 Here, when thy messengers proclaim,
The blessed gospel of thy Son;
Still, by the power of his great name,
Be mighty signs and wonders done.

4 When children's voices raise the song,—
Hosanna to their heavenly King;
Let heaven, with earth, the strain prolong—
"Hosanna!" let the angels sing.

5 But will, indeed, Jehovah deign,
Here to abide,—no transient guest?
Here, will our great Redeemer reign,
And here, the Holy Spirit rest?—

6 Thy glory never hence depart!
Yet choose not, Lord! this house alone;
Thy kingdom come, in every heart,—
In every bosom, fix thy throne.

514. L. M.

Prayer on opening a Church-Edifice.

1 WITHIN thy house, O Lord our God!
In glorious majesty appear;
Make this a place of thine abode,
And shed thy choicest blessings here.

2 When we thy mercy-seat surround,
Thy Spirit, with thy word, impart;
And let thy gospel's joyful sound,
With power divine, reach every heart.

3 Here, let the blind their sight obtain,
Here, give the broken spirit rest;
Let Jesus here triumphant reign,—
Enthroned in every yielding breast.

4 Here, let the voice of sacred joy
And humble supplication rise,
Till higher strains our tongues employ,
In realms of bliss, beyond the skies.

515. C. M.

Dedication of a Church.

1 GOD of the universe! to thee
This sacred fane we rear,
And now, with songs and bended knee,
Invoke thy presence here.

2 Long may this echoing dome resound
The praises of thy name,—
These hallowed walls to all around
The Triune God proclaim.

3 Here, let thy love—thy presence dwell,—
Thy glory here make known;
Thy people's home, Oh! come, and fill,
And seal it as thine own.

4 When sad with care—by sin oppressed,—
Here may the burdened soul,
Beneath thy sheltering wing, find rest;
Here, make the wounded whole.

5 And when the last long Sabbath-morn,
Upon the just, shall rise,
May all, who own thee here, be borne
To mansions in the skies.

MINISTRY.

516.
S. M.
The Heralds of Christ.

1 HOW beauteous are their feet,
Who stand on Zion's hill!
Who bring salvation on their tongues,
And words of peace reveal!

2 How charming is their voice!
How sweet the tidings are!—
"Zion! behold thy Saviour-King,
He reigns and triumphs here!"

3 How happy are our ears
That hear this joyful sound!
Which kings and prophets waited for,
And sought, but never found

4 How blessed are our eyes,
That see this heavenly light!
Prophets and kings desired it long,
But died without the sight.

5 The watchmen join their voice,
And tuneful notes employ;
Jerusalem breaks forth in songs,
And deserts learn the joy.

6 The Lord makes bare his arm,
Through all the earth abroad;
Let every nation now behold
Their Saviour and their God.

517.

L. M.

The great Commission.

1 "GO, preach my gospel!"—saith the Lord,—
"Bid the whole earth my grace receive;
He shall be saved who trusts my word;
He shall be damned who don't believe.

2 "I 'll make your great commission known,
And ye shall prove my gospel true,
By all the works that I have done,
By all the wonders ye shall do.

3 "Teach all the nations my commands,—
I 'm with you till the world shall end;
All power is trusted in my hands,
I can destroy, and I defend."

4 He spake—and light shone round his head;
On a bright cloud, to heaven he rode:
They to the farthest nations spread
The grace of their ascended God.

518.

C. M.

Ministers watch for Souls.

1 LET Zion's watchmen all awake,
And take th' alarm they give;
Now let them, from the mouth of God,
Their awful charge receive.

2 'T is not a cause of small import
The pastor's care demands;
But what might fill an angel's heart;—
It filled a Saviour's hands.

3 They watch for souls, for which the Lord
Did heavenly bliss forego;—
For souls, that must for ever live,
In raptures, or in wo.

4 All to the great tribunal haste,
Th' account to render there;
And shouldst thou strictly mark our faults,
Lord! how should we appear?

5 May they that Jesus, whom they preach,
Their own Redeemer see;
And watch thou daily o'er their souls,
That they may watch for thee.

519.

L. M.

Meeting of Ministers.

1 POUR out thy Spirit from on high;
Lord! thine assembled servants bless;
Graces and gifts to each supply,
And clothe thy priests with righteousness.

2 Within thy temple where we stand,
To teach the truth as taught by thee,
Saviour! like stars, in thy right hand,
The angels of the churches be!

3 Wisdom and zeal, and faith impart,
Firmness with meekness from above,
To bear thy people on our hearts,
And love the souls whom thou dost love:—

4 To watch and pray, and never faint;
By day and night strict guard to keep;
To warn the sinner, cheer the saint,
Nourish thy lambs, and feed thy sheep.

5 Then, when our work is finished here,
In humble hope, our charge resign:
When the chief Shepherd shall appear,
O God! may they and we be thine.

520.

C. M.

The Death of a Minister.

1 NOW let our drooping hearts revive,
And all our tears be dry;
Why should those eyes be drowned in grief
That view a Saviour nigh?

2 Though earthly shepherds dwell in dust,—
The aged and the young;
The watchful eye, in darkness closed,
And mute th' instructive tongue;—

3 Th' eternal shepherd still survives,
New comfort to impart;
His eye still guides us—and his voice
Still animates our heart.

4 "Lo! I am with you," saith the Lord,
"My church shall safe abide;"
The Lord will ne'er forsake his own
Who in his love confide.

5 Through every scene of life and death,
His promise is our trust;
And this shall be our children's song,
When we are cold in dust.

521. S. M.

The Pastor's Death.

1 REST from thy labor, rest;—
Soul of the just, set free!
Blest be thy memory, and blest
Thy bright example be!

2 Faith, perseverance, zeal,
Language of light and power,
Love,—prompt to act, and quick to feel,—
Marked thee, till life's last hour.

3 Now,—toil and conflict o'er,—
Go, take with saints thy place
But go—as each hath gone before,—
A sinner saved by grace.

4 Lord Jesus! to thy hands
Our pastor we resign;
And now we wait thine own commands;—
We were not his, but thine.

5 Thou art thy church's head;
And when the members die,
Thou raisest others in their stead:—
To thee we lift our eye.

6 On thee our hopes depend;
We gather round our Rock;
Send whom thou wilt; but condescend
Thyself to feed thy flock.

522. S. M.

The Death of an aged Minister.

1 "SERVANT of God! well done!
Rest from thy loved employ:
The battle fought,—the vict'ry won,—
Enter thy Master's joy."

2 The voice at midnight came,
He started up to hear;
A mortal arrow pierced his frame,
He fell—but felt no fear.

3 Tranquil amid alarms,
It found him on the field,

A veteran slumbering on his arms,
Beneath his red-cross shield.

4 The pains of death are past,—
Labor and sorrow cease;
And, life's long warfare closed at last,
His soul is found in peace.

5 Soldier of Christ! well-done!
Praise be thy new employ;
And while eternal ages run,
Rest in thy Saviour's joy!

CHRISTIAN MISSIONS.

523.
7s.
Inquiring of a Watchman.

1 WATCHMAN! tell us of the night,
What its signs of promise are?
Traveler! o'er yon mountain's height!
See that glory-beaming star:
Watchman! does its beauteous ray
Aught of hope or joy foretell?
Traveler! yes;—it brings the day,—
Promised day of Israel.

2 Watchman! tell us of the night;—
Higher yet that star ascends;
Traveler! blessedness and light,
Peace and truth, its course portends;
Watchman! will its beams alone
Gild the spot that gave them birth?
Traveler! ages are its own,
See! it bursts o'er all the earth.

3 Watchman! tell us of the night,
For the morning seems to dawn;
Traveler! darkness takes its flight,
Doubt and terror are withdrawn:
Watchman! let thy wanderings cease;
Hie thee to thy quiet home;
Traveler! lo! the Prince of peace,—
Lo! the Son of God is come!

524. H. M.
Christian Effort.

1 RISE, gracious God! and shine
In all thy saving might:
And prosper each design,
To spread thy glorious light:
Let healing streams of mercy flow
That all the earth thy truth may know.

2 Put forth thy glorious power!
The nations then will see,
And earth present her store,
In converts born of thee:
God, our own God, his church will bless,
And earth shall yield her full increase.

525. 8s and 7s.
The Heathen crying for Help.

1 HARK! what mean those lamentations,
Rolling sadly through the sky?
'T is the cry of heathen nations,—
"Come and help us or we die!"

2 Hear the heathen's sad complaining,
Christians! hear their dying cry;
And, the love of Christ constraining,
Haste to help them, ere they die.

526. 7s and 6s.
The Gospel-Banner.

1 NOW be the gospel-banner,
In every land, unfurled;
And be the shout,—"Hosanna!"—
Re-echoed through the world;
Till every isle and nation,
Till every tribe and tongue
Receive the great salvation,
And join the happy throng.

2 What, though th' embattled legions
Of earth and hell combine?
His arm, throughout their regions,
Shall soon resplendent shine:
Ride on, O Lord! victorious,
Immanuel, Prince of peace!
Thy triumph shall be glorious,—
Thy empire still increase.

3 Yes,—thou shalt reign for ever,
O Jesus, King of kings!
Thy light, thy love, thy favor,
Each ransomed captive sings:
The isles for thee are waiting,
The deserts learn thy praise,
The hills and vallies greeting,
The song responsive raise.

527. L. M.

Missionary Meeting.

1 ASSEMBLED at thy great command,
Before thy face, dread King! we stand:
The voice, that marshalled every star,
Has called thy people from afar.

2 We meet, through distant lands, to spread
The truth for which the martyrs bled;
Along the line, to either pole,
The thunder of thy praise to roll.

3 Our prayers assist, accept our praise,
Our hopes revive, our courage raise,
Our counsels aid, to each impart
The single eye, the faithful heart.

4 Forth with thy chosen heralds come,
Recall the wandering spirits home;
From Zion's mount send forth the sound
To spread the spacious earth around.

528. L. M.

The Heralds pointing out the Way.

1 NOW let our faith with joy survey
The glories of the latter day:
Its dawn already seems begun,—
Sure earnest of the rising sun.

2 The friends of truth assembled stand,—
A chosen consecrated band,
The emblem of the cross display,
And cry aloud,—"Behold the way!"

3 Behold the way to Zion's hill,
Where Israel's God delights to dwell:
He fixes there his lofty throne,
And calls the sacred place his own.

4 "Behold the way!" ye heralds! cry;
Spare not, but lift your voices high:

Convey the sound from shore to shore,
And bid the captive sigh no more.

5 Auspicious dawn! thy rising ray,
With joy, we view, and hail the day:
Thou Sun! arise, supremely bright,
And fill the world with purest light.

529.

L. M.

The Heralds of Christ.

1 CAPTAIN of thine exalted host!
Display thy glorious banner high;
The summons send, from coast to coast,
And call a numerous army nigh.

2 A solemn jubilee proclaim,—
Proclaim the great sabbatic day;
Assert the glories of thy name;
Spoil Satan of his wished-for prey.

3 Oh! bid thy heralds publish loud
The peaceful blessings of thy reign;
And when they speak of sprinkled blood,
The mystery to the heart explain.

530.

S. M.

Missionaries encouraged.

1 YE messengers of Christ!
His sovereign voice obey;
Arise, and follow where he leads,
And peace attend your way.

2 The Master, whom you serve,
Will needful strength bestow;
Depending on his promised aid,
With sacred courage go.

3 Go, spread the Saviour's name;
Go, tell his matchless grace;
Proclaim salvation, full and free,
To Adam's guilty race.

4 Mountains shall sink to plains,
And hell in vain oppose;
The cause is God's—and will prevail
In spite of all his foes.

531.

8s, 7s and 4.

Departure of Missionaries.

1 MEN of God! go take your stations;
Darkness reigns o'er all the earth;

Go, proclaim among the nations,
  Joyful news of heavenly birth;
Bear the tidings—
  Tidings of the Saviour's worth.

2 When exposed to fearful dangers,
  Jesus will his own defend:
Borne afar midst foes and strangers,
  Jesus will appear your friend;
And his presence
  Shall be with you to the end.

532. 7s and 6s.
Departure of Missionaries.

1 ROLL on, thou mighty ocean!
  And, as thy billows flow,
Bear messengers of mercy,
  To every vale of wo:
Arise, ye gales! and waft them,
  Safe to their destined shore;
That men may sit in darkness
  And death's black shade no more.

2 O thou eternal Ruler!
  Who holdest in thine arm
The tempests of the ocean,—
  Deliver them from harm:
Thy presence still be with them
  Wherever they may be;
Though far from those who love them,
  Let them be nigh to thee.

533. 8s, 7s and 4.
The Heralds of Salvation.

1 ON the mountain's top appearing,
  Lo! the sacred herald stands;
Welcome news to Zion bearing,—
  Zion long in hostile lands:
    Mourning captive!
  God himself will loose thy bands.

2 Has thy night been long and mournful,
  All thy friends unfaithful proved?
Have thy foes been proud and scornful,
  By thy sighs and tears unmoved?
    Cease thy mourning;—
  Zion still is well-beloved.

3 God, thy God, will now restore thee,
He himself appears thy friend;
All thy foes shall flee before thee.
Here their boasts and triumphs end;
Great deliverance—
Zion's king will quickly send.

4 Peace and joy shall now attend thee,
All thy warfare now is past,
God, thy Saviour, shall defend thee,
Peace and joy are come at last;
All thy conflicts
End in everlasting rest.

534.

7s.

The Messengers of God.

1 GO—ye messengers of God!
Like the beams of morning, fly;
Take the wonder-working rod,
Wave the Banner-Cross on high.

2 Where the towering minaret
Gleams along the morning-skies,
Wave it till the crescent set,
And the "Star of Jacob" rise.

3 Go to many a tropic isle,
In the bosom of the deep,
Where the skies for ever smile,
And th' oppressed for ever weep.

4 O'er the negro's night of care
Pour the living light of heaven;
Chase away the fiend despair,—
Bid him hope to be forgiven.

5 Where the golden gates of day
Open on the palmy east,
Wide the bleeding cross display,—
Spread the gospel's richest feast.

6 Circumnavigate the ball,
Visit every soil and sea:
Preach the cross of Christ to all,—
Christ, whose love is full and free.

535.

C. M.

Promised Aid.

1 GO, and the Saviour's grace proclaim,
Ye favored men of God!

Go, publish, through Immanuel's name,
  Salvation bought with blood.

2 What though your arduous path-way lie
  Through regions dark as death?
What though, your faith and zeal to try,
  Perils beset your path?—

3 Yet, with determined courage, go,
  And armed with power divine:
Your God will needful strength bestow,
  And on your labors shine.

4 He, who has called you to the war,
  Will recompense your pains:
Before Messiah's conquering car,
  Shall mountains sink to plains.

5 Shrink not, though earth and hell oppose,
  But plead your Master's cause;
Assured that e'en your mightiest foes
  Shall bow before his cross.

536. C. M.

Designation of a Missionary.

1 FATHER of mercies! condescend
  To hear our fervent prayer,
While this our brother we commend
  To thy paternal care.

2 Before him set an open door;
  His various efforts bless;
On him thy Holy Spirit pour,
  And crown him with success.

3 Endow him with a heavenly mind;
  Supply his every need;
Make him in spirit meek, resigned,
  But bold in word and deed.

4 In every tempting, trying hour,
  Uphold him, by thy grace;
And guard him, by thy mighty power,
  Till he shall end his race.

5 Then, followed by a numerous train,
  Gathered from heathen lands,
A crown of life may he obtain,
  From his Redeemer's hands.

537.

L. M.

Commission to the Gentiles.

1 GO—messenger of peace and love!
   To nations plunged in shades of night;
Like angels sent from fields above,
   Be thine to shed celestial light.

2 Go, to the hungry food impart;
   To paths of peace the wanderer guide,
And lead the thirsty, panting heart,
   Where streams of living waters glide.

3 Go, bid the bright and morning-star,
   From Bethlehem's plains resplendent shine,
And, piercing through the gloom afar,
   Shed heavenly light and love divine.

4 To India's various castes, proclaim
   The gospel's soft, but powerful voice;
And, at the blest Redeemer's name,
   Let ocean's lonely isles rejoice.

5 From north to south, from east to west,
   Messiah yet shall reign supreme;
His name, by every tongue, confessed,—
   His praise—the universal theme.

538.

S. M.

Prayer for Israel.

1 LORD! send thy servants forth
   To call the Hebrews home;
From east, and west, and south, and north,
   Let all the wanderers come.

2 Where'er, in lands unknown,
   The fugitives remain,
Bid every creature help them on,
   Thy holy mount to gain.

3 An offering to the Lord,
   There let them all be seen,
Sprinkled with water and with blood,
   In soul and body clean.

4 With Israel's myriads sealed,
   Let all the nations meet;
And show the mystery fulfilled,—
   Thy family complete.

539.

8s, 7s and 4.

The Missionary's Farewell.

1 YES,—my native land! I love thee;
All thy scenes I love them well;—
Friends, connexions, happy country!
Can I bid you all farewell?
Can I leave you,
Far in heathen lands to dwell?

2 Home!—thy joys are passing lovely,—
Joys no stranger-heart can tell;
Happy home!—'t is sure I love thee!
Can I—can I say—Farewell?
Can I leave thee,
Far in heathen lands to dwell?

3 Scenes of sacred peace and pleasure,
Holy days and Sabbath-bell,
Richest, brightest, sweetest treasure!
Can I say a last farewell?
Can I leave you,
Far in heathen lands to dwell?

4 Yes! I hasten from you gladly,
From the scenes I love so well;
Far away, ye billows! bear me;
Lovely native land!—farewell!
Pleased I leave thee,
Far in heathen lands to dwell.

5 In the deserts let me labor,
On the mountains let me tell,
How he died—the blessed Saviour—
To redeem a world from hell!
Let me hasten,
Far in heathen lands to dwell.

6 Bear me on, thou restless ocean!
Let the winds my canvass swell:
Heaves my heart with warm emotion,
While I go far hence to dwell:
Glad I bid thee,
Native land!—Farewell!—Farewell!

540.

L. M.

Missionaries remembered.

1 MARKED as the purpose of the skies,
This promise meets our anxious eyes,—

That heathen lands the Lord shall know,
And warm with faith each bosom glow.

2 E'en now the hallowed scenes appear;
E'en now unfolds the promised year:
Lo! distant shores thy heralds trace,
And bear the tidings of thy grace.

3 Mid burning climes and frozen plains,
Where pagan darkness brooding reigns,
Lord! mark their steps, their fears subdue,
And nerve their arm, and clear their view.

4 When, worn by toil, their spirits fail,
Bid them the glorious future hail;
Bid them the crown of life survey,
And onward urge their conquering way.

SPREAD OF THE GOSPEL.

541. L. M.

Prayer for the Millennium.

1 JESUS! we bow before thy throne,
We lift our eyes to seek thy face;
To bleeding hearts thy love make known,
On contrite souls bestow thy grace.

2 See, spread beneath thy gracious eye,
A world o'erwhelmed in guilt and tears,
Where deathless souls in ruin lie,
And no kind voice dispels their fears!

3 Lord! arm thy truth with power divine,
Its conquests spread from shore to shore,
Till suns and stars forget to shine,
And earth and skies shall be no more.

4 Oh! rise, ye ransomed captives! rise,
Peal the loud anthem here below;
Let earth reflect it to the skies,
And heaven with new-born rapture glow.

542. C. M.

Returning to Zion.

1 DAUGHTER of Zion! from the dust
Exalt thy fallen head;

Again in thy Redeemer trust,—
He calls thee from the dead.

2 Awake, awake, put on thy strength,—
Thy beautiful array;
The day of freedom dawns at length,—
The Lord's appointed day.

3 Rebuild thy walls, thy bounds enlarge,
And send thy heralds forth:
Say to the south,—"Give up thy charge,
And keep not back, O north!"

4 They come, they come;—thine exiled bands,
Where'er they rest or roam,
Have heard thy voice in distant lands,
And hasten to their home.

5 Thus, though the universe shall burn,
And God his works destroy,
With songs, thy ransomed shall return,
And everlasting joy.

543.

S. M.

The Gospel-Trumpet.

1 YE trembling captives! hear;
The gospel-trumpet sounds;
No music more can charm the ear,
Or heal your heart-felt wounds.

2 'T is not the trump of war,
Nor Sinai's awful roar;
Salvation's news it spreads afar,
And vengeance is no more.

3 Forgiveness, love, and peace,
Glad heaven aloud proclaims;
And earth, the jubilee's release,
With eager rapture claims.

4. Far, far to distant lands
The saving news shall spread;
And Jesus all his willing bands,
In glorious triumph, lead.

544.

S. M.

Prayer for Success.

1 O LORD, our God! arise,
The cause of truth maintain;

And wide o'er all the peopled world
  Extend her blessed reign.

2 Thou Prince of life! arise,
  Nor let thy glory cease;
Far spread the conquests of thy grace,
  And bless the earth with peace.

3 Thou Holy Ghost! arise,
  Expand thy quickening wing,
And o'er a dark and ruined world
  Let light and order spring.

4 All on the earth! arise,
  To God, the Saviour, sing,
From shore to shore, from earth to heaven,
  Let echoing anthems ring.

545. L. M.

The Time to favor Zion.

1 SOVEREIGN of worlds! display thy power,
Be this thy Zion's favored hour;
Bid the bright morning-star arise,
And point the nations to the skies.

2 Set up thy throne where Satan reigns,
On Afric's shore, on India's plains;
Far let the gospel's sound be known,
And claim the nations for thy own.

3 Speak—and the world shall hear thy voice
Speak,—and the desert shall rejoice;
Scatter the gloom of heathen night;
Bid every nation hail the light.

546. C. M.

Millennial Days.

1 LORD! send thy word, and let it fly,
  Armed with thy Spirit's power;
Ten thousands shall confess its sway,
  And bless the saving hour.

2 Beneath the influence of thy grace
  The barren wastes shall rise,
With sudden green and fruits arrayed—
  A blooming paradise.

3 Peace, with her olive-crown shall stretch
  Her wings from shore to shore;

The nations of the earth shall hear
The sound of war no more.

4 Lord! for those days we wait;—those days
Are in thy word foretold:
Fly swifter, sun and stars! and bring
This promised age of gold.

5 Amen!—with joy divine, let earth's
Unnumbered myriads cry;
Amen!—with joy divine, let heaven's
Unnumbered choirs reply.

547.
S. M.
Prayer for all Lands.

1 O GOD of sovereign grace!
We bow before thy throne;
And plead, for all the human race,
The merits of thy Son.

2 Spread through the earth, O Lord!
The knowledge of thy ways;
And let all lands, with joy, record
The great Redeemer's praise.

548.
7s.
Jesus shall reign.

1 HARK!—the song of jubilee,
Loud as mighty thunders roar,—
Or the fulness of the sea,
When it breaks upon the shore,—
"Hallelujah! for the Lord
God Omnipotent, shall reign!"
Hallelujah! let the word
Echo round the earth and main.

2 "Hallelujah!"—hark!—the sound,
From the centre to the skies,
Wakes, above, beneath, around,
All creation's harmonies:
See Jehovah's banners furled,
Sheathed his sword! he speaks—'t is done,
And the kingdoms of this world
Are the kingdoms of his Son.

3 He shall reign from pole to pole
With illimitable sway:

He shall reign, when, like a scroll,
Yonder heavens have passed away;
Then the end;—beneath his rod,
Man's last enemy shall fall;
Hallelujah!—Christ in God,
God in Christ, is all in all.

549.

L. M.

Prayer for Zion.

1 INDULGENT Sovereign of the skies!
And wilt thou bow thy gracious ear?
While feeble mortals raise their cries,
Wilt thou, the great Jehovah, hear?

2 How shall thy servants give thee rest,
Till Zion's mouldering walls thou raise?
Till thine own power shall stand confessed,
And make Jerusalem a praise?

3 Look down, O God! with pitying eye,
And view the desolations round;
See, what wide realms in darkness lie,
What scenes of wo and crime abound!

4 Loud let the gospel-trumpet blow
And call the nations from afar;
Let all the isles their Saviour know,
And earth's remotest ends draw near

550.

C. M.

Prayer for the Reign of Christ.

1 JESUS, immortal King! arise;
Rise and assert thy sway;
Till earth, subdued, its tribute bring,
And distant lands obey.

2 Ride forth, victorious Conqueror! ride,
Till all thy foes submit;
And all the powers of hell resign
Their trophies at thy feet.

3 Send forth thy word, and let it fly,
This spacious earth around;
Till every soul beneath the sun
Shall hear the joyful sound.

4 From sea to sea, from shore to shore,
May Jesus be adored;

And earth, with all her millions, shout,—
Hosannas to the Lord.

551.

7s and 6s.

The State of the Heathen.

1 FROM Greenland's icy mountains,
From India's coral strand,
Where Afric's sunny fountains
Roll down their golden sand;
From many an ancient river,
From many a palmy plain,
They call us to deliver
Their land from error's chain.

2 What though the spicy breezes
Blow soft o'er Ceylon's isle,—
Though every prospect pleases,
And only man is vile?—
In vain with lavish kindness
The gifts of God are strown;
The heathen, in his blindness,
Bows down to wood and stone.

3 Shall we, whose souls are lighted
With wisdom from on high,—
Shall we, to men benighted,
The lamp of life deny?
Salvation! O Salvation!—
The joyful sound proclaim,
Till earth's remotest nation
Has learned Messiah's name.

4 Waft—waft, ye winds! his story
And you, ye waters! roll,—
Till, like a sea of glory,
It spreads from pole to pole;
Till, o'er our ransomed nature,
The Lamb for sinners slain,
Redeemer, King, Creator,
In bliss returns to reign.

552.

L. M.

Zion encouraged.

1 ZION! awake, thy strength renew,
Put on thy robes of beauteous hue,
And let th' admiring world behold
The king's fair daughter clothed in gold.

2 Church of our God! arise and shine,
Bright with the beams of truth divine:
Then shall thy radiance stream afar,
Wide as the heathen nations are.

3 Gentiles and kings thy light shall view;
All shall admire and love thee too;—
Shall come, like clouds across the sky
Or doves that to their windows fly.

553. C. M.

Prayer for Missionaries.

1 GREAT God! the nations of the earth
Are by creation thine;
And in thy works, from nature's birth,
Thy radiant glories shine.

2 But, Lord! thy greater love hath sent
Thy gospel to our race;
Unveiling thy divine intent
Of rich redeeming grace.

3 Soon may these gracious tidings roll
The spacious earth around,
Till every tribe and every soul
Shall hear the joyful sound.

4 Then, to her sable sons conveyed,
Shall Afric learn thy word,
And vassals, long-enslaved, become
The freemen of the Lord.

5 When shall the scattered wanderers meet,
That now in darkness rove,
And gathered round Immanuel's feet,
Sing of his saving love?

6 O Lord! each faithful effort own,
To spread the gospel-rays;
And rear, on sin's demolished throne,
The temples of thy praise.

554. H. M.

Prophecy fulfilled.

1 ALL hail! incarnate God!
The wondrous things foretold
Of thee, in sacred writ,
With joy our eyes behold;

Still doth thine arm new trophies wear,
And monuments of glory rear.

2 Oh! haste, victorious Prince!
That glorious happy day,
When souls, like drops of dew,
Shall own thy gentle sway:
Oh! may it bless our longing eyes,
And bear our shouts beyond the skies.

3 All hail! triumphant Lord!
Eternal be thy reign;
Behold the nations wait
To wear thy gentle chain:
When earth and time are known no more,
Thy throne shall stand for ever sure.

555.

L. M.

Triumph of the Gospel.

1 ARM of the Lord! awake, awake!
Put on thy strength—the nations shake,
And let the world, adoring, see
Triumphs of mercy wrought by thee.

2 Say to the heathen, from thy throne,—
"I am Jehovah—God alone!"
Thy voice their idols shall confound,
And cast their altars to the ground.

3 Almighty God! thy grace proclaim,
In every land of every name;
Let Zion's time of favor come;
Oh! bring the tribes of Israel home.

4 Arm of the Lord! awake, awake!
Put on thy strength—the nations shake,
Let hostile powers before thee fall,
And crown the Saviour—Lord of all.

556.

8s, 7s and 4.

The Day-Spring.

1 CHRISTIAN! see—the orient morning
Breaks along the heathen sky;
Lo! th' expected day is dawning—
Glorious day-spring from on high:
Hallelujah!—
Hail the day-spring from on high!

2 Heathen at the sight are singing;
Morning wakes the tuneful lays;
Precious offerings they are bringing—
First-fruits of more perfect praise:
Hallelujah!—
Hail the day-spring from on high!

3 Zion's Sun!—salvation beaming,—
Gilding now the radiant hills,—
Rise and shine, till brighter gleamings
All the world thy glory fills:
Hallelujah!—
Hail the day-spring from on high!

4 Lord of every tribe and nation!
Spread thy truth from pole to pole;
Spread the light of thy salvation,
Till it shine on every soul:
Hallelujah!—
Hail the day-spring from on high!

557. L. M.

Christ's Coming to reign.

1 JESUS! thy church with longing eyes
For thine expected coming waits:
When will the promised light arise,
And glory beam on Zion's gates?

2 E'en now, when tempests round us fall,
And wintry clouds o'ercast the sky,
Thy words with pleasure we recall,
And deem that our redemption 's nigh.

3 Oh! come and reign o'er every land;
Let Satan from his throne be hurled,—
All nations bow to thy command,
And grace revive a dying world.

4 Teach us in watchfulness and prayer,
To wait for thine appointed hour;
And fit us, by thy grace, to share
The triumphs of thy conquering power

558. L. M.

The coming Reign of Christ.

1 ASCEND thy throne, almighty King!
And spread thy glories all abroad;

Let thine own arm salvation bring,
  And be thou known the gracious God.

2 Let millions bow before thy seat,—
  Let humble mourners seek thy face;
Bring daring rebels to thy feet,
  Subdued by thy victorious grace.

3 Oh! let the kingdoms of the world
  Become the kingdoms of the Lord;
Let saints and angels praise thy name,—
  Be thou through heaven and earth adored,

559.

7s and 6s.

The final Victory of Christ.

1 WHEN shall the voice of singing
  Flow joyfully along?
When hill and valley, ringing
  With one triumphant song,
Proclaim the contest ended,
  And him, who once was slain,
Again to earth descended,
  In righteousness to reign?

2 Then from the craggy mountains
  The sacred shout shall fly;
And shady vales and fountains
  Shall echo the reply:
High tower and lowly dwelling
  Shall send the chorus round,
All hallelujah swelling
  In one eternal sound.

560.

C. M.

The New-Creation.

1 SPIRIT of power and might! behold
  A world by sin destroyed:
Creator-Spirit!—as of old,
  Move on the formless void.

2 Give thou the word;—that healing sound
  Shall quell the deadly strife;
And earth again, like Eden crowned,
  Produce the tree of life.

3 If sang the morning-stars for joy,
  When nature rose to view

What strains shall angel-harps employ,
When thou shalt all renew?

4 And if the sons of God rejoice
To hear a Saviour's name,
How will the ransomed raise their voice,
To whom that Saviour came?

5 So every kindred, tongue and tribe,
Assembling round the throne,
Thy new-creation shall ascribe
To sovereign love alone.

561. S. M.

Rejoicing in Christ's Reign.

1 NOW living waters flow
To cheer the humble soul;
From sea to sea the rivers go,
And spread from pole to pole.

2 Now righteousness shall spring,
And grow on earth again:
Jesus, Jehovah, be our king,
And o'er the nations reign.

3 Jesus shall rule alone,
The world shall hear his word;
By one blest name shall he be known—
The universal Lord.

562. L. M.

Prayer for the World's Conversion.

1 O SPIRIT of the living God!
In all thy plenitude of grace,
Where'er the foot of man hath trod,
Descend on our apostate race.

2 Give tongues of fire, and hearts of love,
To preach the reconciling word;
Give power and unction from above,
Where'er the joyful sound is heard.

3 Be darkness, at thy coming, light,
Confusion—order, in thy path;
Souls without strength, inspire with might;
Bid mercy triumph over wrath.

4 O Spirit of the Lord! prepare
A sinful world their God to meet:

Breathe thou abroad, like morning-air,
Till hearts of stone begin to beat.

5 Baptize the nations; far and nigh
The triumphs of the cross record;
The name of Jesus glorify,
Till every kindred call him—Lord.

563.

8s, 7s and 4.

Prayer for the Heathen.

1 O'ER the realms of pagan darkness,
Let the eye of pity gaze;
See the kindreds of the people,
Lost in sins bewildering maze;—
Darkness brooding
On the face of all the earth!

2 Light of them who sit in error!
Rise and shine—thy blessings bring;
Light—to lighten all the Gentiles!
Rise with healing in thy wing:
To thy brightness,
Let all kings and nations come.

3 Let the heathen, now adoring
Idol-gods of wood and stone,
Come and, worshiping before him,
Serve the living God alone:
Let thy glory
Fill the earth, as floods the sea.

4 THOU! to whom all power is given,
Speak the word; at thy command,
Let the company of heralds
Spread thy name from land to land:
Lord! be with them,
Always till time's latest end.

564.

L. M.

Spread of the Gospel.

1 THY people, Lord! who trust thy word,
And wait the smilings of thy face,
Assemble round thy mercy-seat,
And plead the promise of thy grace.

2 Hast thou not said—thine only Son
Shall be a light to Gentile lands,

To open the benighted eyes,
  And loose the wretched pris'ners' bands?—

3 From land to land, from sea to sea,
  That his dominion shall extend!—
That every tongue shall call him Lord,
  And every knee before him bend?

4 Now let the happy time appear—
  The time to favor Zion come;
Send forth thy heralds far and near,
  And call the wandering exiles home.

565.

8s, 7s and 4.

Success of the Gospel among the Heathen.

1 O'ER the gloomy hills of darkness,
  Cheered by no celestial ray,
Sun of righteousness! arising,
  Bring the bright, the glorious day;
Send the gospel
  To the earth's remotest bound.

2 Kingdoms wide that sit in darkness,—
  Grant them, Lord! the glorious light,
And, from eastern coast to western,
  May the morning chase the night;
And redemption,
  Freely purchased, win the day.

3 Fly abroad, thou mighty gospel!
  Win and conquer, never cease;
May thy lasting, wide dominions,
  Multiply and still increase;
Sway thy sceptre,
  Saviour! all the world around.

566.

7s.

Triumphs of the Gospel.

1 WHO are these that come from far,
Led by Jacob's rising star?
Strangers now to Zion come,
There to seek a peaceful home.

2 Lo! they gather like a cloud,
Or as doves their windows crowd:
Zion wonders at the sight,—
Zion feels a strange delight.

3 Zion now no more shall sigh,
God will raise her glory high;
He will send a large increase,—
He will give his people peace.

4 Sons of Zion! sing aloud:
See her sun, without a cloud!
God will make her joy complete—
Zion's sun shall never set.

567. C. M.

Kingdom of Christ among Men.

1 LO! what a glorious sight appears,
To our believing eyes!
The earth and seas are passed away,
And the old rolling skies.

2 From the third heaven, where God resides,—
That holy, happy place,—
The New-Jerusalem comes down,
Adorned with shining grace.

3 Attending angels shout for joy,
And the bright armies sing,—
"Mortals! behold the sacred seat
Of your descending King.

4 "The God of glory, down to men,
Removes his blessed abode;—
Men, the dear objects of his grace,
And he their loving God.

5 "His own soft hand shall wipe the tears
From every weeping eye;
And pains, and groans, and griefs, and fears,
And death itself shall die."

6 How long, dear Saviour! Oh! how long
Shall this bright hour delay?
Fly swifter round, ye wheels of time!
And bring the welcome day.

568. 11s.

Zion encouraged.

1 DAUGHTER of Zion! awake from thy sadness;
Awake,—for thy foes shall oppress thee no more:
Bright o'er thy hills dawns the day-star of gladness;
Arise,—for the night of thy sorrow is o'er.

2 Strong were thy foes; but the arm that subdued them,
And scattered their legions, was mightier far;
They fled, like the chaff, from the scourge that pursued them;
Vain were their steeds and their chariots of war.

3 Daughter of Zion! the power, that hath saved thee,
Extolled with the harp and the timbrel should be.
Shout,—for the foe is destroyed that enslaved thee,
Th' oppressor is vanquished, and Zion is free.

569.

C. M.

Universal Praise.

1 O CITY of the Lord! begin
The universal song:
And let the scattered villages
The joyful notes prolong.

2 Let Kedar's wilderness afar
Lift up the lonely voice;
And let the tenants of the rock
In accent rude rejoice.

3 Oh! from the streams of distant lands
To our Jehovah sing;
And joyful, from the mountain-tops,
Shout to the Lord, the king.

4 Let all combined, with one accord,
The Saviour's glories raise,
Till, in the earth's remotest bounds,
The nations sound his praise.

570.

8s, 7s and 4.

Dawning of the Latter-Day.

1 LOOK, ye saints! the day is breaking;
Joyful times are near at hand;
God, the mighty God, is speaking
By his word in every land;
Day advances,—
Darkness flies, at his command.

2 While the foe becomes more daring,
While he enters like a flood,
God, the Saviour, is preparing
Means to spread his truth abroad:
Every language
Soon shall tell the love of God.

3 God of Jacob, high and glorious!
  Let thy people see thy power;
Let the gospel be victorious,
  Through the world for evermore;
Then shall idols
  Perish, while thy saints adore.

571. L. M.
Success anticipated.

1 BEHOLD th' expected time draw near,
The shades disperse, the dawn appear!
Behold the wilderness assume
The beauteous tints of Eden's bloom!

2 Events with prophecies conspire
To raise our faith, our zeal to fire:
The ripening fields, already white,
Present a harvest to the sight.

3 The untaught heathen waits to know
The joy the gospel will bestow;
The exiled captive, to receive
The freedom Jesus has to give.

4 Come, let us, with a grateful heart,
In the blest labor share a part;
Our prayers and offerings gladly bring
To aid the triumphs of our King.

572. C. M.
The Victories of Christ.

1 HOSANNA to our conquering King!
  All hail! incarnate love!
Ten thousand songs and glories wait
  To crown thy head above.

2 Thy vict'ries and thy deathless fame,
  Through the wide world, shall run;
And everlasting ages sing
  The triumph thou hast won.

573. H. M.
The general Jubilee.

1 FAIR shines the morning-star;
  The silver trumpets sound,
Their notes re-echoing far,
  While dawns the day around:
Joy to the earth—the earth is free;
It is the year of jubilee.

2 Pris'ners of hope, in gloom
And silence, left to die!
With Christ's unfolding tomb,
Your portals open fly:
Rise with your Lord—he sets you free;
It is the year of jubilee.

3 Ye who yourselves have sold
For debts to justice due,
Ransomed—but not with gold!
He gave himself for you:
The blood of Christ hath made you free;
It is the year of jubilee.

4 Captives of sin and shame!
O'er earth and ocean, hear
An angel's voice proclaim
The Lord's accepted year:
Let Jacob rise—be Israel free;
It is the year of jubilee.

574. L. M.

The Reign of Christ established.

1 SHOUT,—for the great Redeemer reigns,
Through distant lands his triumphs spread;
Sinners, now freed from Satan's chains,
Own him their Saviour and their head.

2 Oh! may his conquests still increase;
Let every foe his power subdue;
While angels celebrate his praise,
Saints shall his rising glories show.

3 Loud hallelujahs to the Lamb,
From all below and all above;
In lofty songs, exalt his name,—
In songs as lasting as his love.

575. 7s.

The Reign of Christ.

1 WAKE the song of jubilee,
Let it echo o'er the sea!
Now hath come the promised hour;
Jesus reigns with sovereign power.

2 All ye nations! join and sing,—
"Christ, of lords and kings, is King!"
Let it sound from shore to shore,—
"Jesus reigns for evermore!"

3 Now the desert lands rejoice,
And the islands join their voice;
Yea, the whole creation sings,—
"Jesus is the King of kings!"

576. 7s.
The triumphant Reign of Christ

1 SEE the ransomed millions stand,—
Palms of conquest in their hands!
This before the throne their strain,—
"Hell is vanquished—death is slain!—

2 "Blessing, honor, glory, might,
Are the Conqueror's native right;
Thrones and powers before him fall,—
Lamb of God, and Lord of all!"

3 Hasten, Lord! the promised hour;
Come in glory and in power;
Still thy foes are unsubdued—
Nature sighs to be renewed:

4 Time has nearly reached its sum;
All things with the bride, say, "Come!"
Jesus! whom all worlds adore,
Come,—and reign for evermore.

MORNING.

577. 7s.
Morning.

1 IN this calm impressive hour,
Let my prayer ascend on high;
God of mercy! God of power!
Hear me, when to thee I cry:
Hear me from thy lofty throne,
For the sake of Christ, thy Son.

2 With the morning's early ray,
While the shades of night depart
Let thy beams of light convey
Joy and gladness to my heart:
Now o'er all my steps preside,
And for all my wants provide.

3 Oh! what joy that word affords,—
"Thou shalt reign o'er all the earth;"
King of kings, and Lord of lords!
Send thy gospel-heralds forth:
Now begin thy boundless sway,
Usher in the glorious day.

578.

S. M.

Prayer for spiritual Light.

1 WE lift our hearts to thee,
Thou Day-Star from on high!
The sun itself is but thy shade,
Yet, cheers both earth and sky.

2 Oh! let thy rising beams
Dispel the shades of night;
And let the glories of thy love
Come, like the morning-light.

3 How beauteous nature now!
How dark and sad before!—
With joy we view the pleasing change,
And nature's God adore.

4 May we this life improve
To mourn for errors past;
And live, this short revolving day,
As if it were our last.

579.

7s.

Morning-Thanks.

1 THOU that dost my life prolong!
Kindly aid my morning-song;
Thankful, from my couch I rise,
To the God that rules the skies.

2 Thou didst hear my evening-cry;
Thy preserving hand was nigh;
Peaceful slumbers thou hast shed,
Grateful to my weary head.

3 Thou hast kept me through the night,—
'T was thy hand restored the light;
Lord! thy mercies still are new,
Plenteous, as the morning-dew.

4 Still my feet are prone to stray,—
Oh! preserve me through the day;
Dangers every where abound,
Sins and snares beset me round.

5 Gently, with the dawning ray,
On my soul, thy beams display;
Sweeter than the smiling morn,
Let thy cheering light return.

580

S. M.
Morning-Prayer-Meeting.

1 HOW sweet the melting lay
That breaks upon the ear,
When, at the hour of rising day,
Christians unite in prayer!

2 The breezes waft their cries,
Up to Jehovah's throne;
He listens to their bursting sighs,
And sends his blessings down.

3 So Jesus rose to pray,
Before the morning-light;
Once on the chilling mount did stay,
And wrestle all the night.

4 Glory to God on high,
Who sends his blessings down,
To rescue souls condemned to die,
And makes his people one.

581.

S. M.
Morning-Meditations.

1 AWAKE, my drowsy soul!
These airy visions chase;
Awake, my active powers renewed!
To run the heavenly race.

2 See—how the rising sun
Pursues his shining way;
And wide proclaims his Maker's praise,
With every brightening ray!

3 Thus would my rising soul
Her heavenly parent sing;
And to her great original
Her humble tribute bring.

4 Serene, I laid me down
Beneath his guardian care;
I slept, and woke; and still I found
My kind preserver near.

5 Dear Saviour! to thy cross,
I bring my sacrifice;
Tinged with thy blood, it shall ascend,
With fragrance to the skies.

582.
C. M.
A Morning-Song.

1 ONCE more, my soul! the rising day
Salutes thy waking eyes:
Once more, my voice! thy tribute pay
To him who rules the skies.

2 Night unto night his name repeats,
The day renews the sound;
Wide as the heaven, on which he sits
To turn the seasons round.

3 'T is he supports my mortal frame,—
My tongue shall speak his praise;
My sins would rouse his wrath to flame,
And yet his wrath delays.

4 A thousand wretched souls are fled,
Since the last setting sun;
And yet he lengthens out my thread,—
And yet my moments run.

5 Great God! let all my hours be thine,
Whilst I enjoy the light;
Then shall my sun in smiles decline,
And bring a peaceful night.

583.
L. M.
Morning-Gratitude.

1 IN sleep's serene oblivion laid,
I safely passed the silent night;
Again I see the breaking shade,—
I drink again the morning-light.

2 New-born, I bless the 'waking hour,
Once more, with awe, rejoice to be;
My conscious soul resumes her power,
And springs, my guardian God! to thee.

3 Oh! guide me through the various maze,
My doubtful feet may this day tread;
And spread thy shield's protecting blaze,
Where dangers press around my head.

4 A deeper shade will soon impend,—
  A deeper sleep mine eyes oppress;
Yet, then thy strength shall still defend,—
  Thy goodness still delight to bless.

5 That deeper shade shall break away,
  That deeper sleep shall leave mine eyes;
Thy light shall give eternal day;
  Thy love—the rapture of the skies.

584. L. M.

Praise to the God of the Morning.

1 GOD of the morning! at thy voice
  The cheerful sun makes haste to rise,
And like a giant doth rejoice,
  To run his journey through the skies;—

2 From the fair chambers of the east,
  The circuit of his race begins,
And without weariness or rest,
  Round the whole earth, he flies and shines,

3 Oh! like the sun may I fulfill
  Th' appointed duties of the day;
With ready mind, and active will,
  March on, and keep my heavenly way.

4 Lord! thy commands are clean and pure,
  Enlightening our beclouded eyes;
Thy threatenings just, thy promise sure,
  Thy gospel makes the simple wise.

5 Give me thy counsel for my guide,
  And then receive me to thy bliss:
All my desires and hopes beside
  Are faint, and cold, compared with this.

EVENING.

585. L. M.

An Evening-Sacrifice.

1 GREAT God! to thee my evening-song,
  With humble gratitude I raise,
Oh! let thy mercy tune my tongue,
  And fill my heart with lively praise.

2 My days unclouded, as they pass,
And every gently rolling hour,
Are monuments of wondrous grace,
And witness to thy love and power.

3 Seal my forgiveness in the blood
Of Jesus ;—his dear name alone
I plead for pardon, gracious God!
And kind acceptance, at thy throne.

4 Let this blest hope mine eyelids close ;
With sleep refresh my feeble frame ;
Safe in thy care may I repose,
And wake with praises to thy name.

586. 7s
Evening-Contemplation.

1 SOFTLY, now, the light of day
Fades upon my sight away ;
Free from care, from labor free,
Lord! I would commune with thee.

2 Soon for me, the light of day
Shall for ever pass away ;
Then, from sin and sorrow free,
Take me, Lord! to dwell with thee.

587. C. M.
Evening-Prayer and Praise.

1 INDULGENT Father! by whose care,
I 've passed another day,—
Let me, this night, thy mercy share ;—
Oh! teach me how to pray.

2 Show me my sins, and how to mourn
My guilt before thy face ;
Direct me, Lord! to Christ alone
And save me by thy grace.

3 Let each returning night declare
The tokens of thy love ;
And, every hour, thy grace prepare
My soul for joys above.

4 And when, on earth, I close mine eyes,
To sleep in death's embrace,
Let me, to heaven and glory, rise,
To see thy smiling face.

588.

8s and 7s. Peculiar.

An Evening-Offering.

1 THROUGH the day thy love has spared us.
Now we lay us down to rest;
Through the silent watches guard us,
Let no foe our peace molest;
Jesus! thou our guardian be,
Sweet it is to trust in thee.

2 Pilgrims here on earth, and strangers,
Dwelling in the midst of foes,—
Us and ours preserve from dangers,
In thine arms, let us repose,
And, when life's short day is past,
Rest with thee, in heaven, at last.

589.

7s.

Repose and Devotion.

1 NOW from labor and from care,
Evening-shades have set me free;
In the work of praise and prayer,
Lord! I would converse with thee:
Oh! behold me from above,
Fill me with a Saviour's love.

2 Sin and sorrow, guilt and wo,
Wither all my earthly joys;
Naught can charm me here below,
But my Saviour's melting voice:
Lord! forgive—thy grace restore,
Make me thine for evermore.

3 For the blessings of this day,
For the mercies of this hour,
For the gospel's cheering ray,
For the Spirit's quickening power,—
Grateful notes to thee I raise;
Oh! accept my song of praise.

590.

C. M.

An Evening-Song.

1 DREAD Sovereign, let my evening-song,
Like holy incense rise;
Assist the offerings of my tongue,
To reach the lofty skies.

2 Through all the dangers of the day,
Thy hand was still my guard;

And still, to drive my wants away,
Thy mercy stood prepared.

3 Perpetual blessings from above
Encompass me around;
But, Oh! how few returns of love
Hath my Creator found!

4 What have I done for him who died
To save my wretched soul?
How are my follies multiplied,
Fast as the minutes roll!

5 Lord! with this guilty heart of mine,
To thy dear cross I flee;
And to thy grace my soul resign,
To be renewed by thee.

6 Sprinkled afresh with pard'ning blood,
I lay me down to rest,—
As in th' embraces of my God,
Or on my Saviour's breast.

591. C. M.

Evening-Prayer and Praise.

1 INDULGENT God! whose bounteous care
O'er all thy works is shown,—
Oh! let my grateful praise and prayer
Arise before thy throne.

2 What mercies has this day bestowed!
How largely hast thou blest!
My cup with plenty overflowed,
With cheerfulness—my breast.

3 Now may soft slumber close my eyes,
From pain and sickness free;
And let my waking thoughts arise
To meditate on thee.

4 Thus bless each future day and night,
Till life's vain scene is o'er;
And then, to realms of endless light,
Oh! let my spirit soar.

592. C. M.

Secret Prayer at Twilight.

1 I LOVE to steal awhile away,
From every cumbering care,

And spend the hours of setting day
In humble, grateful prayer.

2 I love, in solitude, to shed
The penitential tear;
And all his promises to plead,
When none but God is near.

3 I love to think on mercies past,
And future good implore;
My cares and sorrows all to cast,
On him whom I adore.

4 I love, by faith, to take a view
Of brighter scenes in heaven;
The prospect doth my strength renew;
While here by tempests driven.

5 And, when life's toilsome day is o'er,
May its departing ray
Be calm, as this impressive hour,
And lead to endless day.

593. C. M.

Evening-Worship in the Family.

1 O LORD! another day is flown,
And we, a lonely band,
Are met once more before thy throne,
To bless thy fostering hand.

2 And wilt thou bend a listening ear
To praises low as ours?
Thou wilt!—for thou dost love to hear
The song which meekness pours.

3 And, Jesus! thou thy smiles wilt deign,
As we before thee pray;
For thou didst bless the infant train,
And we are less than they.

4 Thy heavenly grace to each impart;
All evil far remove;
And shed abroad in every heart
Thine everlasting love.

5 Thus cleansed from sin and wholly thine,
A flock by Jesus led,
The Sun of righteousness shall shine
In glory on our head.

6 Oh! still restore our wandering feet,
And still direct our way;
Till worlds shall fade, and faith shall greet
The dawn of endless day.

594.

L. M.

An Evening-Hymn.

1 THUS far the Lord has led me on,
Thus far his power prolongs my days;
And every evening shall make known
Some fresh memorial of his grace.

2 Much of my time has run to waste,
And I, perhaps, am near my home;
But he forgives my follies past,
He gives me strength for days to come.

3 I lay my body down to sleep,—
Peace is the pillow for my head;
While well-appointed angels keep
Their watchful stations round my bed.

4 Thus, when the night of death shall come,
My flesh shall rest beneath the ground,
And wait thy voice to rouse my tomb,
With sweet salvation in the sound.

595.

L. M. 6 Lines.

For such as keep Saturday-Evening

1 SWEET is the last, the parting ray,
Which ushers placid evening in;
When, with the still, expiring day,
The Sabbath's peaceful hours begin:
How grateful to the anxious breast
The sacred hours of holy rest!

2 Hushed is the tumult of the day,
And worldly cares and business cease,—
While soft the vesper-breezes play,
To hymn the glad return of peace:
Delightful season! kindly given
To turn the wandering thoughts to heaven.

3 Oft as this peaceful hour shall come,
Lord! raise my thoughts from earthly things,
And bear them to my heavenly home,
On faith and hope's celestial wings;

Till the last gleam of life decay,
In one eternal Sabbath-day.

596.
S. M.
Saturday-Evening.

1 THE hours of evening close;
  Its lengthened shadows, drawn
O'er scenes of earth, invite repose,
  And wait the Sabbath-dawn.

2 So let its calm prevail
  O'er forms of outward care;
Nor thought for "many things" assail,
  The still retreat of prayer.

3 Our guardian Shepherd near
  His watchful eye will keep;
And, safe from violence and fear,
  Will fold his flock to sleep.

4 So may a holier light,
  Than earth's, our spirits rouse,
And call us, strengthened by his might,
  To pay the Lord our vows.

MORNING, OR EVENING.

597.
L. M.
A Song for Morning and Evening.

1 MY God! how endless is thy love!
  Thy gifts are every evening new;
And morning-mercies from above,
  Gently distill, like early dew.

2 Thou spread'st the curtains of the night,
  Great Guardian of my sleeping hours!
Thy sovereign word restores the light,
  And quickens all my drowsy powers.

3 I yield my powers to thy command;
  To thee I consecrate my days;
Perpetual blessings, from thy hand,
  Demand perpetual songs of praise.

598.

C. M.

Morning or Evening-Worship.

1 ON thee, each morning, O my God!
  My waking thoughts attend;
In thee are founded all my hopes,
  In thee my wishes end.

2 My soul, in pleasing wonder lost,
  Thy boundless love surveys;
And, fired with grateful zeal, prepares
  A sacrifice of praise.

3 When evening-slumbers press my eyes,
  With his protection blest,
In peace and safety, I commit
  My wearied limbs to rest.

4 My spirit in his hand, serene,
  Fears no approaching ill;
For, whether waking or asleep,
  Thou, Lord! art with me still.

599.

C. M.

Morning and Evening-Offering.

1 HOSANNA, with a cheerful sound,
  To God's upholding hand!
Ten thousand snares attend us round,
  And yet secure we stand.

2 That was a most amazing power
  That raised us with a word;
And, every day, and every hour,
  We lean upon the Lord.

3 The rising morn cannot assure,—
  That we shall end the day;
For death stands ready at the door
  To hurry us away.

4 Our life is forfeited, by sin,
  To God's avenging law;
We own thy grace, immortal King!
  In every breath we draw.

5 God is our sun—whose daily light
  Our joy and safety brings;
Our feeble frame lies safe, at night,
  Beneath his shady wings.

600.

L. M. 6 Lines.

Morning and Evening.

1 WHEN, streaming from the eastern skies,
The morning-light salutes mine eyes,
O Sun of righteousness divine!
On me, with beams of mercy, shine;
Chase the dark clouds of guilt away,
And turn my darkness into day.

2 When each day's scenes and labors close,
And wearied nature seeks repose,
With pard'ning mercy richly blest,
Guard me, my Saviour! while I rest;
And, as each morning-sun shall rise,
Oh! lead me onward to the skies.

3 And, at my life's last setting sun,
My conflicts o'er, my labors done,
Jesus! thy heavenly radiance shed,
To cheer and bless my dying-bed;
And from death's gloom my spirit raise,
To see thy face, and sing thy praise.

THE YEAR.

601.

11s and 5s.

The New-Year.

1 COME let us anew
Our journey pursue,
Roll round with the year,
And never stand still till the master appear;
His adorable will
Let us gladly fulfill,
And our talents improve,
By the patience of hope, and the labor of love.

2 Our life is a dream;
Our time, as a stream,
Glides swiftly away,
And the fugitive moment refuses to stay:
The arrow is flown—
The moment is gone—
The millenial year
Rushes on to our view, and eternity 's here!

3 Oh! that each in the day
Of his coming may say,—
"I have fought my way through—
I have finished the work which thou gav'st me to do!"
Oh! that each, from his Lord,
May receive the glad word,—
"Well and faithfully done.
Enter into my joy, and sit down on my throne!"

602.

L. M.

The changing Seasons.

1 GREAT God! let all our tuneful powers
Awake, and sing thy mighty name:
Thy hand revolves our circling hours,—
Thy hand from which our being came.

2 Seasons and moons still rolling round,
In beauteous order speak thy praise;
And years, with smiling mercy crowned,
To thee successive honors raise.

3 To thee we raise the annual song,
To thee the grateful tribute give;
Our God doth still our years prolong,
And, midst unnumbered deaths, we live.

4 Our life, our health, our friends, we owe
All to thy vast, unbounded love;
Ten thousand precious gifts below,
And hope of nobler joys above.

5 Thus will we sing, till nature cease,
Till sense and language are no more,
And, after death, thy boundless grace,
Through everlasting years, adore.

603.

C. M.

New-Year:—Providential Goodness.

1 GOD of our lives! thy various praise
Our voices shall resound:
Thy hand directs our fleeting days,
And brings the seasons round.

2 To thee shall grateful songs arise,
Our Father and our Friend!
Whose constant mercies, from the skies,
In genial streams descend.

3 In every scene of life, thy care,
In every age, we see:
And, constant as thy favors are,
So let our praises be.

4 Still may thy love, in every scene,
In every age, appear;
And let the same companions deign
To bless the opening year.

5 If mercy smile, let mercy bring
Our wandering souls to God;
In our affliction, we shall sing,
If thou wilt bless the rod.

604. L. M.

New-Year:—God, our Helper.

1 OUR helper, God! we bless thy name,
Whose love for ever is the same;
The tokens of thy gracious care
Open, and crown, and close the year.

2 Amid ten thousand snares we stand,
Supported by thy guardian hand;
And see, when we review our ways,
Ten thousand monuments of praise.

3 Thus far thine arm has led us on;
Thus far we make thy mercy known;
And while we tread this desert land,
New mercies shall new songs demand.

4 Our grateful souls, on Jordan's shore,
Shall raise one sacred pillar more;
Then bear, in thy bright courts above,
Inscriptions of immortal love.

605. C. M.

New-Year:—Prayer for a Blessing.

1 NOW, gracious Lord! thine arm reveal,
And make thy glory known;
Now let us all thy presence feel,
And soften hearts of stone.

2 From all the guilt of former sin,
May mercy set us free;
And let this year, we now begin,
Begin and end with thee.

3 Send down thy Spirit from above,
That saints may love thee more;
And sinners now may learn to love,
Who never loved before.

4 And, when, before thee, we appear,
In our eternal home,
May growing numbers worship here,
And praise thee in our room.

606.

L. M.

A Song for the opening Year.

1 GREAT God! we sing that mighty hand,
By which supported still we stand;
The opening year thy mercy shows,—
Let mercy crown it till it close.

2 By day, by night—at home, abroad,
Still we are guarded by our God;
By his incessant bounty fed,
By his unerring counsel led.

3 With grateful hearts the past we own;
The future—all to us unknown—
We to thy guardian care commit,
And peaceful leave before thy feet,

4 In scenes exalted or depressed,
Be thou our joy—and thou our rest;
Thy goodness all our hopes shall raise,
Adored, through all our changing days.

5 When death shall close our earthly songs
And seal, in silence, mortal tongues,
Our helper, God, in whom we trust,
Shall keep our souls, and guard our dust.

607.

7s.

The opening Year.

1 BLESS, O Lord! the opening year
To the souls assembled here;
Clothe thy word with power divine,
Make us willing to be thine.

2 When thou hast thy work begun,
Give new strength the race to run;
Scatter darkness, doubts, and fears;
Wipe away the mourner's tears.

3 Bless us all both old and young —
Call forth praise from every tongue:
Let our whole assembly prove
All thy power and all thy love.

608.

7s and 6s.

A Winter's Day.

1 TIME is winging us away,
To our eternal home;
Life is but a winter's day,
A journey to the tomb;
Youth and vigor soon will flee,
Blooming beauty lose its charms;
All that 's mortal soon will be
Enclosed in death's cold arms.

2 Time is winging us away
To our eternal home;
Life is but a winter's day,
A journey to the tomb:
But the Christian shall enjoy
Health and beauty soon above;
Far beyond the world's alloy—
Secure in Jesus' love.

609.

C. M. Double.

Spring of the Year

1 WHILE beauty clothes the fertile vale,
And blossoms on the spray;
And fragrance breathes in every gale,
How sweet the vernal day!
Hark! how the feathered warblers sing!
'T is nature's cheerful voice;
Soft music hails the lovely spring,
And woods and fields rejoice.

2 How kind the influence of the skies,
While showers, with blessing fraught,
Bid verdure, beauty, fragrance, rise,
And fix the roving thought!
Oh! let my wandering heart confess,
With gratitude and love,
The bounteous hand that deigns to bless
Each smiling field and grove.

3 That hand, in this hard heart of mine,
Can bid each virtue live;

While gentle showers of grace divine,
  Life, beauty, fragrance give:
O God of nature, God of grace!
  Thy heavenly gifts impart,
And bid sweet meditation trace
  Spring blooming in my heart.

610.

S. M. D.

The Spring.

1 SWEET is the time of spring,
  When nature's charms appear;
The birds with ceaseless pleasure sing,
  And hail the opening year:
But sweeter far the spring
  Of wisdom and of grace,
When children bless and praise their King,
  Who loves the youthful race.

2 Sweet is the dawn of day,
  When light just streaks the sky;
When shades and darkness pass away,
  And morning's beams are nigh:
But sweeter far the dawn
  Of piety in youth;
When doubt and darkness are withdrawn,
  Before the light of truth.

3 Sweet is the early dew,
  Which gilds the mountain's tops,
And decks each plant and flower we view,
  With pearly glittering drops:
But sweeter far the scene
  On Zion's holy hill,
When there the dew of youth is seen
  Its freshness to distill.

611.

7s.

Spring, natural and spiritual

1 PLEASING spring again is here;
Trees and fields in bloom appear;
Hark! the birds, with artless lays,
Warble their Creator's praise.

2 Lord! afford a spring to me;
Let me feel like what I see:
Ah! my winter has been long,—
Chilled my hopes, suppressed my song.

3 How the soul in winter mourns,
Till the Lord, the Sun, returns!
Till the Spirit's gentle rain
Bids the heart revive again!

4 O beloved Saviour! haste,
Tell me—all the storms are past:
Speak, and by thy gracious voice,
Make my drooping soul rejoice.

612.

L. M.

The Year crowned with Goodness.

1 ETERNAL Source of every joy!
Well may thy praise our lips employ,—
While, in thy temple, we appear,
Whose goodness crowns the circling year.

2 While,—as the wheels of nature roll,—
Thy hand supports the steady pole;
The sun is taught by thee to rise,
And darkness, when to veil the skies.

3 The flowery spring, at thy command,
Embalms the air and paints the land;
The summer-rays, with vigor, shine
To raise the corn, and cheer the vine.

4 Thy hand, in autumn, richly pours,
Through all our coasts, redundant stores.
And winters, softened by thy care,
No more a face of horror wear.

5 Seasons, and months, and weeks, and days,
Demand successive songs of praise;
Still be the cheerful homage paid,
With morning-light and evening-shade.

613.

C. M.

Summer and Harvest.

1 TO praise the ever-bounteous Lord,
My soul! wake all thy powers:
He calls—and at his voice come forth
The smiling harvest-hours.

2 His covenant with the earth he keeps;
My tongue! his goodness sing;
Summer and winter know their time—
The harvest crowns the spring.

3 Well-pleased the husbandmen behold
The waving yellow crop;
With joy they bear the sheaves away,
And sow again in hope.

4 Thus teach me, gracious God! to sow
The seeds of righteousness;
Smile on my soul, and, with thy beams
The ripening harvest bless.

614. C. M.

Seed-time and Harvest.

1 FOUNTAIN of mercy, God of love!
How rich thy bounties are;
The changing seasons, as they move,
Proclaim thy constant care.

2 When, in the bosom of the earth,
The sower hid the grain,
Thy goodness marked its secret birth,
And sent the early rain.

3 The spring's sweet influence, Lord! was thine—
The plants in beauty grew;
Thou gav'st refulgent suns to shine,
And soft refreshing dew.

4 These varied mercies, from above,
Matured the swelling grain:
A kindly harvest crowns thy love,
And plenty fills the plain.

5 We own and bless thy gracious sway—
Thy hand all nature hails:
Seed-time nor harvest, night nor day,
Summer nor winter, fails.

615. C. M.

Fruitful Seasons from God.

1 O THOU who givest all their food!—
Causing thy sun to shine
Upon the evil and the good,—
Earth's teeming stores are thine.

2 Thy covenant to man secures
The harvest of his toil;
Thy faithful word, while earth endures,
With plenty clothes the soil.

3 The wintry frost, the flowery prime,
Alike thy laws obey:

Each herb and blossom knows its time,
And feels the quickening ray.

4 Revolving seasons still proclaim
Thine all-sustaining word:
Seed-time and harvest speak thy name,—
The promise-keeping Lord.

616.
C. M.
Close of the Year.

1 AWAKE, ye saints! and raise your eyes,
And raise your voices high;
Awake, and praise that sovereign love
That shows salvation nigh.

2 On all the wings of time it flies,
Each moment brings it near;
Then welcome each declining day,
Welcome each closing year.

3 Not many years their rounds shall run,
Nor many mornings rise,
Ere all its glories stand revealed
To our admiring eyes.

4 Ye wheels of nature! speed your course;
Ye mortal powers! decay;
Fast as ye bring the night of death,
Ye bring eternal day.

617.
C. M.
Time short—Man frail.

1 THEE we adore, eternal Name!
And humbly own to thee,
How feeble is our mortal frame,
What dying worms are we!

2 The year rolls round, and steals away
The breath that first it gave;
Whate'er we do, where'er we be,
We 're traveling to the grave.

3 Good God! on what a slender thread
Hang everlasting things!
Th' eternal state of all the dead,
Upon life's feeble strings.

4 Infinite joy, or endless wo,
Attends on every breath,—
And yet how unconcerned we go,
Upon the brink of death!

5 Waken, O Lord! our drowsy sense,
To walk this dangerous road;
And, if our souls are hurried hence,
May they be found with God.

DEATH.

618.
L. M.
Death and Burial of Saints.

1 UNVEIL thy bosom, faithful tomb!
Take this new treasure to thy trust,
And give these sacred relics room
To seek a slumber in the dust.

2 Nor pain, nor grief, nor anxious fear,
Invade thy bounds;—no mortal woes
Can reach the peaceful sleeper here,
While angels watch the soft repose.

3 So Jesus slept;—God's dying Son [bed!
Passed through the grave, and blessed the
Rest here, blest saint!—till, from his throne,
The morning break, and pierce the shade.

4 Break from his throne, illustrious morn!
Attend, O earth! his sovereign word;
Restore thy trust;—a glorious form
Shall then arise to meet the Lord.

619.
8s and 7s.
Mourners Comforted.

1 CEASE, ye mourners! cease to languish,
O'er the grave of those you love;
Pain, and death, and night, and anguish,
Enter not the world above.

2 While our silent steps are straying,
Lonely, through night's deepening shade,
Glory's brightest beams are playing
Round th' immortal spirit's head.

3 Light and peace at once deriving,
From the hand of God most high,
In his glorious presence living,
They shall never—never die.

4 Endless pleasure, pain excluding,
  Sickness there, no more can come;
There, no fear of wo, intruding,
  Sheds o'er heaven a moment's gloom.

5 Now, ye mourners! cease to languish,
  O'er the grave of those you love;
Far removed from pain and anguish,
  They are chanting hymns above.

620.

C. M.

Dying in the Lord.

1 HEAR what the voice from heaven proclams,
  For all the pious dead;—
"Sweet is the savor of their names,
  And soft their sleeping-bed.

2 "They die in Jesus, and are blessed,—
  How kind their slumbers are!
From sufferings, and from sins, released,
  And freed from every snare.

3 "Far from this world of toil and strife,
  They 're present with the Lord;
The labors of their mortal life
  End in a large reward."

621.

C. M.

Mourning with Hope.

1 WHY should our tears in sorrow flow
  When God recalls his own;
And bids them leave a world of wo,
  For an immortal crown?

2 Is not e'en death a gain to those
  Whose life to God was given?
Gladly to earth their eyes they close
  To open them in heaven.

3 Their toils are past—their work is done,
  And they are fully blest;
They fought the fight, the vict'ry won,
  And entered into rest.

4 Then let our sorrows cease to flow,—
  God has recalled his own;
But let our hearts, in every woe,
  Still say,—"Thy will be done!"

622.

C. M.

Prayer in view of Death.

1 WHEN, bending o'er the brink of life,
My trembling soul shall stand,
Waiting to pass death's awful flood,
Great God! at thy command;—

2 When every long-loved scene of life
Stands ready to depart;
When the last sigh that shakes the frame
Shall rend this bursting heart;—

3 O thou great Source of joy supreme!
Whose arm alone can save,—
Dispel the darkness that surrounds
The entrance to the grave.

4 Lay thy supporting, gentle hand
Beneath my sinking head;
And, with a ray of love divine,
Illume my dying bed.

5 Leaning on thy dear faithful breast,
May I resign my breath,
And in thy fond embraces lose
"The bitterness of death."

623.

S. M.

Reflections on past Generations.

1 HOW swift the torrent rolls,
That bears us to the sea!
The tide which hurries thoughtless souls
To vast eternity!

2 Our fathers!—where are they,
With all they called their own?—
Their joys and griefs—and hopes and cares,
And wealth and honor—gone!

3 But joy or grief succeeds
Beyond our mortal thought,
While still the remnant of their dust
Lies in the grave forgot.

4 There, where the fathers lie,
Must all the children dwell;
Nor other heritage possess,
But such a gloomy cell.

5 God of our fathers! hear,—
Thou everlasting friend!—
While we, as on life's utmost verge,
Our souls to thee commend.

6 Of all the pious dead
May we the footsteps trace,
Till with them, in the land of light,
We dwell before thy face.

624.

L. M.

Death of the Righteous.

1 HOW blest the righteous when he dies,—
When sinks a weary soul to rest!
How mildly beam the closing eyes!
How gently heaves th' expiring breast!

2 So fades a summer-cloud away;
So sinks the gale when storms are o'er;
So gently shuts the eye of day;
So dies a wave along the shore.

3 A holy quiet reigns around,—
A calm which life nor death destroys,
Nothing disturbs that peace profound,
Which his unfettered soul enjoys.

4 Farewell, conflicting hopes and fears!
Where lights and shades alternate dwell;
How bright th' unchanging morn appears!
Farewell, inconstant world! farewell!

5 Life's duty done, as sinks the clay,
Light from its load the spirit flies;
While heaven and earth combine to say,—
"How blest the righteous when he dies!"

625.

8s and 7s.

The dying Saint comforted.

1 HAPPY soul! thy days are ending,—
All thy mourning days below:
Go, the angel-guards attending—
To the sight of Jesus go!
Waiting to receive thy spirit,
Lo! the Saviour stands above;
Shows the fulness of his merit—
Reaches out the crown of love.

2 For the joy he sets before thee,
Bear a momentary pain;
Die—to live a life of glory;
Suffer—with thy Lord to reign:
Struggle, through thy latest passion,
To thy dear Redeemer's breast,—
To his uttermost salvation,—
To his everlasting rest.

626.

7s and 4.

Support in Death.

1 WHEN the vale of death appears,—
Faint and cold this mortal clay,—
Kind Forerunner! soothe my fears,
Light me through the darksome way;
Break the shadows,—
Usher in eternal day.

2 Upward from this dying state,
Bid my waiting soul aspire;
Open thou the chrystal gate;
To thy praise attune my lyre:
Then, triumphant,—
I will join th' immortal choir

3 When the mighty trumpet blown,
Shall the judgment-dawn proclaim;
From the central, burning throne,
Mid creation's final flame;
With the ransomed,—
Thou wilt own my worthless name.

627.

C. M.

Mourning with Hope.

1 THAT once-loved form, now cold and dead,
Each mournful thought employs;
And nature weeps, her comforts fled,
And withered all her joys.

2 Hope looks beyond the bounds of time,—
When what we now deplore
Shall rise in full immortal prime,
And bloom to fade no more.

3 Then cease, fond nature! cease thy tears,
Religion points on high;

There everlasting spring appears,
  And joys that cannot die.

628.

L. M.

Death of an Infant.

1 SO fades the lovely, blooming flower,—
Frail smiling solace of an hour!
So soon our transient comforts fly,
And pleasure only blooms to die.

2 Is there no kind,—no lenient art,
To heal the anguish of the heart?
Spirit of grace! be ever nigh,
Thy comforts are not made to die.

3 Bid gentle patience smile on pain,
Till dying hope shall live again;
Hope wipes the tear from sorrow s eye,
And faith points upward to the sky.

629.

C. M.

The Grave peaceful.

1 HOW still and peaceful is the grave,
  Where,—life's vain tumults past,—
Th' appointed house, by heaven's decree,
  Receives us all at last!

2 The wicked there from troubling cease,
  Their passions rage no more;
And there the weary pilgrim rests
  From all the toils he bore.

3 All, leveled by the hand of death,
  Lie sleeping in the tomb,
Till God, in judgment, call them forth
  To meet their final doom.

630.

C. M.

Prospect of Death.

1 MY soul! come, meditate the day,
  And think how near it stands,
When thou must quit this house of clay
  And fly to unknown lands.

2 And you, my eyes! look down and view
  The hollow gaping tomb;
This gloomy prison waits for you,
  Whene'er the summons come.

3 Oh! could we die with those that die,
And place us in their stead;
Then would our spirits learn to fly,
And converse with the dead.

4 Then should we see the saints above,
In their own glorious forms,
And wonder, why our souls should love
To dwell with mortal worms.

5 We should almost forsake our clay
Before the summons come,
And pray, and wish our souls away,
To their eternal home.

631.

8s and 7s.

The Spirit of a dying Christian.

1 PARTING soul! the flood awaits thee,
And the billows round thee roar;
Yet rejoice,—the holy city
Stands on yon celestial shore.

2 There are crowns and thrones of glory,
There the living waters glide;
There the just in shining raiment,
Standing by Immanuel's side.

3 Linger not,—the stream is narrow,
Though its cold dark waters rise;
He, who passed the flood before thee,
Guides thy path to yonder skies.

632.

L. M.

Death disarmed.

1 WHY should we start, and fear to die?
What tim'rous worms we mortals are!
Death is the gate of endless joy,
And yet we dread to enter there.

2 The pains, the groans, the dying strife,
Fright our approaching souls away;
Still we shrink back again to life,
Fond of our prison and our clay.

3 Oh! if my Lord would come and meet,
My soul would stretch her wings in haste.
Fly fearless through death's iron gate—
Nor feel the terrors as she passed.

4 Jesus can make a dying bed
   Feel soft as downy pillows are,
While on his breast I lean my head,
   And breathe my life out sweetly there.

633. C. M.

Comfort in the Death of Friends.

1 WHY do we mourn departing friends,
   Or shake at death's alarms?
'T is but the voice that Jesus sends,
   To call them to his arms.

2 Are we not tending upward too,
   As fast as time can move?
Nor should we wish the hours more slow
   To keep us from our love.

3 Why should we tremble to convey
   Their bodies to the tomb?
There the dear flesh of Jesus lay,
   And left a long perfume.

4 The graves of all the saints he blessed,
   And softened every bed:
Where should the dying members rest,
   But with their dying Head?

5 Thence he arose, ascended high,
   And showed our feet the way;
Up to the Lord his saints shall fly,
   At the great rising day.

6 Then let the last loud trumpet sound,
   And bid our kindred rise;
Awake, ye nations under ground!
   Ye saints! ascend the skies.

634. C. M.

Silent Submission.

1 PEACE! 't is the Lord Jehovah's hand,
   That blasts our joys in death;
Changes the visage once so dear,
   And gathers back our breath.

2 'T is he, the Potentate supreme
   Of all the worlds above,
Whose steady counsels wisely rule,
   Nor from their purpose move.

3 'T is he, whose justice might demand
Our souls a sacrifice ;
Yet scatters, with unwearied hand,
A thousand rich supplies.

4 Our covenant-God and Father he,
In Christ, our bleeding Lord ;
Whose grace can heal the bursting heart,
With one reviving word.

5 Silent we own Jehovah's name,—
We kiss thy chastening hand ;
And yield our comforts and our life,
To thy supreme command.

635.
C. M.
Triumph over Death.

1 GREAT God ! I own the sentence just,
And nature must decay ;
I yield my body to the dust,
To dwell with fellow-clay.

2 Yet faith may triumph o'er the grave;
And trample on the tombs ;
My Jesus, my Redeemer, lives,
My God, my Saviour, comes.

3 The mighty Conqueror shall appear,
High on a royal seat ;
And death, the last of all his foes,
Lie vanquished at his feet.

4 Then shall I see thy lovely face,
With strong, immortal eyes ;
And feast upon thine unknown grace,
With pleasure and surprise.

636.
12s and 11s.
A Funeral Hymn.

1 THOU art gone to the grave—but we will not deplore thee,
Though sorrows and darkness encompass the tomb ;
The Saviour has passed through its portals before thee,
And the lamp of his love is thy guide through the gloom.

2 Thou art gone to the grave—we no longer behold thee,
Nor tread the rough paths of the world by thy side;
But the wide arms of mercy are spread to enfold thee,
And sinners may hope, since the Sinless hath died.

3 Thou art gone to the grave—and, its mansion forsaking,
Perchance thy weak spirit in doubt lingered long;
But the sunshine of heaven beamed bright on thy waking,
And the sound thou didst hear was the seraphim's song.

4 Thou art gone to the grave—but we will not deplore thee,
Since God was thy ransom, thy guardian, thy guide;
He gave thee, he took thee, and he will restore thee,
And death hath no sting, since the Saviour hath died.

637.

C. M.

Victory over Death.

1 OH! for an overcoming faith,
To cheer my dying hours;
To triumph o'er the monster, death,
And all his frightful powers!

2 Joyful, with all the strength I have,
My quivering lips should sing,—
"Where is thy boasted vict'ry, grave?
O death! where is thy sting?"

3 If sin be pardoned, I'm secure;
Death has no sting beside:
The law gives sin its damning power,
But Christ, my ransom, died.

4 Now to the God of victory
Immortal thanks be paid;—
Who makes us conquerors, while we die,
Through Christ, our living head.

638.
C. M.
The Death of Children.

1 YE mourning saints! whose streaming tears
Flow o'er your children dead,—
Say not in transports of despair,
That all your hopes are fled.

2 While, cleaving to that darling dust,
In fond distress ye lie,
Rise, and with joy, and reverence, view
A heavenly parent nigh.

3 Though—your young branches torn away,—
Like withered trunks ye stand;
With fairer verdure shall ye bloom,
Touched by th' Almighty's hand.

4 "I 'll give the mourner," saith the Lord,
"In my own house a place;
No names of daughters and of sons
Could yield so high a grace.

5 "Transient and vain is every hope
A rising race can give;
In endless honor and delight,
My children all shall live."

6 We welcome, Lord! those rising tears,
Through which thy face we see; [hearts,
And bless those wounds which, through our
Prepare a way for thee.

639.
L. M.
The Christian's parting Hour.

1 HOW sweet the hour of closing day,
When all is peaceful and serene;
And the broad sun's retiring ray
Sheds a mild lustre o'er the scene!

2 Such is the Christian's parting hour,—
So peacefully he sinks to rest;
When faith, endued from heaven with power,
Strengthens and cheers his languid breast.

3 Mark but that radiance of his eye,—
That smile, upon his wasted cheek!
They tell us of his glory nigh,
In language which no tongue can speak.

4 A beam from heaven is sent to cheer
The pilgrim on his gloomy road;
And angels are attending near,
To bear him to their bright abode.

5 Who would not wish to die, like those
Whom God's own Spirit deigns to bless;
To sink into that soft repose,
Then wake to perfect happiness!

640.

C. M.

The Christian's Farewell.

1 YE golden lamps of heaven! farewell,
With all your feeble light;
Farewell, thou ever-changing moon!
Pale empress of the night.

2 And thou, refulgent orb of day!
In brighter flames arrayed,—
My soul, that springs beyond thy sphere,
No more demands thy aid.

3 Ye stars are but the shining dust
Of my divine abode;
The pavement of those heavenly courts,
Where I shall see my God.

4 The Father of eternal light
Shall there his beams display;
Nor shall one moment's darkness mix,
With that unvaried day.

5 No more the drops of piercing grief
Shall swell into mine eyes;
Nor the meridian sun decline
Amid those brighter skies.

6 There all the millions of his saints
Shall in one song unite;
And each the bliss of all shall view,
With infinite delight.

641.

C. M.

The Moment after Death.

1 IN vain the fancy strives to paint
The moment after death,—
The glories that surround a saint,
When yielding up his breath.

2 One gentle sigh the fetters breaks;
We scarce can say,—He 's gone!—
Before the willing spirit takes
Its mansion near the throne.

3 Faith strives—but all its efforts fail,—
To trace the spirit's flight;
No eye can pierce within the veil
Which hides the world of light.

4 Thus much—and 't is enough to know—
Saints are completely blest;
Have done with sin, and care, and wo,
And with their Saviour rest.

5 On harps of gold, they praise his name,
And see him face to face:
Oh! let us catch the heavenly flame,
And live in his embrace.

642. C. M.

The earthly and heavenly House.

1 THERE is a house not made with hands,
Eternal, and on high;
And here my spirit, waiting, stands,
Till God shall bid it fly.

2 Shortly this prison of my clay
Must be dissolved and fall;
Then, O my soul! with joy obey
Thy heavenly Father's call.

3 'T is he, by his almighty grace,
Who forms thee fit for heaven;
And, as an earnest of the place,
Hath his own Spirit given.

4 We walk by faith of joys to come;
Faith lives upon his word;
But while the body is our home,
We 're absent from the Lord.

5 'T is pleasant to believe thy grace,
But we had rather see;
We would be absent from the flesh,
And present, Lord! with thee.

643. C. M.

A Voice from the Tomb.

1 HARK! from the tombs a doleful sound!
My ears! attend the cry—

"Ye living men! come view the ground,
Where you must shortly lie.

2 "Princes! this clay must be your bed,
In spite of all your towers;
The tall, the wise, the reverend head,
Must lie as low as ours."

3 Great God! is this our certain doom?
And are we still secure?
Still walking downward to the tomb,
And yet prepare no more!

4 Grant us the power of quickening grace,
To fit our souls to fly;
Then, when we drop this dying flesh,
We 'll rise above the sky.

644. S. M.
Death and the Resurrection.

1 AND must this body die?—
This mortal frame decay?
And must these active limbs of mine
Lie mouldering in the clay?

2 God, my Redeemer, lives,
And often from the skies
Looks down and watches all my dust,—
Till he shall bid it rise.

3 Arrayed in glorious grace,
Shall these vile bodies shine;
And every shape, and every face,
Look heavenly and divine.

4 These lively hopes we owe
To Jesus' dying love;
We would adore his grace below,
And sing his power above.

5 Dear Lord! accept the praise
Of these our humble songs;
Till tunes of nobler sound we raise,
With our immortal tongues.

645. S. L. M.
The Death-Bed of the Righteous.

1 THIS place is holy ground;
World! w th thy cares, away!

Silence and darkness reign around;
But lo! the break of day!
What bright and sudden dawn appears,
To shine upon this scene of tears!

2 Behold the bed of death,—
This pale and lovely clay!
Heard ye the sob of parting breath!
Marked ye the eyes' last ray?—
No!—life so sweetly ceased to be,
It lapsed in immortality.

3 Could tears revive the dead,
Rivers should swell our eyes;
Could sighs recall the spirit fled,
We would not quench our sighs,
Till love relumed this altered mien,
And all th' embodied soul were seen.

4 Bury the dead,—and weep,
In stillness, o'er the loss;
Bury the dead,—in Christ they sleep,
Who bore on earth his cross,
And, from the grave, their dust shall rise
In his own image to the skies.

646. C. M.

Funeral.

1 BENEATH our feet and o'er our head,
Is equal warning given;
Beneath us lie the countless dead,—
Above us, is the heaven.

2 Death rides on every passing breeze,
And lurks in every flower;
Each season has its own disease,
Its peril—every hour.

3 Our eyes have seen the rosy light
Of youth's soft cheek decay,
And fate descend, in sudden night,
On manhood's middle day.

4 Our eyes have seen the steps of age
Halt feebly to the tomb;
And yet shall earth our hearts engage,
And dreams of days to come?

5 Turn, mortal! turn; thy danger know;
  Where'er thy foot can tread,
The earth rings hollow from below,
  And warns thee of her dead.

6 Turn, Christian! turn; thy soul apply
  To truths divinely given;
The forms, which underneath thee lie,
  Shall live, for hell, or heaven.

647.

C. M.

Death and Eternity.

1 STOOP down, my thoughts! that used to rise;
  Converse a while with death;
Think—how a gasping mortal lies,
  And pants away his breath.

2 His quivering lip hangs feebly down,
  His pulse is faint and few;
Then, speechless, with a doleful groan,
  He bids the world adieu!

3 But Oh! the soul that never dies!
  At once it leaves the clay:
Ye thoughts! pursue it where it flies,
  And track its wondrous way:—

4 Up to the courts where angels dwell,
  It mounts, triumphant there;—
Or devils plunge it down to hell,
  In infinite despair.

5 And must this body faint and die?
  And must this soul remove?
Oh! for some guardian angel nigh,
  To bear it safe above!

6 Jesus! to thy dear faithful hand,
  My naked soul I trust;
And my flesh waits for thy command,
  To drop into my dust.

648.

L. M.

Prayer for the dying Christian.

1 GENTLY, my Saviour! let me down,
  To slumber in the arms of death:
I rest my soul on thee alone,
  E'en till my last expiring breath.

2 Soon will the storm of life be o'er,
And I shall enter endless rest:
There I shall live to sin no more,
And bless thy name for ever blest.

3 Bid me possess sweet peace within;
Let childlike patience keep my heart;
Then shall I feel my heaven begin,
Before my spirit hence depart.

4 Hasten thy chariot, God of love!
And fetch me from this world of wo;
I long to reach those joys above,
And bid farewell to all below.

5 There shall my raptured spirit raise
Still louder notes than angels sing,—
High glories to Immanuel's grace,—
My God, my Saviour, and my King!

649. L. M.

Mourning with Submission.

1 THE God of love will sure indulge
The flowing tear, the heaving sigh,
When righteous persons fall around,—
When tender friends and kindred die.

2 Yet not one anxious, murm'ring thought
Should with our mourning passions blend;
Nor would our bleeding hearts forget
Th' almighty, ever-living Friend.

3 Beneath a numerous train of ills,
Our feeble flesh and heart may fail;
Yet shall our hope in thee, our God,
O'er every gloomy fear prevail.

4 Our Father-God! to thee we look,
Our Rock, our Portion and our Friend;
And on thy covenant-love and truth,
Our sinking souls shall still depend.

650. C. M.

The Death of a Youth.

1 WHEN blooming youth is snatcthed away,
By death's resistless hand,
Our hearts the mournful tribute pay,
That pity must demand.

2 While pity prompts the rising sigh,
Oh ! may this truth, impressed
With awful power,—"I too must die !"
Sink deep in every breast.

3 Let this vain world engage no more ;
Behold the gaping tomb !
It bids us seize the present hour,—
To-morrow death may come.

4 Oh ! let us fly—to Jesus fly—
Whose powerful arm can save ;
Then shall our hopes ascend on high,
And triumph o'er the grave.

5 Great God ! thy sovereign grace impart,
With cleansing, healing power ;
This only can prepare the heart,
For death's surprising hour.

651. C. M.

Death and the Resurrection.

1 THROUGH sorrow's night, and danger's path,
Amid the deepening gloom,
We, soldiers of an injured king,
Are marching to the tomb.

2 There, when the turmoil is no more,
And all our powers decay,
Our cold remains, in solitude,
Shall sleep the years away.

3 Our labors done securely laid
In this our last retreat,
Unheeded, o'er our silent dust,
The storms of life shall beat.

4 Yet not thus lifeless, thus inane,
The vital spark shall lie ;
For, o'er life's wreck, that spark shall rise
To seek its kindred sky.

5 These ashes too,—this little dust,—
Our Father's care shall keep,
Till the last angel rise and break
The long and dreary sleep.

6 Then love's soft dew, o'er every eye,
Shall shed its mildest rays,

And the long-silent dust shall burst,
  With shouts of endless praise.

652.
C. M.
Death dreadful or delightful.

1 DEATH !—'t is a melancholy day,
  To those who have no God,—
When the poor soul is forced away
  To seek her last abode.

2 In vain, to heaven she lifts her eyes,—
  But guilt a heavy chain,
Still drags her downward from the skies,
  To darkness, fire, and pain.

3 Awake, and mourn, ye heirs of wo !
  Let stubborn sinners fear ;
Why will ye sink to flames below,
  And dwell for ever there ?

4 See how the pit gapes wide for you,
  And flashes in your face ;
And thou, my soul ! look downward too,
  And sing recovering grace.

653.
C. M.
Death and Judgment appointed to all.

1 HEAVEN has confirmed the dread decree,
  That Adam's race must die ;
One general ruin sweeps them down,
  And low in dust they lie.

2 Ye living men ! the tomb survey,
  Where you must shortly dwell ;
Hark ! how the awful summons sounds,
  In every funeral-knell !

3 Once you must die—and once for all,—
  The solemn purport weigh ;
For know, that heaven and hell are hung,
  On that important day.

4 Those eyes, so long in darkness veiled,
  Must wake the Judge to see ;
And every word, and every thought,
  Must pass his scrutiny.

5 Oh! may I, in the Judge, behold
My Saviour and my Friend;
And, far above the reach of death,
With all thy saints ascend.

JUDGMENT.

654. 7s.
Christ coming to save his People

1 HARK—that shout of rapturous joy,
Bursting forth from yonder cloud!
Jesus comes—and, through the sky
Angels tell their joy aloud.

2 Hark!—the trumpet's awful voice
Sounds abroad through sea and land;
Let his people now rejoice,
Their redemption is at hand.

3 See!—the Lord appears in view;
Heaven and earth before him fly;
Rise, ye saints! he comes for you,—
Rise, to meet him in the sky.

4 Go and dwell with him above,
Where no foe can e'er molest;
Happy in the Saviour's love,
Ever blessing, ever blest.

655. C. M.
God, the awful Judge.

1 SING to the Lord, ye heavenly hosts!
And thou, O earth! adore;
Let death and hell, through all their coasts,
Stand trembling at his power.

2 His sounding chariot shakes the sky,
He makes the clouds his throne:
There all his stores of lightning lie,
Till vengeance darts them down.

3 Think, O my soul! the dreadful day,
When this incensed God
Shall rend the sky, and burn the sea,
And send his wrath abroad.

4 What shall the wretch, the sinner do?
He once defied the Lord;
But he shall dread the thunderer now
And sink beneath his word.

5 Tempests of angry fire shall roll
To blast the rebel-worm,
And beat upon his naked soul,
In one eternal storm.

656.

8s, 7s and 4.

Christ coming to Judgment.

1 LO! he comes, in clouds descending,
Once for favored sinners slain;
Thousand thousand saints attending
Swell the triumph of his train:
Hallelujah;—
Jesus shall for ever reign.

2 Every eye shall now behold him,
Robed in dreadful majesty;
Those who set at nought, and sold him,
Pierced and nailed him to the tree,
Deeply wailing,—
Shall the great Messiah see.

3 Every island, sea, and mountain,
Heaven, and earth shall flee away;
All who hate him, must, confounded,
Hear the trump proclaim the day;
Come to judgment!—
Come to judgment,—come away.

4 Now the Saviour, long-expected,
See, in solemn pomp, appear!
All his saints, by man rejected,
Now shall meet him in the air.
Hallelujah!—
See the day of God appear.

657.

8s, 7s and 4.

The Judgment welcomed.

1 LO! he cometh,—countless trumpets
Wake to life the slumbering dead;
Mid ten thousand saints and angels,
See their great exalted Head:
Hallelujah!—
Welcome, welcome, Son of God!

2 Full of joyful expectation,
Saints behold the Judge appear:
Truth and justice go before him—
Now the joyful sentence hear;
Hallelujah!—
Welcome, welcome, Judge divine!

3 "Come, ye blessed of my Father!
Enter into life and joy;
Banish all your fears and sorrows;
Endless praise be your employ:"
Hallelujah!—
Welcome, welcome to the skies.

658.

C. M.

Everlasting Absence of God intolerable.

1 THAT awful day will surely come,
Th' appointed hour makes haste,—
When I must stand before my judge,
And pass the solemn test.

2 Thou lovely Chief of all my joys!
Thou Sovereign of my heart!
How could I bear to hear thy voice
Pronounce the sound—Depart!

3 Oh! wretched state of deep despair—
To see my God remove,
And fix my doleful station, where
I must not taste his love!

4 Jesus! I throw my arms around,
And hang upon thy breast;
Without one gracious smile from thee,
My spirit cannot rest.

5 Oh! tell me that my worthless name
Is graven on thy hands;
Show me some promise in thy book,
Where my salvation stands.

659.

C. M.

The Judgment anticipated.

1 WHEN, rising from the bed of death,
O'erwhelmed with guilt and fear,
I see my Maker face to face,—
Oh! how shall I appear?

2 If now, while pardon may be found,
And mercy may be sought,
My heart with inward horror shrinks,
And trembles at the thought;—

3 When thou, O Lord! shalt stand disclosed,
In majesty severe,
And sit in judgment on my soul,—
Oh! how shall I appear?

4 Then see my sorrows, gracious Lord!
Let mercy set me free;
While, in the confidence of prayer,
My heart takes hold of thee.

5 For never shall my soul despair
Thy mercy to procure;
Since thy beloved Son has died
To make that mercy sure.

660.

8s, 7s and 4.

The Judgment-Trumpet.

1 HARK!—the judgment-trumpet sounding
Rends the skies and shakes the poles;
Lo! the day, with wrath abounding,
Breaks upon astonished souls:
Every creature
Now the awful Judge beholds.

2 Jesus, captain of salvation,
Leads his armies down the skies;
Every kindred, tribe and nation,
From the sleep of death, arise:
Heaven's loud summons
Fills the world with dread surprise.

3 Zion's king, his throne ascending,
Calls his saints before his face;
Crowns, with glory never-ending,
All the children of his grace:
Heaven shall echo;—
Songs of triumph fill the place.

4 Look beneath, where hell is burning!
There the sons of darkness lie;
Hope to black despair is turning;
There the worm shall never die:
Careless sinner!—
Oh! to Jesus quickly fly.

661.

L. M.

The Judgment-Scene.

1 THE Lord shall come,—the earth shall quake,
The mountains to their centre shake;
And, withering from the vault of night,
The stars shall pale their feeble light.

2 The Lord shall come,—but not the same
As once, in lowliness, he came,—
A silent lamb before his foes,—
A weary man, and full of woes.

3 The Lord shall come,—a dreadful form,
With rainbow-wreath, and robes of storm,
On cherub-wings and wings of wind,—
Appointed judge of all mankind.

4 Can this be he, who wont to stray
A pilgrim on the world's highway;
Oppressed by power, and mocked by pride,
The Nazarene—the Crucified?

5 While sinners in despair shall call,—
"Rocks,—hide us!—mountains! on us fall!"
The saints, ascending from the tomb,
Shall joyful sing,—"The Lord is come!"

662.

8s, 7s and 4.

Saints and Sinners judged.

1 DAY of judgment! day of wonders!
Hark!—the trumpet's awful sound,
Louder than a thousand thunders,
Shakes the vast creation round:
How the summons
Will the sinner's heart confound!

2 See the Judge, our nature wearing,
Clothed in majesty divine!
You, who long for his appearing,
Then shall say,—"This God is mine!"
Gracious Saviour!
Own me in that day for thine.

3 At his call, the dead awaken,
Rise to life from earth and sea;
All the powers of nature, shaken,
By his looks, prepare to flee·
Careless sinner!
What will then become of thee?

4 But to those who have confessed,
Loved and served the Lord below,
He will say,—"Come near, ye blessed!
See the kingdom I bestow!
You for ever
Shall my love and glory know."

663.
8s and 7s. Irregular.
Christ, coming to Judgment.

1 GREAT God! what do I see and hear?—
The end of things created!
Behold the Judge of man appear,
On clouds of glory seated!
The trumpet sounds—the graves restore
The dead which they contained before!—
Prepare, my soul! to meet him.

2 The dead in Christ shall first arise,
At the last trumpet's sounding,
Caught up to meet him in the skies,
With joy their Lord surrounding:
No gloomy fears their souls dismay,
His presence sheds eternal day,
On those prepared to meet him.

3 Great God! what do I see and hear?—
The end of things created!
Behold the Judge of man appear,
On clouds of glory seated!
Low at his cross I view the day,
When heaven and earth shall pass away,
And thus prepare to meet him.

664.
S. M.
The Judgment in Prospect.

1 AND will the Judge descend?
And must the dead arise?
And not a single soul escape
His all-discerning eyes?

2 How will my heart endure
The terrors of that day,
When earth and heaven before his face,
Astonished, shrink away?

3 But ere that trumpet shakes
The mansions of the dead,

Hark!—from the gospel's cheering sound
What joyful tidings spread!

4 Ye sinners! seek his grace,—
His wrath ye cannot bear;
Fly to the shelter of his cross,
And find salvation there.

5 So shall that curse remove,
By which the Saviour bled;
And the last awful day shall pour
His blessings on your head.

665.

C. P. M.

The Saint at Christ's right Hand.

1 WHEN thou, my righteous Judge! shalt come
To fetch thy ransomed people home,
Shall I among them stand?
Shall such a worthless worm as I,
Who sometimes am afraid to die,
Be found at thy right hand?

2 Blest Saviour! grant it by thy grace;
Be thou my only hiding-place,
In this th' accepted day;
Thy pard'ning voice, Oh! let me hear,
To still my unbelieving fear,
Nor let me fall, I pray.

3 Among thy saints let me be found;
Whene'er th' archangel's trump shall sound
To see thy smiling face;
Then filled with rapture shall I sing,
While heaven's resounding mansions ring
With shouts of sovereign grace.

666.

8s, 7s and 4.

The Sinner's Doom.

1 SEE th' eternal Judge descending,
View him seated on his throne!
Now, poor sinner! now lamenting,
Stand and hear thine awful doom;—
Trumpets call thee!—
Stand and hear thine awful doom.

2 Hear the cries he now is venting,
Filled with dread of fiercer pain;

While in anguish thus lamenting,
That he ne'er was born again!
Greatly mourning,—
That he ne'er was born again!—

3 "Yonder sits my slighted Saviour,
With the marks of dying love;
Oh! that I had sought his favor,
When I felt his Spirit move!
Golden moments,—
When I felt his Spirit move."

4 Now, despisers! look and wonder;
Hope and sinners here must part;
Louder than a peal of thunder,
Hear the dreadful sound,—"Depart!"
Lost forever,—
Hear the dreadful sound,—"Depart!"

667. L. M.
The Day of Wrath.

1 THAT day of wrath!—that dreadful day,
When heaven and earth shall pass away!—
What power shall be the sinner's stay?
How shall he meet that dreadful day,—

2 When, shrivelling like a parched scroll,
The flaming heavens together roll;
And louder yet—and yet more dread,—
Swells the high trump that wakes the dead?

3 Oh! on that day—that wrathful day,
When man to judgment wakes from clay,
Be thou, O Christ! the sinner's stay,—
Though heaven and earth shall pass away.

668. S. M.
The Lord, coming to Judgment.

1 BEHOLD! the day is come,
The righteous Judge is near;
And sinners, trembling at their doom,
Shall soon their sentence hear.

2 Angels, in bright attire,
Conduct him through the skies;
Darkness and tempests, smoke and fire,
Attend him as he flies.

3 How awful is the sight!
How loud the thunders roar!
The sun forbears to give his light,
And stars are seen no more.

4 The whole creation groans,
But saints arise and sing;
They are the ransomed of the Lord,
And he their God and King

HEAVEN.

669. C. M.

The cheering Prospect of Heaven.

1 THERE is a land of pure delight,
Where saints immortal reign,
Infinite day excludes the night,
And pleasures banish pain.

2 There everlasting spring abides,
And never-withering flowers;
Death, like a narrow sea, divides
This heavenly land from ours.

3 Sweet fields, beyond the swelling flood,
Stand dressed in living green;
So to the Jews old Canaan stood,
While Jordan rolled between.

4 But tim'rous mortals start and shrink
To cross this narrow sea;
And linger, shivering on the brink,
And fear to launch away.

5 Oh! could we make our doubts remove,—
Those gloomy doubts that rise,—
And see the Canaan that we love,
With unbeclouded eyes;—

6 Could we but climb where Moses stood,
And view the landscape o'er,—
Not Jordan's streams, nor death's cold flood,
Should fright us from the shore.

670.
L. M.
The Worship of Heaven.

1 OH! for a sweet, inspiring ray,
To animate our feeble strains,
From the bright realms of endless day,—
The blissful realms, where Jesus reigns.

2 There, low before his glorious throne,
Adoring saints and angels fall;
And, with delightful worship, own
His smile their bliss, their heaven, their all.

3 Immortal glories crown his head,
While tuneful hallelujahs rise,
And love, and joy, and triumph spread
Through all th' assemblies of the skies.

4 He smiles,—and seraphs tune their songs
To boundless rapture, while they gaze;
Ten thousand, thousand joyful tongues
Resound his everlasting praise.

5 There all the foll'wers of the Lamb
Shall join at last the heavenly choir;
Oh! may the joy-inspiring theme
Awake our faith and warm desire.

6 Dear Saviour! let thy Spirit seal
Our interest in that blissful place;
Till death remove this mortal veil,
And we behold thy lovely face.

671.
7s.
The Songs and Bliss of Heaven.

1 HIGH in yonder realms of light,
Dwell the raptured saints above;
Far beyond our feeble sight,
Happy in Immanuel's love:
Pilgrims in this vale of tears,
Once they knew, like us below,
Gloomy doubts, distressing fears,
Torturing pain, and heavy wo.

2 Mid the chorus of the skies,
Mid th' angelic lyres above,
Hark! their songs melodious rise,
Songs of praise to Jesus' love:
Happy spirits! ye are fled,
Where no grief can entrance find,—

Lulled to rest, the aching head,
Soothed, the anguish of the mind.

3 All is tranquil and serene,—
Calm and undisturbed repose;
There no cloud can intervene,
There no angry tempest blows:
Every tear is wiped away,
Sighs no more shall heave the breast;
Night is lost in endless day,
Sorrow, in eternal rest.

672. S. M.

Rest for the weary Soul.

1 OH! where shall rest be found,—
Rest for the weary soul?
'T were vain the ocean-depths to sound,
Or pierce to either pole.

2 The world can never give
The bliss for which we sigh;
'T is not the whole of life to live,
Nor all of death to die.

3 Beyond this vale of tears,
There is a life above,
Unmeasured by the flight of years;
And all that life is love.

4 There is a death, whose pang
Outlasts the fleeting breath;
Oh! what eternal horrors hang
Around the second death!

5 Lord God of truth and grace!
Teach us that death to shun;
Lest we be banished from thy face,
And evermore undone.

673. C. M.

Freedom from Sin and Sorrow.

1 HOW happy are the souls above,
From sin and sorrow free!
With Jesus they are now at rest,
And all his glory see.

2 "Worthy the Lamb," aloud they cry,
"That brought us near to God:"
In ceaseless hymns of praise, they shout
The virtue of his blood.

3 Sweet gratitude inspires their songs,
Ambitious to proclaim,
Before the Father's awful throne,
The honors of the Lamb.

4 With wondering joy, they recollect,
Their fears and dangers past;
And bless the wisdom, power, and love,
Which brought them safe at last.

5 Lord! let the merit of thy death
To me be likewise given;
And I, with them, will shout thy praise,
Through all the courts of heaven.

674.

8s and 6s. Irregular.

Things temporal and eternal.

1 OH! weep not for the joys that fade,
Like evening-lights away,—
For hopes, that, like the stars decayed,
Have left thy mortal day;
For clouds of sorrow will depart,
And brilliant skies be given;
And though on earth the tear may start,
Yet bliss awaits the holy heart,
Amid the bowers of heaven.

2 Oh! weep not for the friends that pass
Into the lonely grave,
As breezes sweep the withered grass
Along the restless wave;
For though thy pleasures may depart,
And mournful days be given,
And lonely though on earth thou art,
Yet bliss awaits the holy heart,
When friends rejoin in heaven.

675.

C. M.

Heaven anticipated.

1 COME, Lord! and warm each languid heart,
Inspire each lifeless tongue,
And let the joys of heaven impart
Their influence to our song.

2 Then to the shining realms of bliss
The wings of faith shall soar,
And all the charms of paradise
Our raptured thoughts explore.

3 There shall the foll'wers of the Lamb
Join in immortal songs;
And endless honors to his name
Employ their tuneful tongues.

4 Lord! tune our hearts to praise and love,—
Our feeble notes inspire;
Till in thy blissful courts above,
We join the heavenly choir.

676.

8s and 6s. Irregular.

Heaven anticipated.

1 THERE is an hour of peaceful rest,
To mourning wanderers given:
There is a joy for souls distressed,
A balm for every wounded breast,
'T is found above—in heaven.

2 There is a home for weary souls,
By sin and sorrow driven;
When tossed on life's tempestuous shoals,
Where storms arise and ocean rolls,
And all is drear but heaven.

3 There, faith lifts up her cheerful eye,
To brighter prospects given;
And views the tempest passing by,
The evening-shadows quickly fly,
And all serene in heaven.

4 There, fragrant flowers immortal bloom,
And joys supreme are given;
There, rays divine disperse the gloom;—
Beyond the confines of the tomb,
Appears the dawn of heaven.

677.

C. M.

The Peace and Repose of Heaven.

1 THERE is an hour of hallowed peace
For those with cares oppressed,
When sighs and sorr'wing tears shall cease
And all be hushed to rest.

2 'T is then the soul is freed from fears
And doubts which here annoy;
Then they, who oft have sown in tears,
Shall reap again in joy.

3 There is a home of sweet repose,
Where storms assail no more;

The stream of endless pleasure flows,
On that celestial shore.

4 There, purity with love appears,
And bliss without alloy;
There, they, who oft had sown in tears,
Shall reap again in joy.

678.

C. M.

Heaven unseen and immortal.

1 HOW far beyond our mortal sight
The Lord of glory dwells!
A veil of interposing night
His radiant face conceals.

2 Oh! could my longing spirit rise
On strong, immortal wing,
And reach thy palace in the skies,
My Saviour and my King!—

3 There, thousands worship at thy feet,
And there—divine employ—
Thy love triumphant they repeat
In songs of endless joy.

4 Thy presence beams eternal day,
O'er all the blissful place:
Who would not leave this house of clay,
And fly to thine embrace?

679.

C. M.

Union of Saints in Heaven and on Earth.

1 COME, let us join our friends above,
Who have obtained the prize,
And, on the eagle-wings of love,
To joy celestial rise.

2 Let saints below in concert sing
With those to glory gone,
For all the servants of our King
In heaven and earth are one:—

3 One family,—we dwell in him;
One church,—above, beneath;
Though now divided by the stream—
The narrow stream of death.

4 One army of the living God,
To his command we bow;

Part of the host have crossed the flood,
And part are crossing now.

5 Ev'n now to their eternal home
Some happy spirits fly;
And we are to the margin come,
And soon expect to die!

6 Dear Saviour! be our constant guide;
Then, when the word is given,
Bid Jordan's narrow stream divide,
And land us safe in heaven.

680.

L M

Rising to God.

1 NOW let our souls, on wings sublime,
Rise from the vanities of time;
Draw back the parting veil, and see
The glories of eternity.

2 Born by a new celestial birth,
Why should we grovel here on earth?
Why grasp at transitory toys,
So near to heaven's eternal joys?

3 Should aught beguile us on the road,
When we are walking back to God?
For strangers into life we come,
And dying is but going home.

4 Welcome, sweet hour of full discharge!
That sets our longing souls at large,
Unbinds our chains, breaks up our cell,
And gives us with our God to dwell.

5 To dwell with God—to feel his love,
Is the full heaven enjoyed above;
And the sweet expectation now
Is the young dawn of heaven below.

681.

C. M.

The Heavenly City.

1 JERUSALEM!—my happy home!
Name ever dear to me,—
When shall my labors have an end,
In joy, and peace, and thee?

2 When shall these eyes thy heaven-built walls
And pearly gates behold?

Thy bulwarks, with salvation strong,
  And streets of shining gold?

3 Oh! when, thou city of my God!
  Shall I thy courts ascend?—
Where congregations ne'er break up,
  And Sabbaths never end.

4 Why should I shrink at pain or wo,
  Or feel, at death, dismay?
Jerusalem I soon shall view,
  In realms of endless day.

5 Redeemed saints and angels, there,
  Around my Saviour stand;
And soon my friends in Christ, below,
  Will join the glorious band.

6 Jerusalem!—my happy home!
  My soul still pants for thee;
Then shall my labors have an end,
  When I thy joys shall see.

682.

S. L. M.

The Perpetuity of Heaven.

1 FRIEND after friend departs:
  Who hath not lost a friend?
There is no union here of hearts
  That finds not here an end:
Were this frail world our final rest,
Living or dying, none were blest.

2 Beyond the flight of time,
  Beyond the reign of death,
There surely is some blessed clime
  Where life is not a breath;
Nor life's affections, transient fire,
Whose sparks fly upwards and expire.

3 There is a world above,
  Where parting is unknown;
A long eternity of love,
  Formed for the good alone;
And faith beholds the dying here,
Translated to that glorious sphere.

4 Thus star by star declines,
  Till all have passed away;

As morning high and higher shines,
To pure and perfect day;
Nor sink those stars in empty night,
But hide themselves in heaven's own light.

683.

C. M.

Heaven:—for Sunday-Schools.

1 THERE is a glorious world of light,
Above the starry sky;
Where saints departed, clothed in white,
Adore the Lord most high.

2 And hark!—amid the sacred songs
Those heavenly voices raise,
Ten thousand, thousand infant tongues
Unite in perfect praise.

3 Those are the hymns that we shall know,
If Jesus we obey;
That is the place where we shall go,
If found in wisdom's way.

4 This is the joy we ought to seek,
And make our chief concern;
For this we come, from week to week,
To read, and hear, and learn.

5 Soon will our earthly race be run,
Our mortal frame decay;
Children and teachers, one by one,
Must pass from earth away.

6 Great God! impress the serious thought
This day, on every breast;
That both the teachers and the taught
May enter to thy rest.

684.

C. M.

The Joys unseen.

1 NOR eye hath seen, nor ear hath heard
Nor sense nor reason known,
What joys the Father has prepared,
For those who love the Son.

2 But the good Spirit of the Lord
Reveals a heaven to come:
The beams of glory, in his word,
Allure and guide us home.

3 Pure are the joys above the sky,
  And all the region peace;
No wanton lip, nor envious eye,
  Can see or taste the bliss.

4 Those holy gates for ever bar
  Pollution, sin, and shame;
None shall obtain admittance there,
  But foll'wers of the Lamb.

685. L. M.

Heaven alone unfading.

1 HOW vain is all beneath the skies!
  How transient every earthly bliss!
How slender all the fondest ties
  That bind us to a world like this!

2 The evening-cloud, the morning-dew,
  The withering grass, the fading flower,
Of earthly hopes are emblems true,—
  The glory of a passing hour.

3 But, though earth's fairest blossoms die,
  And all beneath the skies is vain,
There is a land whose confines lie
  Beyond the reach of care and pain.

4 Then let the hope of joys to come
  Dispel our cares, and chase our fears:
If God be ours, we 're traveling home,
  Though passing through a vale of tears.

686. C. L. M.

The everlasting Bliss of Heaven.

1 HEAVEN is the land where troubles cease,
  Where toils and tears are o'er;—
The blissful clime of rest and peace,
  Where cares distract no more;
And not the shadow of distress
Dims its unsullied blessedness.

2 Heaven is the place where Jesus lives
  To plead his dying blood;
While, to his prayers, his Father gives
  An unknown multitude, [days,
Whose harps and tongues, through endless
Shall crown his head with songs of praise.

3 Heaven is the dwelling-place of joy,
The home of light and love,
Where faith and hope in rapture die,
And ransomed souls above
Enjoy, before th' eternal throne,
Bliss everlasting and unknown.

687.

C. M.

The unseen and blessed World.

1 FAR from these narrow scenes of night
Unbounded glories rise,
And realms of infinite delight,
Unknown to mortal eyes.

2 Fair distant land! could mortal eyes
But half its charms explore,
How would our spirits long to rise,
And dwell on earth no more!

3 No cloud those blissful regions know,—
Realms ever bright and fair;
For sin, the source of mortal wo,
Can never enter there.

4 Oh! may the heavenly prospect fire
Our hearts with ardent love,
Till wings of faith and strong desire
Bear every thought above.

5 Prepare us, Lord! by grace divine,
For thy bright courts on high;
Then bid our spirits rise and join
The chorus of the sky.

688.

8s and 6s. Irregular.

Nothing like Heaven.

1 THIS world is poor from shore to shore,
And, like a baseless vision,
Its lofty domes and brilliant ore,
Its gems and crowns, are vain and poor;—
There 's nothing rich but heaven.

2 Empires decay and nations die,
Our hopes to winds are given;
The vernal blooms in ruin lie,
Death reigns o'er all beneath the sky;—
There 's nothing sure but heaven.

3 Creation's mighty fabric all
Shall be to atoms riven,—
The skies consume, the planets fall,
Convulsions rock this earthly ball;—
There's nothing firm but heaven.

4 A stranger, lonely here I roam,
From place to place am driven;
My friends are gone, and I'm in gloom,
This earth is all a dismal tomb;—
I have no home but heaven.

5 The clouds disperse—the light appears,
My sins are all forgiven,
Triumphant grace hath quelled my fears;—
Roll on, thou sun! fly swift, my years!
I'm on my way to heaven.

689.

C. M.

Heaven in Prospect.

1 ON Jordan's stormy banks I stand,
And cast a wishful eye
To Canaan's fair and happy land,
Where my possessions lie.

2 Oh! the transporting, rapturous scene,
That rises to my sight!
Sweet fields, arrayed in living green,
And rivers of delight!

3 O'er all those wide-extended plains
Shines one eternal day;
There, God, the Son, for ever reigns,
And scatters night away.

4 No chilling winds—no pois'nous breath,
Can reach that healthful shore;
Sickness and sorrow, pain and death,
Are felt and feared no more.

5 When shall I reach that happy place,
And be for ever blest?
When shall I see my Father's face,
And in his bosom rest?

6 Filled with delight, my raptured soul
Would here no longer stay;
Though Jordan's waves should round me roll,—
Fearless I'd launch away.

690.

8s and 7s.

The Christian's Flight to Heaven.

1 WHAT is life? 't is but a vapor;
Soon it vanishes away;
Life is but a dying taper;
O my soul! why wish to stay?
Why not spread thy wings and fly,
Straight to yonder world of joy?

2 See that glory—how resplendent!
Brighter far than fancy paints;
There, in majesty transcendent,
Jesus reigns—the King of saints:—
Spread thy wings, my soul! and fly
Straight to yonder world of joy.

3 Joyful crowds, his throne surrounding,
Sing with rapture of his love;
Through the heavens his praises sounding,
Filling all the courts above:
Spread thy wings, my soul! and fly
Straight to yonder world of joy.

4 Go, and share his people's glory,
Mid the ransomed crowd appear;—
Thine a joyful, wondrous story,
One that angels love to hear:
Spread thy wings, my soul! and fly
Straight to yonder world of joy.

691.

C. M.

The blessed Society in Heaven.

1 RAISE thee, my soul! fly up, and run
Through every heavenly street;
And say,—there 's nought below the sun,
That 's worthy of thy feet.

2 There, on a high majestic throne,
Th' almighty Father reigns;
And sheds his glorious goodness down,
On all the blissful plains.

3 Bright, like the sun, the Saviour sits,
And spreads eternal noon:
No evenings there, nor gloomy nights,
To want the feeble moon.

4 Amid those ever-shining skies,
Behold the sacred Dove!
While, banished sin, with sorrow, flies
From all the realms of love.

5 The glorious tenants of the place
Stand bending round the throne;
And saints and seraphs sing and praise
The infinite Three-One.

6 Jesus!—and when shall that dear day,—
That joyful hour, appear,
When I shall leave this house of clay,
To dwell among them there!

692.

C. M.

The everlasting Song.

1 EARTH has engrossed my love too long;
'T is time, I lift mine eyes
Upward, dear Father! to thy throne,
And to my native skies.

2 There, the blest man, my Saviour, sits;—
The God!—how bright he shines!
And scatters infinite delights
On all the happy minds.

3 Seraphs, with elevated strains,
Circle the throne around;
And move and charm the starry plains
With an immortal sound.

4 Jesus, the Lord, their harps employs,—
Jesus, my love, they sing!
Jesus, the life of all our joys,
Sounds sweet from every string.

5 Now let me mount, and join their song,
And be an angel too;
My heart! my hand! my ear! my tongue!
Here 's joyful work for you.

6 I would begin the music here,
And so my soul should rise;—
Oh! for some heavenly notes to bear
My passions to the skies!

693.

C. M.

Victory through the Lamb.

1 GIVE me the wings of faith, to rise
Within the veil, and see
The saints above,—how great their joys,—
How bright their glories be.

2 I ask them,—whence their vict'ry came?
They, with united breath,
Ascribe their conquest to the Lamb,—
Their triumph to his death.

3 They marked the footsteps he had trod;
His zeal inspired their breast;
And, foll'wing their incarnate God,
Possess the promised rest.

4 Our glorious Leader claims our praise,
For his own pattern given,—
While the long cloud of witnesses
Show the same path to heaven.

694.

C. M.

The Worship of Earth and Heaven.

1 FATHER! I long, I faint, to see
The place of thine abode;
I'd leave thine earthly courts, and flee
Up to thy seat, my God!

2 Here I behold thy distant face,
And 't is a pleasing sight;
But, to abide in thine embrace
Is infinite delight.

3 I'd part with all the joys of sense,
To gaze upon thy throne;
Pleasure springs fresh for ever thence,
Unspeakable, unknown.

4 There all the heavenly hosts are seen;
In shining ranks they move;
And drink immortal vigor in,
With wonder and with love.

5 Then at thy feet with awful fear,
Th' adoring armies fall;
With joy they shrink to nothing there,
Before th' eternal All.

6 Father! I long, I faint to see
The place of thine abode;
I 'd leave thine earthly courts to be
For ever with my God.

695.

11s.
Longing for Heaven.

1 I WOULD not live always—I ask not to stay,
Where storm after storm rises dark o'er the way;
The few lucid mornings that dawn on us here,
Are followed by gloom, and beclouded by fear.

2 I would not live always—no,—welcome the tomb;
Since Jesus hath lain there, I dread not its gloom;
There, sweet be my rest, till he bid me arise
To hail him in triumph descending the skies.

3 Who—who would live always—away from his God;—
Away from yon heaven, that blissful abode,
Where the rivers of pleasure flow o'er the bright plains,
And the noontide of glory eternally reigns?

4 There saints of all ages, in harmony meet,
Their Saviour and brethren transported to greet;
While anthems of rapture unceasingly roll,
And the smile of the Lord is the feast of the soul.

696.

C. M.
The Martyrs glorified.

1 "THESE glorious minds,—how bright they shine!
Whence all their white array?
How came they to the happy seats
Of everlasting day?"

2 From torturing pains to endless joys,
On fiery wheels they rode;
And strangely washed their raiment white,
In Jesus' dying blood.

3 Now they approach a spotless God,
And bow before his throne;
Their warbling harps, and sacred songs,
Adore the Holy One.

4 The unveiled glories of his face
  Among his saints reside,
While the rich treasures of his grace
  See all their wants supplied.

5 Hunger and thirst for ever flee—
  Their joys for ever last:
The fruit of life's immortal tree
  Shall be their sweet repast.

6 The Lamb shall lead his heavenly flock
  Where living fountains rise;
And love divine shall wipe away
  The sorrows of their eyes.

697.

7s.

The Redeemed in Heaven.

1 WHAT are these in bright array,
  This innumerable throng,
Round the altar night and day,
  Hymning one triumphant song?—
"Worthy is the Lamb once slain,
  Blessing, honor, glory, power,
Wisdom, riches, to obtain,
  New dominion, every hour!"

2 These through fiery trials trod,—
  These from great affliction came;
Now before the throne of God,
  Sealed with his almighty name,
Clad in raiment pure and white,
  Victor-palms in every hand,
Through their dear Redeemer's might,
  More than conquerors they stand.

3 Hunger, thirst, disease unknown,
  On immortal fruits they feed;
Them, the Lamb, amidst the throne,
  Shall to living fountains lead;
Joy and gladness banish sighs,
  Perfect love dispel all fears,
And for ever from their eyes,
  God shall wipe away the tears.

698.

9s and 6s.

Prospect of Heaven.

1 COME away to the skies—
  My beloved! arise,
And rejoice in the day thou wert born;

On this festival day,
Come exulting away,
And, with singing, to Zion return.

2 We have laid up our love,
With our treasure, above,
Though our bodies continue below,
The redeemed of the Lord—
We remember his word,
And, with singing, to paradise go.

3 For thy glory we were
First created, to share
Both thy nature and kingdom divine;
Now created again,
That our souls may remain,
Both in time and eternity, thine.

4 With thanks we approve
The design of thy love,
Which hath joined us in Christ's precious name;
So united in heart
That we never can part—
We shall meet at the feast of the Lamb.

5 There, Oh! there, at his feet,
We shall joyfully meet,
And be parted, in body, no more;
We shall sing to our lyres,
With the heavenly choirs,
And our Saviour, in glory, adore.

6 "Hallelujah!"—we sing,
To our Father and King,
And his rapturous praises repeat;
To the Lamb that was slain,
"Hallelujah!"—again—
Sing all heaven, and fall at his feet.

699.

8s.

Longing to be with Christ.

1 TO Jesus, the crown of my hope,
My soul is in haste to be gone;
Oh! bear me, ye cherubim! up,
And waft me away to his throne.

2 My Saviour! whom absent I love;
Whom, not having seen, I adore;
Whose name is exalted above
All glory, dominion, and power;—

3 Dissolve thou these bonds, that detain
My soul from her portion in thee;
Ah! strike off this adamant-chain,
And make me eternally free.

4 When that happy era begins,
Arrayed in thy glories I 'll shine,
Nor grieve any more, by my sins,
The bosom on which I recline.

700.

7s.

The Victory of the Saints.

1 PALMS of glory, raiment bright,
Crowns that never fade away,
Gird and deck the saints in light,—
Priests, and kings, and conquerors they

2 Yet the conquerors bring their palms
To the Lamb amidst the throne,
And proclaim, in joyful psalms,
Vict'ry through his cross alone.

3 Kings for harps their crowns resign,
Crying as they strike the chords,—
"Take the kingdom—it is thine,—
King of kings, and Lord of lords!"

4 Round the altar, priests confess,—
If their robes are white as snow,
'T was their Saviour's righteousness
And his blood that made them so.

5 Who were these?—On earth they dwelt,
Sinners once of Adam's race,—
Guilt, and fear, and suffering felt,
But were saved by sovereign grace.

6 They were mortal, too, like us:—
Ah! when we like them shall die,
May our souls, translated thus,
Triumph, reign, and shine on high!

701.

C. M.

The New-Song before the Throne.

1 WHAT blissful harmonies above,
In vocal thunders swell?
The perfecting of joy and love,
What raptured legions tell?

2 The glorious apostolic band,—
Do they in triumph sing?
Do prophets from the holy land
Their inspiration bring?

3 Or from the noble army breaks
The deep, adoring strain,
Who won their way from fiery stakes
And were for conscience slain?

4 Is it the patriarchal race
That breathe the sacred song?
Or to the heirs of gospel-grace
Do the full choirs belong?

5 For each, for all, the Word is found
Almighty to atone:
All,—all in shining hosts surround
The bright celestial throne.

6 Peoples, and languages, and tongues
The choral anthem raise:
To every voice and speech belongs
The work of heavenly praise.

702.

C. M.

Earthly and heavenly Good.

1 HOW vain a thought is bliss below!
'T is all an airy dream;
How empty are the joys that flow
On pleasure's smiling stream!

2 Oh! let my nobler wishes soar
Beyond these realms of night;
In heaven substantial bliss explore,
And permanent delight.

3 No fleeting landscape cheers the gaze,
Nor airy form beguiles;
But everlasting bliss displays
Her undissembled smiles.

4 Adieu to all below the skies!
  Celestial Guardian! come;
On thy kind wing, my soul would rise
  To her celestial home.

DISMISSIONS AND DOXOLOGIES.

703.
L. M.
Dismission.

1 DISMISS us, with thy blessing, Lord!
Help us to feed upon thy word;
All that has been amiss forgive,
And let thy truth within us live.

2 Though we are guilty, thou art good;—
Wash all our works in Jesus' blood;
Give every burdened soul release,
And bid us all depart in peace.

704.
L. M.
Praise to the co-equal Three.

1 BLESSING and honor, praise and love,
  Co-equal, Co-eternal Three!
In earth below, in heaven above,
  By all thy works, be paid to thee.

2 Thrice Holy! thine the kingdom is;
  The power omnipotent is thine;
And when created nature dies,
  Thy never-ceasing glories shine.

705.
L. M.
Praise from all Creatures.

1 PRAISE God, from whom all blessings flow;
Praise him, all creatures here below!
Praise him above, ye heavenly host!
Praise Father, Son, and Holy Ghost.

706.
L. M.
Praise to the Trinity.

1 TO God, the Father—God, the Son,—
And God, the Spirit—three in one,
Be honor, praise, and glory given,
By all on earth, and all in heaven.

707.
L. P. M.
The sacred Three.

1 NOW to the great and sacred Three
The Father, Son, and Spirit be
Eternal praise and glory given—
Through all the worlds where God is known,
By all the angels near the throne,
And all the saints in earth and heaven.

708.
C. M.
The Trinity adored.

1 LET God,—the Father, and the Son,
And Spirit,—be adored,
Where there are works to make him known,
Or saints to love the Lord.

709.
C. M.
A grateful Song to the Trinity.

1 IN hope to join th' angelic host
And all the ransomed throng,
To Father, Son, and Holy Ghost,
We raise the grateful song.

710.
C. M. D.
Praise to the Trinity.

1 THE God of mercy be adored,
Who calls our souls from death,
Who saves by his redeeming word
And new-creating breath;
To praise the Father and the Son
And Spirit all-divine,—
The one in three, and three in one,—
Let saints and angels join.

711.

C. P. M.
The Source of all Blessings.

1 TO Father, Son, and Holy Ghost,
Be praise amid the heavenly host,
And in the church below;
From whom all creatures draw their breath,
By whom redemption blessed the earth,
From whom all comforts flow.

712.

S. M.
Ascriptions of Angels and Saints.

1 YE angels round the throne!
And saints that dwell below!
Worship the Father, praise the Son,
And bless the Spirit too.

713.

H. M.
Honor, Glory, and Praise

1 TO God the Father's throne,
Your highest honors raise;
Glory to God, the Son,—
To God, the Spirit, praise:
With all our powers,
Eternal King!
Thy name we sing,
While faith adores.

714.

8s and 7s.
A Benediction implored.

1 MAY the grace of Christ, our Saviour,
And the Father's boundless love,
With the Holy Spirit's favor,
Rest upon us from above!
Let us thus abide in union
With each other, and the Lord;
And possess, in sweet communion,
Joys which earth cannot afford.

715.

8s and 7s.
Praise to the Three in One.

1 PRAISE the God of all creation;
Praise the Father's boundless love:
Praise the Lamb, our expiation,—
Priest and King enthroned above:

Praise the Fountain of salvation,—
Him by whom our Spirits live;
Undivided adoration
To the one Jehovah give.

716.

8s and 7s.
Praise to the Lamb.

1 GLORY, honor, praise and power
To the Lamb be ever paid;
Let new blessings, every hour,
Rest on his adored head.

717.

7s.
Eternal Praises to the Trinity.

1 SING we to our God above,
Praise eternal as his love:
Praise him—all ye heavenly host!
Father, Son and Holy Ghost.

718.

8s, 7s and 4.
A parting Blessing implored.

1 LORD! dismiss us with thy blessing;
Fill our hearts with joy and peace:
Let us all, thy love possessing,
Triumph in redeeming grace:
Oh! refresh us—
Traveling through this wilderness.

2 Thanks we give and adoration,
For thy gospel's joyful sound;
Let the fruits of thy salvation
In our hearts and lives abound;
May thy presence
With us evermore be found.

3 So, whene'er the signal 's given
Us from earth to call away,
Borne on angels' wings to heaven,
Glad to leave this cumbrous clay,
May we ever
Reign with Christ in endless day.

719.

8s, 7s and 4.
The Trinity enthroned.

GREAT Jehovah! we adore thee,
God, the Father—God, the Son—

God, the Spirit—joined in glory,
On the same eternal throne;
Endless praises
To Jehovah, three in one.

720.

7s and 6s.
Endless Praises.

1 WE 'LL praise thy name for ever,—
Thou glorious King of kings!
Thy wondrous love and favor
Each ransomed spirit sings:
We 'll celebrate thy glory,
With all thy saints above,
And shout the joyful story
Of thy redeeming love.

721.

5s and 6s.
Praise from Angels and Saints.

1 BY angels in heaven
Of every degree,
And saints upon earth,
All praise be addressed
To God in three persons,—
One God ever-blessed:
As hath been, and now is,
And always shall be.

722.

6s and 4s.
Boundless Praise.

1 TO God—the Father, Son,
And Spirit—three in one,
All praise be given!
Crown him, in every song;
To him your hearts belong;
Let all his praise prolong—
On earth—in heaven.

INDEX OF THE FIRST LINES.

INDEX OF SUBJECTS.

www.ingramcontent.com/pod-product-compliance
Lightning Source LLC
LaVergne TN
LVHW020114110826
845151LV00001B/154
9781425543075